MACROECONOMICS FOR PROFESSIONALS

Understanding macroeconomic developments and policies in the twenty-first century is daunting: policymakers face the combined challenges of supporting economic activity and employment, keeping inflation low and risks of financial crises at bay, and navigating the ever-tighter linkages of globalization. Many professionals face demands to evaluate the implications of developments and policies for their business, financial, or public policy decisions. *Macroeconomics for Professionals* provides a concise, rigorous, yet intuitive framework for assessing a country's macroeconomic outlook and policies. Drawing on years of experience at the International Monetary Fund, Leslie Lipschitz and Susan Schadler have created an operating manual for professional applied economists and all those required to evaluate economic analysis.

Leslie Lipschitz was an economist at the International Monetary Fund for more than thirty-five years. He served as Director of the IMF Institute, taught at the School of Advanced International Studies at Johns Hopkins University and at Bowdoin College, was a guest scholar at the Brookings Institution, worked and consulted with private financial institutions, and has written, spoken, and published widely on open-economy macroeconomics.

Susan Schadler was an economist at the International Monetary Fund for over thirty years. Her published articles and books cover exchange rate policies, economic growth and crises, how countries adjust in crises, and the integration of Eastern and Western Europe. Since leaving the IMF, she has been a senior member of St Antony's College, Oxford University, senior fellow at the Atlantic Council and the Centre for International Governance Innovation, and consultant for the IMF's Independent Evaluation Office.

Macroeconomics for Professionals

A Guide for Analysts and Those Who Need to
Understand Them

LESLIE LIPSCHITZ

Bowdoin College

SUSAN SCHADLER

Center for International Governance Innovation

CAMBRIDGE
UNIVERSITY PRESS

CAMBRIDGE
UNIVERSITY PRESS

University Printing House, Cambridge CB2 8BS, United Kingdom

One Liberty Plaza, 20th Floor, New York, NY 10006, USA

477 Williamstown Road, Port Melbourne, VIC 3207, Australia

314-321, 3rd Floor, Plot 3, Splendor Forum, Jasola District Centre, New Delhi - 110025, India

79 Anson Road, #06-04/06, Singapore 079906

Cambridge University Press is part of the University of Cambridge.

It furthers the University's mission by disseminating knowledge in the pursuit of education, learning and research at the highest international levels of excellence.

www.cambridge.org
Information on this title: www.cambridge.org/9781108449830
DOI: 10.1017/9781108598293

First published 2019

A catalogue record for this publication is available from the British Library

Library of Congress Cataloging in Publication data
NAMES: Lipschitz, Leslie, author. | Schadler, Susan, author.
TITLE: Macroeconomics for professionals : a guide for analysts and those who need to understand them / Leslie Lipschitz, Bowdoin College, Maine, Susan Schadler, Center for International Governance Innovation.
DESCRIPTION: New York : Cambridge University Press, [2018] | Includes bibliographical references and index.
IDENTIFIERS: LCCN 2018025214| ISBN 9781316515891 (hbk. : alk. paper) | ISBN 9781108449830 (pbk. : alk. paper)
SUBJECTS: LCSH: Macroeconomics.
CLASSIFICATION: LCC HB172.5 .L57 2018 | DDC 339–dc23
LC record available at https://lccn.loc.gov/2018025214

ISBN 978-1-316-51589-1 Hardback
ISBN 978-1-108-44983-0 Paperback

For Charlotte, Jessica, and Vanessa. After the years of enduring (and sometimes being moved to engage in) ferocious dinner-table debate on issues of political economy, much of what's in this book may seem like old hat.

And for our former colleagues at the IMF who honed our commitment to getting the macroeconomic diagnosis and policy prescription right.

Contents

Acknowledgments

The authors owe a debt of gratitude to too many former colleagues at the IMF and to economists in government statistical agencies to mention individually; some are acknowledged in the specific areas where they provided data or input. Bas Bakker (at the International Monetary Fund) and David Vines and Adam Bennett (at Oxford University) read an early draft of the manuscript and provided insightful suggestions. Claudio Borio and Ingo Fender (at the Bank for International Settlements) helped improve Chapter 6. Anonymous reviewers, students at Bowdoin College and in an MBA class taught by one of the reviewers, and (perhaps unwittingly) colleagues at Investec Asset Management also helped shape the book. Elizabeth Weston of the Bowdoin College Economics department provided excellent technical and editorial assistance. The authors alone are responsible for any remaining errors.

Glossary of symbols and acronyms

Upper and lower-case letters

Except for interest rates (which are always in small-case letters), most variables are written in capital letters for levels of the variable and small letters for growth rates (or percentage changes) or for ratios of variables to GDP. Which of the two is in use for any specific small letter symbol should explicit in the text or clear from the context.

Subscripts

g   designates government (as opposed to private)
i   designates one component of an aggregate measure
n   designates a nominal or current price (as opposed to a real or constant price) measure, except when it is used on "P" when it designates the price of nontraded goods
p   designates private (as opposed to government)
r   designates a real or constant price (as opposed to nominal or current price) measure
$t, t+1$ designate time periods

Superscripts

*   designates a target value (e.g., for the inflation rate), a potential value (e.g., for potential output or growth), or a cyclically neutral value (e.g., for the cyclically neutral interest rate, structural, or cyclically-adjusted, fiscal aggregates)
$ designates that the variable is measured in US dollars

e   designates an expected value. Thus E^e_{t+1} is the value of the exchange
        rate expected one period in the future
d   designates domestic variables, such that i^d is the domestic interest
        rate and D^d the stock of government debt in domestic currency
f   designates foreign, such that i^f is the foreign interest rate and D^f the
        stock of government debt in foreign currency
w   designates that a variable is measured in US dollars

Greek symbols

α = share of capital in production and income
$1-\alpha$ = share of labor in production and income
β = share of traded goods in the CPI
$1-\beta$ = share of nontraded goods in CPI
ε = percentage change in the exchange rate, such that a positive
               number is a depreciation of the home currency
γ_r = the elasticity of revenue to nominal income
γ_e = the elasticity of expenditure to nominal income
π = the aggregate inflation rate (abstracting from the particular price
               index)

Symbols and acronyms

A = TFP   = total factor productivity
ABS   = absorption
ARA   = IMF's analysis of reserve adequacy metric
AT1   = additional tier 1 capital
BCBS   = Basel Committee on Banking Supervision
BIS   = Bank for International Settlements
BOP   = balance of payments
C   = consumption
CAB   = current account balance = X – M + NFI + TR
CAD   = -CAB = current account deficit of the balance of payments
CB   = central bank loans to the banking system
CET1   = common equity tier 1 capital
CiB   = currency in banks
CiC   = currency in circulation
CFM   = capital flow management (policies)
CO   = other claims of the banking system (i.e., those on the private
             nonbank sector). A suffix "1" refers to the central bank, a suffix

"2" refers to the commercial banks, and no suffix is used for the consolidated banking system (or where the context is unambiguous)

CoB	= currency outside banks
CPI	= consumer price index
D	= the stock of government debt or of debt to non-residents (external debt)[1]
DD	= demand deposits
Def	= the overall government deficit (equal to -OB)
DEP	= bank deposits
DIs	= depository institutions (chiefly banks) in the accounts of the US Federal Reserve System
DSA	= debt sustainability analysis (whether of public sector debt in Chapter 5 or external debt in Chapter 7
DSGE	= dynamic stochastic general equilibrium model
E	= exchange rate (domestic currency units per US dollar)
E&O	= errors and omissions (in the balance of payments)
EBA	= external balance assessment
EFA	= the external financial account of the balance of payments
EM	= emerging market country
ER	= excess reserves (i.e., deposits) of the banking system with the central bank
Exp	= government expenditure
F	= forward exchange rate such that F_t^{t+1} is the forward exchange rate for time t+1 quoted at time t
FA	= foreign assets
FB	= foreign balance = X – M
FCL	= Flexible Credit Line of the IMF
FDI	= foreign direct investment
FL	= foreign liabilities
FDD	= final domestic demand = C +IF = TDD – IN
FSAP	= financial sector assessment program (of the IMF and World Bank)
FX	= any financial aggregate denominated in foreign exchange
FXD	= deposits (of residents) in foreign currency
FXH	= foreign exchange holdings of the monetary authorities
GDA	= gross domestic absorption, identical to TDD

---

[1]   We use the same symbols for these two different measures of indebtedness with D referring to public debt in Chapter 5 and to external debt in Chapter 7.

GDP = gross domestic product

GFSM = Government Finance Statistics Manual of the IMF

GNDI = gross national disposable income

GNI = GNP = gross national income which is sometimes called gross national product

GOB = gross operating balance, identical to S_g (= Rev – C_g) if C_g *excludes* capital consumption (i.e., depreciation)

gr_n = the rate of growth of nominal income (that is $\Delta Y_{n\ t}/Y_{n\ t\text{-}1}$)

gr_r = the rate of growth of real income

GS = government surplus = $S_g – I_g$

GSIBs = global systemic important banks (generally identical to TITF)

i = nominal interest rate

I = total investment = IF + IN

IF = fixed investment

IMF = International Monetary Fund

IN = inventory investment

IT = inflation targeting

K = index of capital inputs into production

KAB = capital account balance

L = labor hours worked per period

LI = Laspeyres Index

LOANS = net foreign borrowing component of the net financial balance (NFB)

M = imports of goods and services

M_1 = narrow money

M_2 = broad money

MAC = market access country (country grouping including EMs and advanced countries)

MB = the monetary base (sometimes referred to as reserve money)

MG = monetary gold holdings

MPC = monetary policy committee

mpc = marginal propensity to consume out of income

NAIRU = non-accelerating inflation rate of unemployment

NCG = net credit to government. A suffix "1" refers to the central bank, a suffix "2" refers to the commercial banks, and no suffix is used for the consolidated banking system (or where the context is unambiguous)

NDA = the net domestic assets of the central bank

NDCAB   = non-interest current account balance plus net non-debt-creating financial inflows, all measured in dollars

NFA   = net foreign assets in the monetary balance sheet (FA – FL). A suffix "1" refers to the central bank, a suffix "2" refers to the commercial banks, and no suffix refers to the consolidated banking system (or where the context is unambiguous)

NFB   = net financial balance

NFI   = net factor income from abroad

NIIP   = net international investment position

NOB   = net operating balance, equal to GOB minus capital consumption; identical to S_g (= Rev – C_g) if C_g *includes* capital consumption

NPI   = net primary income

O_i = gross output of sector i

OA   = other short-term assets in foreign currency held by the monetary authority

OECD   = Organization for Economic Cooperation and Development

OIN   = other items net in the balance sheet (defined as an asset). A suffix "1" refers to the central bank, a suffix "2" refers to the commercial banks, and no suffix is used for the consolidated banking system (or where the context is unambiguous). Sometimes OIN is included under a broad conception of NDA

OTH   = other influences on the level of government debt

P   = the price level (when the specific index used is not specified)

P_i = price of value added component i of GDP

P_n = price index of nontraded goods (and services).

P_w = world price index (for a traded good) measured in US$

P_y = GDP deflator

PExp   = primary expenditure

PGFR   = public gross financing requirement

PI   = Paasche Index

PL   = private credit

PL(DC)   = private credit in domestic currency

PL(FX)   = private credit in foreign currency

PPF   = production possibility frontier

PPP   = purchasing power parity

PRIM   = primary balance

prim	= the primary balance as a ratio to nominal income (that is, $PRIM/Y_n$)
PROD	= productivity (output per person-hour)
OB	= overall balance or net lending (defined as Rev − Exp)
OEB	= overall external balance
OMC	= US Federal Reserve Open Market Committee
OMOs	= open market operations
Q_i	= quantity of value added component i of GDP
QE	= quantitative easing
r	= real interest rate
R	= rental cost of capital
REER	= multilateral real effective exchange rate (a weighted index of RERs vis-à-vis a group of countries)
RER	= bilateral real exchange rate
Rev	= government revenue
rp	= currency risk premium (this has the dimension of an interest rate)[2]
RPF	= reserve position in the IMF (foreign currency amounts that a member country may draw from the IMF at short notice)
RT	= net foreign exchange reserve transactions of the central bank = reserve loss
S	= gross national saving (comprising private and government components)
SDR	= special drawing rights issued to the country by the IMF or obtained from another country through the IMF
SEI	= seigniorage
TD	= time deposits
TDD	= total domestic demand = C + IF + IN sometimes also referred to as Gross Domestic Absorption (GDA)
TFP	= total factor productivity
TITF	= too important to fail (a class of large, interconnected banks)
TOT	= external terms of trade = $price of export/$price of imports
TR	= net transfers from abroad
ULC	= unit labor cost. Lower case used to indicate a rate of change.
UKC	= unit capital cost

---

[2] E.g., $\{(1 + i_{mex\ t})/(1 + rp_t)\} - 1$ is the interest rate on Mexican bonds adjusted for the risk premium on the peso.

VAR   = value at risk (a class of models relevant for setting capital
             adequacy standards)
VAT   = value added tax
W   = wage rate
WEO   = IMF's World Economic Outlook
X   = exports of goods and services
Y   = aggregate output often used when we are not distinguishing
             between various related output measures (e.g., GDP, GNI,
             etc.)

Preface

The business of macroeconomics is essentially practical. It entails analyzing economies usually open to international influences and buffeted by developments at home and abroad. The objective is sensible policy advice or investment decisions. The emphasis in teaching macroeconomics, however, is usually initially theoretical (focusing on the analytic foundations of different models of the economy), and then empirical in the sense of testing models against data. Often even those who have studied macroeconomics are not fully clear on how to apply what they have learned to real-world questions: for example, how do practitioners actually assess the global competitiveness of an economy? What concretely do practitioners mean when they identify an economy as vulnerable to crisis? How do practitioners balance short-term cyclical considerations and long-term sustainability considerations in assessing monetary and fiscal policies?

In our book, *Understanding Macroeconomics*, we aim to help analysts (and those who need to understand them) answer these and many other operational questions. In under 300 pages – including real-world examples, figures, and exercises – we provide a guide to the practical tools of macroeconomic analysis. The text reflects decades of working as economists at the International Monetary Fund (IMF) and subsequent work in the private financial sector, think tanks, and academia. The aim is clear-cut exposition with minimal mathematical complexity.

For many economists the initial material in each chapter will be old hat: definitions of well-understood concepts and details on how to read basic presentations of macroeconomic data. They will be able to move quickly over these parts of the book. However, precision on definitions and an understanding of data catchment systems is essential to the next part of each chapter: how to parse the data for diagnostic content, assess policies in place, and understand commentary on a government's policy intentions.

The exercises at the end of each chapter relate to frequently encountered real-world problems; they should be manageable given good comprehension of the chapter. However, because they simulate real-world problems, they cannot avoid overlapping with some concepts explained in later chapters. Instructors may decide to assign exercises immediately after each chapter (for a quick assessment of the understanding of key concepts), to postpone assigning some exercises in early chapters until later in the course (to facilitate richer, more complete answers), or to revisit exercises that students found especially interesting or taxing. Those using the book as a self-study guide or reference book can use the exercises to help consolidate the content of each chapter.

Online Teaching and Learning Resources

A companion online workbook volume, available to instructors using the book in their courses, can be accessed at www.cambridge.org/Lipschitz. Those using the book for reference or self-study can obtain the companion volume by following instructions on the website www.macroeconomicsfor professionals.com. This volume contains complete answers to all the exercises and three case studies with model answers. The case studies are ideal for helping readers integrate the material presented throughout the book.

Each case study describes an actual country that has faced a macroeconomic crisis or serious economic weakness that readers must diagnose and address. Each presents a narrative on the background to the crisis or issues, a cache of actual data, and an outline for the structure of the analysis that is needed. As in the real world, there is no "correct" strategy; the questions posed have no clear-cut right or wrong answers. What is important is the cogency of the argumentation behind the assessment and advice.

The first case study covers the Latvian financial crisis of 2008, and the exercise is an ex post analysis (by a fictional team at the Bank for International Settlements) to cull wisdom from the history on policies that might have forestalled the crisis or lessened its intensity.

The second case study deals with the 2010 sovereign debt crisis in Greece and asks readers to take the perspective of an asset management company with exposure to Greek sovereign debt. This is a fiscal crisis with some unique characteristics. The exercise entails an analysis of the relevant developments and data in order to advise on a strategy with respect to holdings of Greek sovereign debt.

The third case study deals with South Africa in 2013 from the perspective of a fictional consulting team engaged by the government and monetary authorities. No crisis is imminent. However, economic policies confront extreme inequality, dire unemployment, poverty, sluggish output growth, and challenges to longer-term financial stability. Readers are asked to prepare an annotated agenda for a first meeting with the authorities that displays an analytical understanding of the background and an appreciation of the economic and political imperatives.

When the book is used in academic courses, the case studies are useful assignments. The authors have found that having class participants – whether university students or professionals – work in teams, each on one of the case studies, is an excellent end to a course. If the case studies are assigned early in the term, they facilitate in-depth, cooperative team work and provide a specific real-world context for understanding the content of the book.

CHAPTER 1

Introduction, Motivation, and Overview

Macroeconomics is ubiquitous and nobody questions its importance. Media commentary on breaking economic data – perhaps the gross domestic product (GDP) and its growth, employment, inflation, or the balance of payments – is almost inescapable. Political campaigns often revolve around starkly conflicting views on exchange rates, movements of jobs across borders, or concerns about government deficits and debt. For a discipline that is called a science, macroeconomics displays a confusing divergence of views on real-world developments.

Understanding economic developments – making sense of the mass of data, debate, and commentary produced every day – is difficult even for experts. It is especially challenging for those whose jobs or studies require that they can critically evaluate macroeconomic developments and policies, who have some university-level training, but who have not had practical experience in economic analysis. Our premise is that reporting and debate on macroeconomics can be made understandable if the underlying issues are placed in a broad analytical framework on which economists generally agree and which has immediate relevance to real-world settings.

The aim of this book is to provide such a framework. It is designed for use in courses on applied macroeconomics or for professionals in finance, management, or government and public policy who need to understand macroeconomics.

The manuscript has been filtered through a variety of professional experiences. The inspiration for it started at the International Monetary Fund (IMF) where we were involved in various ways with answering the question "What analytical tools are essential for assessing a country's macroeconomic outlook and policies and communicating this assessment in the simplest possible terms?" It evolved through work in the private financial sector with portfolio managers who were highly motivated, severely time constrained, and focused on opportunities, vulnerabilities, and risks in the countries in which they were investing. It was subsequently reorganized, broadened, and made more accessible in seminars on *Applied Macroeconomics* for Economics majors at Bowdoin College.

Our conviction throughout has been that good macroeconomic analysis requires both an understanding of key conceptual constructs and exposure to real-world situations where positions must be taken and decisions made under uncertainty. In this spirit, the book occupies a somewhat unusual niche: it assumes some familiarity with basic macroeconomic models and does not cover the same ground as most textbooks, it eschews the higher-level mathematics and technical material of current academic debate, and it focuses on the practical application of macroeconomics to frequently encountered situations. Thus, for each segment of macroeconomic analysis addressed, the book summarizes key analytical tools and presents thought experiments and exercises that require readers to make decisions and formulate advice in simulations of real-world situations. At the end of the book, readers should be able to evaluate the assumptions and contingencies on which various positions are founded, and the strengths and weaknesses of alternative policy prescriptions.

A few essential requirements for analysis cut across all of the specific topics addressed in the book:

Reading the data. Critical evaluation of real-world developments and policies is impossible without an ability to read the main macroeconomic accounts: the national income accounts as well as the balance sheets and flow accounts of the government, the central bank, the banking sector, and the country as a whole in its transactions with the rest of the world (the balance of payments and the international investment position). Each of these accounts has its own conventions. Once these are understood, the store of data becomes a stepping stone to an appreciation of what is transpiring in and between economies.

Understanding macroeconomic constraints. There are many hard-and-fast relationships among macroeconomic variables drawn from the different accounts. In the language of economists, these are the definitional identities and adding-up constraints that discipline analysis, policy prescription, and forecasting. Unlike many behavioral models, these relationships are not contentious, and they are essential to an understanding of the economy.

Respecting the demands of macroeconomic sustainability. "Sustainability" (a term that will be used in many contexts through the book) essentially refers to a configuration of policies and economic developments – typically related to economic growth, inflation, credit expansion, the government budget, and the balance of payments – that does not inherently presage a need for substantial and discontinuous future adjustment. In other words, sustainable policies or developments are those that can reasonably be expected to be steady and predictable in the absence of shocks. Judgments about whether any given set of macroeconomic policies is sustainable must inform all responsible analysis and prescription. Such judgments start with a view of the potential output of the economy – when capital and labor are fully employed but not stretched to a point of continuously rising inflation – which is in a sense the envelope for the macroeconomy. But they also encompass, among other things, the government finances and the external balance of payments accounts. They influence risk premia in financial markets, and they impinge on a wide swath of private and government decisions. At each level, clear methodologies exist for reaching at least qualitative judgments about sustainability. These form another layer of essential constraints on macroeconomic policies.

Considering policy choices. Policy options in the face of economic cycles are a theme throughout the book. We include a great deal of discussion of cyclical positions (booms and recessions) and the efficacy of policies aimed at reducing the amplitude of cycles (countercyclical policies). The debate on policy options almost always uses tools – like those for assessing potential output or financial sustainability – that are based on (sometimes heroic) assumptions that need to be examined critically. Our experience is that the political process will almost always drive governments to adopt countercyclical policies, and that such policies can do good. But when they are based on an incorrect reading of the data or on unrealistic objectives, they can be harmful and make the economy vulnerable to crisis.

Identifying vulnerabilities and crisis triggers. The policy objective of forestalling economic crises runs through the book. Crises are usually triggered when a shock event exposes a vulnerability in the fiscal or financial system. It is impossible to predict trigger events, but it is possible for policies to make a country's finances more robust and less vulnerable to these shocks. Significant portions of the coverage of monetary policy, government financing, microprudential and macroprudential policies, and risks in a country's macroeconomic interactions with the rest of the world (in Chapters 4, 5, 6, and 7) are motivated by this policy objective.

Characterizing cross-border economic linkages. The perspective that runs through the book is global. In all of the presentations of data catchment systems and tools for analysis, we emphasize international economic linkages through both trade and global financial markets – how they must be read in the data and how they constrain economic developments and policies in both large and small countries.

We have sought to create as simple a framework as possible by being ruthlessly selective in what we present while acknowledging real-world complexity. Many of the intense debates among academic economists of different persuasions reflect differences in assumptions about how the agents in an economy (i.e., consumers and investors, workers, managers, owners, and entrepreneurs) respond to market signals and government policies. The arguments are often couched in stylized models that facilitate elegant mathematical analysis. To the extent that we give these debates and models relatively short shrift, it is because a vast academic literature covers these topics but there is less emphasis on the basic analytic prerequisites that lie behind them and are our main focus. The essence of arguments is usually accessible using the tools we provide.

Each of the following six chapters covers one broad area of macroeconomic analysis:

Chapter 2: the real economy from the perspectives of both potential output and aggregate demand
Chapter 3: prices, inflation, interest rates, exchange rates, and expectations
Chapter 4: the monetary accounts and monetary policy
Chapter 5: the government accounts and fiscal policy
Chapter 6: financial stability, the financial system, and regulation (including microprudential and macroprudential policies)
Chapter 7: the external accounts (the flow balance of payments and the stock international investment position)

Each chapter starts by outlining the principal concepts covered and ends with exercises to test comprehension. Analytic and diagnostic techniques are presented with numerous detours to illustrate how they have been used to understand or address actual macroeconomic issues. Throughout the book (and especially the exercises) readers are forced to adopt the perspective of a decision-maker or advisor: they are called upon to diagnose developments and advocate policies or assess opportunities.

A companion online volume provides answers to the exercises and presents three full-length case studies that allow the reader to use the tools of the main volume to interpret the problems and consider the policy choices in the actual historical circumstances of the case-study countries.[1]

The book is necessarily sequential in its coverage. But it is impossible to discuss demand and supply (covered in Chapter 2) or monetary developments (in Chapter 4) without acknowledging the influence of government operations and international economic relations on them, even though the fiscal and external accounts are only covered fully later in the book. The summary and intuitive treatment of these topics in chapters before they are covered in depth should suffice for the level of analysis required; readers, however, will gain a richer appreciation of some of the material treated lightly in these earlier chapters when they get to the more in-depth subsequent coverage. Also, it is suggested that readers return to some of the exercises in earlier chapters as they progress through the book and become capable of more comprehensive analysis.

Finally, this book is intended as a guide, not an academic treatise or a textbook.[2] Even though the book obviously draws on the broad body of economics literature, we provide few citations or references, limiting these to instances where we have drawn directly from a publication. In the main, the economics behind our analytics is so much a part of the standard curriculum that it defies specific attribution. We are enormously indebted to colleagues at the IMF who over the years taught us most of what we know. We hope we have gotten it right.

---

[1] This online volume is available without charge. For instructors using the book in their courses, it can be accessed at www.cambridge.org/Lipschitz. For those using the book for reference or self-study, it can obtained by following instructions on the website www.macroeconomicsfor professionals.com. The three case studies cover the Latvian financial crisis of 2008, the crisis in Greece in 2010, and the economic difficulties and policy conundrums in South Africa in 2013. In each the reader is cast in an advisory role and asked to provide advice based on an examination of the relevant data and economic circumstances.

[2] Readers may need at times to refer to one of the widely-used textbooks on macroeconomics. Three excellent options are:

Dornbusch, Rudiger, Fischer, Stanley, Startz, Richard, *Macroeconomics* (12th edition), New York: McGraw Hill Education, 2013.
Mankiw, M. Gregory, *Macroeconomics* (9th edition), New York: Worth Publishers, 2015.
Mishkin, Frederic, *Economics of Money, Banking, and Financial Markets* (11th edition), Boston: The Pearson Series in Economics, 2016.

CHAPTER 2

Real Economic Activity

This chapter covers the measurement and analysis of a country's aggregate economic activity, a term typically used synonymously with total output. The chapter is concerned with "real" measures and concepts – i.e., measures that do not include changes in prices. Five basic concepts are covered:

1 *The determination of actual and potential output of a country (the difference between the two being critical to policy analysis in subsequent chapters).*
2 *Decisions on labor and capital inputs to production (which determine employment and investment and affect international capital flows).*
3 *Factors that influence whether output levels across countries converge (i.e., whether poorer countries catch up with richer ones).*
4 *The National Accounts data catchment system, and how it can be partitioned in different ways to diagnose demand shocks and help formulate policies.*

A country's aggregate economic activity during any period, its gross domestic product (GDP), can be measured in three ways – as aggregate output (or the supply) of goods and services, as aggregate demand for those goods and services, or as income generated from the production of those goods and services.[1] The critical aspect of GDP is that regardless of which of the three measures is used, it represents the *value-added* produced by the economy.[2]

---

[1]   We use GDP here because it is the most commonly used measure. But, as shown in section 2 of this chapter, alternative broad measures of economic activity may be more appropriate in particular circumstances.

[2]   The concept of output in GDP is not gross output but value-added. (The term "gross" in the name refers to the fact that depreciation of capital is not excluded from the measure.) If a manufacturer requires a raw material input to produce output, the contribution to GDP would be only the value-added by capital and labor to that raw material input. If the raw material is produced by domestic mines, its production would be included in GDP as

Although, in principle, all three measures produce the same statement of activity, each provides a different perspective on the underlying influences. This chapter reviews the measurement and conceptual underpinnings of aggregate activity from both the production and expenditure perspectives. While we will frequently use the terms "output," "production," and "activity," these will all refer to GDP. Even those familiar with these concepts should find useful the numerous examples of how they are used in real-world analysis.

Aside from wars and natural disasters, the conditions of supply change relatively slowly. This is why we usually approach secular questions about an economy's productive potential (i.e., the amount that the country could produce if its labor and capital were fully employed) from the perspective of the production or supply side. Cyclical fluctuations, however, usually originate in demand (i.e., actual expenditure), so much of the discussion about short- to medium-term movements in the real economy centers on the analysis of demand.[3] Over time, demand and potential supply should converge, but they are not identical at any point in time.

Figure 2.1 shows a stylized relationship between *potential output* and *actual output* (which responds quickly to demand). The former tends to follow a trend reflecting the growth of labor and capital inputs and changing productive efficiency. The latter reflects actual changes in demand (which are subject to more frequent shocks) and therefore varies around the trend.

Figure 2.1 shows a business cycle perspective for a roughly 10-year period. In this example, potential growth is a steady 3 percent a year (represented by the slope of the smooth blue line), and actual growth (the changing slope of the red line) varies between a high (during the initial boom years and final recovery years) of 5 to 7 percent per year and a low (during the middle recessionary years) of 0 to –1 percent.

The gap between the actual output line and the potential output line (the "output gap") defines the business cycle (positive in the boom and early slowdown period and negative in the recessionary and recovery years). When demand exceeds sustainable capacity – so that inventories fall, imports rise, and producers add extra hours for existing employees or hire more workers – changes in prices and other variables usually push demand

the capital and labor value-added in the mining process. If the raw material is imported, it is excluded from GDP.

[3]   This is the conventional view. But, as will be seen in later chapters, sudden changes in risk premia, and thus interest rates and exchange rates, may be as much supply shocks as demand shocks.

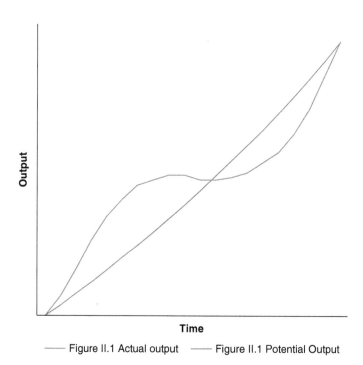

Figure II.1 Actual output — Figure II.1 Potential Output

FIGURE 2.1 Macroeconomic cycles: potential and actual output

back down to the level of potential output. When demand falls short of supply – inventories rise, imports fall, and producers cut back on labor input – a similar (but opposite) set of endogenous changes is put in train that leads eventually to a rise in demand. But these automatic adjustments may be slow (or, put differently, prices may be sticky) so that booms and recessions may be protracted. The objective of countercyclical macroeconomic policies (often also called demand management policies) is to shorten the periods when an economy is experiencing output gaps. Thus, the analysis of aggregate activity and output gaps in this chapter feeds directly into the analysis of monetary policy in Chapter 4 and fiscal policy in Chapter 5.

Some of the most fundamental questions that macroeconomic policymakers must answer on economic activity are these:

- What is a country's potential level of output?
- What components of demand are driving a country's actual level of output, and can they feed back to affect potential output?

- Is there an "output gap" at any point in time?
- How can the sources of shocks to demand be identified in ways that help fashion appropriate policy responses?
- How is a country's productive capacity likely to grow over the medium to long term (that is, how steep is the slope of the red line in Figure 2.1) and what will determine this growth rate?

The first four questions relate mainly to where a country is in its business cycle and how demand shocks play out. Answering them is the first step in addressing a range of issues, from whether economic conditions and institutions are in some way preventing the economy from fully employing its labor force to whether countercyclical policies are needed and how strongly they should be applied. The fifth bullet concerns the underlying growth rate of the economy.

To address the cyclical questions as well as the long-term growth question, we need supply-side analysis to estimate potential output. Such analysis focuses, in the first instance, on a country's inputs to production – its labor supply and capital stock. More broadly, however, it needs to encompass a country's institutional and technological environment and the "structural policies"– i.e., policies that influence this environment over the medium and long term. Cyclical questions also require demand-side analysis – i.e., analysis of the shorter-term fluctuations in the components of demand (consumption, investment, and trade). As will be clear from this chapter and those that follow, sound analysis of both supply and demand is critical to getting economic policies right.

1 The Supply Side

The centerpiece of supply-side analysis is estimating an economy's potential output – a task that is conceptually straightforward but exceedingly difficult in practice. Although the input variables that determine potential output tend to move slowly and be less volatile than those that influence demand, there can be structural breaks in potential output due, for example, to sudden shifts in technology, governmental institutions, or trading conditions. But a more important difficulty in assessing potential output is the fact that past and current levels of potential output – as opposed to actual output – are unobservable; potential output is a concept rather than a variable for which there are data. And initial errors in assessing potential output tend to carry over into future diagnostic and policy errors.

Good estimates of potential output are essential to two types of macroeconomic analysis: calculating output gaps and projecting GDP with a focus on a three- to five-year horizon so as to understand whether there are any structural impediments to medium- and long-term growth.

a A Framework for Understanding the Drivers of Potential Output

Macroeconomists borrow a production function framework from microeconomists to consider the drivers of potential output. The production function, in this application, represents the capacity to produce goods and services by combining inputs (defined broadly as labor and physical capital) in a given institutional environment and state of technology.[4]

$$Y = Af(K, L) \qquad (2.1)$$

Y = aggregate real output (or GDP) per year
K = an index of the capital input per year
L = hours worked per year
A is a summary of the efficiency with which capital and labor are combined. It is also referred to as total factor productivity (TFP).[5]

Whereas microeconomists specify the production function to explain the value-added in an individual firm or industry, in macroeconomic analysis the production function is specified as one aggregate process for all goods and services. That is, it is a characterization of a country's average production process even though every good and service individually has different input proportions of K, L, and A, and the specific characteristics of capital and labor employed differ for different goods and services produced. The aggregation is heroic but the production function mechanics nevertheless provide a useful conceptual framework.

Actually using the production function to assess a country's potential output requires specifying a functional form and parameters relating inputs

---

[4] Note that aggregating capital over different vintages and labor over different skill levels is problematic, but a more elaborate function to deal with these complications would detract from the clarity of exposition without adding analytic value.

[5] The concept of A or TFP is much debated among economists. In their macroeconomic application, Y, L, and K are aggregates of products or inputs that are not in fact homogeneous. But they are more measurable than A, which does not even have any conceptual units of measurement. Rather, A is typically calculated as a residual in equation 2.1 given data for Y, L, and K.

and TFP to output. The simplest workhorse for these is called the Cobb–Douglas production function.[6]

$$Y = AK^{\alpha}L^{1-\alpha} \tag{2.2}$$

α = proportionate contribution of K to total inputs, usually assumed at about 0.3

This representation of the production technology embodies three important features that define how output responds to increases in inputs. We will come back to these features repeatedly as we consider the aggregate demand for capital and labor and the incentives for international capital flows, so it is worth spelling them out here.

- *Constant returns to scale.* If K and L are increased in the same combination, output rises proportionately. In other words, it is not possible to achieve more efficiency by raising or lowering the scale of production. Operationally, the importance of this feature is that production units (firms) of any size are able to compete.
- *Marginal products of K and L are positive.* This means that output increases when the input of K or L is increased by one unit while the input of the other is held constant. In other words, if the application of either input is increased by one unit, output will rise.[7]
- *However, the marginal product of each input decreases as more of that input is added* with an unchanged amount of the other input. For example, the more capital is added to a fixed supply of labor, the less output rises.[8]

b Estimating Potential Output

While the concept of potential output is rather simple, actually estimating it is complex and infuriatingly inexact. In this section we review how estimates are often done in practice, taking in turn the cases of richer "advanced countries" and then poorer "emerging market and developing countries."[9]

---

[6] There are other functional forms for production functions that impose fewer restrictive assumptions about the relationship between inputs and output. However, for a workable balance between capturing characteristics of actual production decisions and ease of use for understanding basic economics, the Cobb–Douglas formulation is a good analytical tool.

[7] Algebraically, this feature is represented as $\delta Y/\delta K = \alpha AK^{\alpha-1}L^{1-\alpha} = \alpha A(K/L)^{\alpha-1} > 0$

[8] Algebraically, this feature is represented as $\delta^2 Y/\delta K^2 = \alpha(\alpha-1)AK^{\alpha-2}L^{1-\alpha} < 0$

[9] The IMF divides its coverage of 193 countries into two groups: 39 are classified as "advanced countries" and 154 as "emerging market and developing countries." A decade ago a distinction was generally made between "emerging market countries" (EMs) and

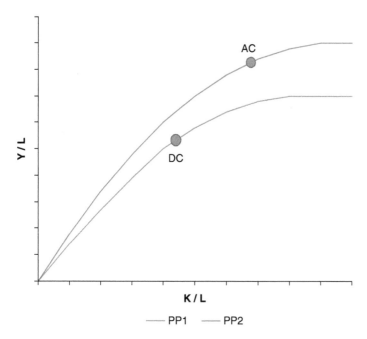

FIGURE 2.2 Output per worker, capital-labor ratios, and TFP

The distinction reflects two differences: "advanced countries" have more capital per worker (higher K/L) and a better technological and institutional environment for production (higher TFP). Figure 2.2 represents the position of an advanced country on the red line and a developing country on the blue one. (The figure plots Y/L against K/L, a relationship that simply involves dividing both sides of equation (2.2) by L. Each PP line shows the combinations of K/L and Y/L that are possible for the current state of technology or TFP.) The gap between the two lines represents the difference in TFP. Movement along either line represents increases in capital per worker.

"developing countries" – the former were seen as less developed than advanced countries (with lower per capita incomes, capital/labor ratios, and TFP) but with growing access to global financial markets. Some EMs could borrow in global financial markets only in hard currencies (like the US dollar or the euro) but an increasing number were able to borrow in their own currencies. More recently, however, the distinction between developing countries and EMs has largely been abandoned or blurred as more and more countries have gained access to global financial markets. Clearly, however, the poorest countries – those classified by the IMF as "highly indebted poor countries" or "low-income developing countries" – can hardly yet be deemed to be EMs. In this chapter we refer to "developing countries" to cover EMs and developing countries, but in subsequent chapters we will often focus on EMs.

The potential output per worker for the advanced country will be at a point like AC on PP2; it represents the level of output per worker achievable with a given capital/labor ratio (higher than that in the developing country) and with what might be thought of as state-of-the-art TFP. The potential output per worker for the developing country will be at a point like DC on PP1 with both less capital per worker and a lower level of TFP.

(i) Estimating Potential Output in Advanced Countries

For the advanced country, the future path of potential output per worker depends on a higher K/L ratio ("capital deepening"– that is, movement along the PP1 curve) and technological and institutional innovations that lift the whole curve. Capital deepening is also important for the developing country, but its overall growth trajectory will be lifted to the extent that it is able to catch up with more advanced countries in terms of total factor productivity.

Applying the production function framework to estimating potential output requires quantifying inputs and TFP. This presents many challenges, the most significant being that A, which is a single variable representing a wide and not precisely specified range of influences, cannot be measured directly. Rather, it needs to be calculated as a residual by rearranging equation (2.2) and putting variables for which data exist on the right side.

$$A_t = Y_t / \left(K_t^a L_t^{1-a} \right) \qquad (2.3)$$

Data for L are most simply represented by the hours that would be worked if a country were able to employ its working-age population (adjusted for frictional unemployment and other sources of "equilibrium" unemployment). Data for capital services, K, are proxied by the actual capital stock with the assumption that capital services are proportional to it. (Box 2.1 goes into more detail on how inputs of L and K can be measured for a potential output estimate.) Combining these time series data on inputs with a cyclically-adjusted time series on GDP (Y) in equation (2.3) allows us to construct estimates for a historical series for A.[10]

Although the production function is always at the heart of any considera-tion of potential output, sometimes as a quick and dirty approximation, economists draw a trend line of actual GDP, say for 5–10 recent years, and

[10] Obviously, this method is somewhat circular in that cyclically-adjusted GDP is approxi-mately the same as past levels of potential output. So why go through the complication of the production function if we could simply calculate cyclically-adjusted output through some simple process of cleansing GDP of its cycle? The answer is that projections of potential output require a base estimate of A, which can then be used with projections for it, L, and K to maximize the information content of the estimates of future potential output.

Box 2.1 What Do We Mean by Inputs of Labor and Capital to Potential Output?

In any period (let's call it a year), actual L and K (in the aggregate) are measured respectively as the number of person-hours worked during the year and the capital services used during the year as proxied by the nonresidential capital stock. But when we are trying to estimate potential output, we obviously do not want (or for future periods have) the actual measures of the inputs, but rather we want the amount of each input that is available if all inputs were used to their potential. Measuring "potential" inputs, therefore, requires sorting out cyclical from underlying influences.

In principle, a country's available labor supply might be thought of as the normal working hours of its working-age population (WAP, commonly defined as 15- to 64-year-old residents). The actual "labor force" (those employed or actively looking for employment) in high-income countries tends to be 60–80 percent of the WAP. This gap reflects those in the WAP who are in full-time education, are unable or unwilling to work, or do not work outside the home.

Not all of this 60–80 percent is employed even at "full employment", broadly for two reasons:

- *Frictional unemployment* (workers in transition between jobs). This varies between countries owing to differences in unemployment compensation systems that influence how long people spend looking for work when they are unemployed but wish to work.
- *Structural impediments* that effectively exclude willing workers from employment – e.g., a minimum wage set above some workers' marginal product, or high firing costs that discourage hiring when firms are unsure of their longer-term workforce requirements.

Taking all of these influences into account, economists define a "structural unemployment rate" or a "non-accelerating inflation rate of unemployment" (NAIRU).[1] The notion behind the NAIRU (elaborated in Chapter 3) is that the unemployment rate (1 minus the ratio of those employed to the labor force) will seldom fall below the NAIRU unless stimulative policies or an overly ebullient private sector are pushing demand beyond

(*continued*)

Box 2.1 (*continued*)

potential output. Then wage inflation will increase to elicit faster growth of the labor supply than is consistent with normal preferences (reflecting the influences listed above). The higher wage inflation will lead to higher overall inflation, setting in train a process of accelerating inflation as long as the demand for workers exceeds the normal supply. Therefore, in a potential output estimation L is typically measured as the hours of work provided when the labor force is employed up to the point of the NAIRU, estimated from past data.[2]

Potential capital inputs are typically proxied by the nonresidential capital stock based on a "continuous inventory" estimate. The intuition is that the current capital stock is equal to the sum of past investment over many – say 20 – years adjusted for a reasonable assumed depreciation rate. More sophisticated estimates explicitly consider the vintage of the capital stock because older machines provide less service than newer ones, even after adjusting for depreciation.

[1]   In the United States, that level is thought to be about 4–4.5 percent but in a country with large structural impediments to employment, like South Africa, estimates can be well over 20 percent.

[2]   Labor inputs could also be differentiated by skill level.

assume that future potential output is some extrapolation of that trend.[11] An extension of the trend line in Figure 2.1 would represent such a calculation. The premise is that the average growth rate over a historical period – including both cyclically strong and cyclically weak parts – should capture the capacity of an economy to grow on a sustained basis without overheating. Provided the historical period chosen for the calculation genuinely includes cyclically strong and weak periods, it should not be biased by episodes of overheating or recession. However, the trend method is obviously sensitive to the starting point chosen (ideally not a cyclical peak or trough) and is not robust to the problem of structural changes creating

[11]   A linear or (more usually) log-linear trend line is the easiest extrapolation device to get rid of cyclical deviations. But there are more sophisticated algebraic formulations – see, for example, Hodrick–Prescott filters – devised to filter out the cyclical components of output. Even these, however, require assumptions and judgment calls about the parameters used for filtering.

breaks between past and future growth. These pitfalls aside, an attraction of this trend method is that it is relatively easy to carry out.

The production function approach goes many steps further. It systematically relates unmeasurable potential output to measurable parts of the economy (capital and labor inputs) and even the more difficult variable A, which we know is affected by identifiable institutional and technological changes. In other words, the production function approach allows us to use all information on recent or highly likely changes in L, K, or A that have not yet affected Y. Thus, information on changing demographics, labor force participation trends, recent investment in plant and machinery and depreciation rates, recent savings rates (which affect future investment), and recent technological innovations can be used to refine the estimates of potential output.

Let's think through an example. In most advanced countries, birth rates have been falling substantially in recent decades, and now baby boomers are entering retirement age. It has been important to anticipate the deceleration in the working-age population in estimates of current and future potential output. Such events are far easier to pick up and incorporate in a production function approach than in a simple trend approach. (Box 2.2 summarizes an analysis by the staff of the IMF of postcrisis potential growth. It illustrates the importance of information on changes in capital accumulation, employment, and TFP for potential growth estimates in advanced countries but also its limitations.) Thus, while it is more cumbersome to use, the production function approach is likely to give us better estimates of potential output – underscoring the tradeoff between trend analysis, which is easy to use, and techniques that require more analytical effort.

All macroeconomic forecasts are fraught with uncertainties but those stemming from two sources are particularly important for potential output estimates. The first is separating noise and bubbles (which sometimes can persist well beyond the short term) from sustainable trends in past data. A stunning example is the analysis of the United Kingdom surrounding the 2008 financial crisis. The United Kingdom had experienced a rapid

---

Box 2.2 Why Use the Production Function Approach to Estimate Potential Output?

The production function approach incorporates projected departures from historical trends in demographics, investment, and technology that influence potential output. Simple smoothing and extrapolation techniques cannot do this. A recent IMF study in the IMF's World

(continued)

Box 2.2 (*continued*)

Economic Outlook (WEO) of potential output in 10 advanced countries since the late 1990s illustrates the importance of this difference.[1]

In broad terms most advanced countries experienced two economic cycles during 2000-2015. Starting from a strong dot.com-fueled peak in 2000, output growth slowed sharply, but then picked up again during 2004-2007. During the global recession (2008-2009) output actually dropped. A recovery began in 2010. IMF estimates of potential growth (made in 2015 using a production function approach) depart significantly from what would have been estimated based on a simple trend analysis (Figure 2.3).

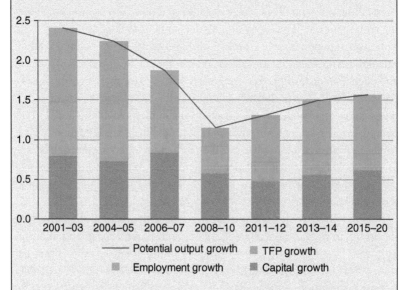

FIGURE 2.3 Contributions of components of potential output growth in 10 advanced countries, 2001–2020 (in percent of aggregate GDP)

First, several developments starting around the turn of the century set in motion a gradual reduction in potential growth even as actual growth rose. Potential growth is estimated to have fallen from about 2.4 percent during 2000–2003 to below 2 percent in 2006–2007. About 80 percent of the slowing was attributable to falling TFP growth as the effects of the exceptionally strong gains in communications and information technology in the late 1990s waned, resources were

(*continued*)

Box 2.2 (*continued*)

shifted into lower-productivity sectors, and human capital growth diminished. The remainder of the slowing came from demographic influences: falling growth of the working-age population and a declining trend in labor force participation.

Second, the 2008 financial crisis caused a fall in the *level* of potential output reflecting a drop in all three of its components and some sectoral reallocation of resources during the actual crisis.[2] A key question was this: would the postcrisis economy (a) grow rapidly to reestablish the precrisis level and trend, (b) revert to the precrisis growth rate but from the new lower base, or (c) grow from this new lower base at a rate below that before the crisis? Estimates of the components of potential growth help answer this question. The IMF estimates that during and right after the crisis (2008–2012), potential growth fell by about 0.5–1 percentage point owing to the negative effects of the crisis on investment, as well as TFP growth (though this effect waned rather rapidly) and potential employment.

Third, some influences on potential growth during 2008–2011 were temporary. TFP growth recovered by the mid-teens, and crisis-related effects on potential employment also faded. Still, the IMF estimates that the crisis had persistent dampening effects on investment and thus the capital stock. Together with continuing adverse demographics, the IMF's estimate for potential growth during 2015–2020 is about 0.5–1 percentage point below the precrisis rate.

[1] This box draws on IMF, Where Are We Headed? Perspectives on Potential Output, *World Economic Outlook* (April 2015), 69–110. Advanced countries covered are Australia, Canada, France, Germany, Italy, Japan, Korea, Spain, the United Kingdom, and the United States.

[2] The level of potential output can fall while the prospective growth of potential output is positive. This is because any estimate of potential growth starts from the current level of potential output.

expansion of its banking industry and real-estate sector for many years. These developments, which drove a considerable acceleration of GDP, were gradually built into the estimates of potential GDP (effectively into A) as a permanent component of output. It is not hard to imagine that after a country has had years of very rapid growth with low inflation and moderate external imbalances, projections of TFP are revised upward.

A common perception was that UK banks were simply startlingly productive rather than that they were feeding and benefiting from asset market bubbles. But when the crash occurred, many banks had to cut back on their lending activity and housing prices plummeted. It quickly became apparent that past estimates of potential output had been inflated by the financial bubble.

The second major uncertainty comes when a country has experienced a large structural change that will affect potential output. An extreme example was in the countries of Central and Eastern Europe in the early 1990s. Under communism, these countries had endured stultifying economic policies and low growth for years. After the collapse of the Soviet order around 1990, an enormous transition from socialism to market economics started. With the opening of trade with foreign markets, liberalization of prices, improvements in legal structures, and stabilization of macroeconomic conditions, output growth was expected to pick up substantially. But given the rapid changes in institutions and major imports of new technology, there was no historical reference point for establishing a base level of TFP or even a starting point for the capital stock (much of which was redundant) and productive capacity. In such circumstances estimates of potential output had to rely on imagination and assumptions drawn from experiences of other countries that had undertaken different, but in some ways comparable, changes.

The production function approach to estimating potential output has many of the same problems as extrapolating trend output, especially if estimates of future TFP are largely projections of past trends. This often occurs because of the uncertainties about the quantitative significance of recent and imminent structural changes. In practice, policymakers typically rely on both trend GDP and production function approaches to come up with concrete estimates of potential output. Final estimates are usually based on a combination of analytical and empirical results with a significant input of judgment.

The conclusion of this discussion about estimating potential output and the cyclical positions is that such calculations, while essential to analysis and policy formulation, are subject to considerable uncertainty, not infrequent errors, and ex post revision. Uncertainty and disagreement about potential output is often at the heart of debates on the right conduct of monetary, fiscal, and financial sector policies.

(ii) Employment and Investment from a Supply-Side Perspective

Producers of goods and services are the supply side of markets for goods and final services. But they are the demand side of markets for factor inputs to the production process – the labor market and the market for capital goods (investment in plant and equipment). In other words, they make the decisions about how much labor and capital to employ.[12] It is important, therefore, to understand and characterize the influences that drive producers' input decisions. These are derived directly from the production function along with the assumption that producers' decisions on inputs are driven by the objective of maximizing profits.

Individual producers hire labor, add to capital stock, and increase production up to the point where they can make profits given the going real wage rate and real cost of capital (typically assumed to equal the real interest rate). Let's look at the process of a firm deciding on the amount of labor to employ. As we saw earlier, for a given capital stock and state of technology, the amount each new worker produces (the marginal product of labor) falls as the amount of labor input rises. Thus a profit-maximizing firm increases its labor input (either the number of employees or the hours each employee works) to the point where the production due to the last hour of labor added equals the real cost of the labor input (that is, compensation measured in terms of output).[13] In Figure 2.4, this decision is characterized in the classic downward sloping marginal product curve. A firm demands labor up to the point where the curve meets the going real wage.

An identical process takes place for decisions on capital inputs, where demand for capital occurs up to the point where the marginal product of capital is equivalent to the cost of capital (often proxied by the real interest rate) in terms of output.

Though this marginal product analysis is a microeconomic construct, aggregating across all firms points to a constraint that has important implications for the macroeconomy, in particular for employment growth: for any given capital stock and state of technology, an increase in the structure of real wages (say because of pressure from labor unions) puts more firms in a position where the real wage they must pay is above labor's marginal product in their firm or industry. In other words, starting from equilibrium where the average real wage equals the marginal product of firms' workers in the aggregate, an increase in the real wage means that firms will cut back on employment or hours employees work so as to avoid making losses at the margin. We will come back to these concepts in Chapter 3 when we discuss wage and price behavior and international competitiveness.

---

[12] We will not go fully into a framework for determining employment and investment. As with any good or service, aggregate labor and capital markets have a supply and demand side. For most individual firms, however, the labor supply curve will appear horizontal at the going real wage.

[13] In the world of real (as opposed to monetary) variables, we use the term "marginal product" of labor and we measure the input cost in terms of units of output. When we are measuring output and wages in money, we use the term "marginal revenue product" of labor.

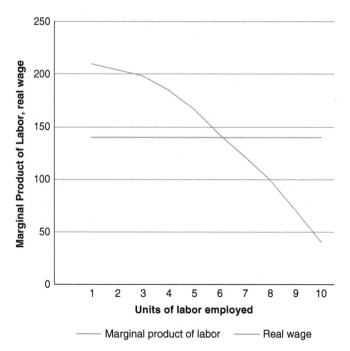

FIGURE 2.4 Marginal product and wages

(iii) The Supply-Side Framework and Potential Output in Developing Countries

Estimating potential output in developing countries follows broadly the same process as for advanced countries. But there is an obvious and important extra dimension: considering whether and how quickly the sources of the disparity in per capita output vis-à-vis advanced countries can be eliminated.[14] In other words, for advanced countries potential growth is about pushing the frontiers of TFP and K/L, while in developing countries it is much more about catching up – or converging – to advanced country levels of K/L and TFP. Obviously, if a developing country can accelerate the increase in its K/L and improve its TFP to levels of advanced countries, it could expect its per capita GDP to rise very rapidly.

In this section we will look at the income convergence issue from two perspectives: first, in the context of a country that is relatively closed to

[14] In the remainder of this section we will focus on per capita GDP (GDP divided by the population of a country), which is the output variable that is comparable across countries insofar as more populous countries would, all other things being equal, have higher absolute GDP.

international capital flows (as was the case for most developing countries during the postwar period until sometime between 1970 and 1990, and continues to be the case for some developing countries) and therefore must rely on domestic saving to raise K/L; and, second, in the context of a country that is open to inflows of capital (as more and more developing countries are) and can make use of foreign saving to raise K/L.

INCOME CATCHUP IN ECONOMIES RELATIVELY CLOSED TO CAPITAL INFLOWS

Recall Figure 2.2, which shows the positions of an advanced country and a developing country in terms of the relationship between Y/L and K/L. We saw that the two main sources of the income gap between advanced countries and developing countries are the latter's lower production possibility curve (PP1 compared to PP2) because of lower TFP and lower capital per worker (K/L) to the left of that in an advanced country.

Another frequent contributor to the income gap is lower employment relative to the working-age population in developing than in advanced countries. There are two channels through which increasing employment raises per capita GDP (although neither can be shown in the two-dimensional figure): first, although at a fixed capital stock, higher employment leads to lower K/L and therefore lower Y/L, output per capita (Y/population) will rise because Y actually increases while the population is unchanged; second, as total income rises saving increases – financing investment, increasing the capital stock, and thereby boosting K/L back to, or possibly beyond, the starting level.

For a country relatively closed to foreign investment, there are three avenues for income convergence with more advanced economies: raising the domestic saving rate so as to increase K/L; increasing the share of the working-age population that actually works (e.g., by eliminating disincentives to firms' hiring and by changing attitudes to female labor force participation); and raising TFP.[15]

Without capital inflows (investment from abroad) the capital stock is constrained by the scope for increasing domestic saving. Even with concerted policy actions to raise the domestic saving rate, this channel to convergence is likely to be slow. Similarly, even if greater labor force

---

[15] A common growth pattern – albeit one that requires consideration in a two-sector (that is, a less aggregated) model – is one where low-productivity, underemployed people move from the rural agricultural sector into a manufacturing sector where there is substantial growth potential through new technology and access to global markets. This process increases both labor force participation and TFP.

participation can be achieved, a slow-growing capital stock will reduce the marginal product of labor and constrain growth. Increases in TFP, therefore, are likely to be critical to income convergence.

It is worth saying more about TFP. It is a portmanteau variable that is influenced by all of the technological, institutional, and structural characteristics of a country. This amalgamation of influences not only affects output directly, but also influences the marginal product of capital and labor, thus exerting a positive influence on decisions to invest and employ workers. It is easy to show this formally by differentiating output with respect to capital and to labor inputs.

$$\delta Y / \delta K = \alpha A K^{-(1-\alpha)} L^{1-\alpha} = \alpha A (K/L)^{-(1-\alpha)} \tag{2.4}$$

$$\delta Y / \delta L = (1 - \alpha) A K^{\alpha} L^{-\alpha} = \alpha A (K/L)^{\alpha} \tag{2.5}$$

When TFP rises, the marginal product (or rate of return) on capital rises so there is a greater inducement to invest. Similarly, the marginal product of labor rises, the equilibrium real wage increases, and more of the working-age population is drawn into the labor force.

The specific influences on TFP are many and varied (see Box 2.3). Obviously looming large is the state of technology – determined, in a low-income country, mainly by technology transfer from richer countries, usually through direct foreign investment. The characteristics of a country's geography and infrastructure (some of which may be excluded from the capital stock) are also key determinants of TFP. Then there is a range of more subtle but equally important influences that can be roughly grouped under the headings of human capital (the skills and energy of the workforce) and governance. The latter is especially varied and ranges from the institutional setting for firms' operations, to corruption, to any excessive regulation of (or government interference in) the productive activities of firms, to the predictability of macroeconomic and legal conditions in a country.

These latter components of TFP are often referred to as "structural" conditions, a term that is frequently criticized for being vague. But insofar as it captures a wide range of influences it probably cannot be labeled more precisely. Understanding the particular structural impediments to growth in a country is critical to formulating sensible policies. In some countries the most egregious structural problems are easily discerned; in others they are less obvious. But in many cases these institutional characteristics are deeply embedded in the cultural fabric, protected by powerful lobbies, and can only be changed by far-sighted and determined governments.

Box 2.3 What Influences Total Factor Productivity (TFP)?

In one unmeasurable variable, TFP encompasses all the institutional and technological characteristics of an economy that determine how efficiently labor and capital can be combined to produce output. Four important components of TFP are discussed below:

Technology: High-income countries are typically at the technological forefront. Proxies for changes in technology in those countries often place heavy weight on indices of educational attainment or specific technologies available in a country. Lower-income countries typically receive transfers of technology through foreign direct investment. The growth of this source of investment is sometimes taken as a proxy for technology growth in those countries.

Infrastructure: A country's infrastructure is not always fully included in its capital stock insofar as it is not used directly in the production of goods and services. But the quality of infrastructure – especially in transportation, telecommunications, energy/power, information technology, and finance – has a substantial influence on production.

Human capital: Some applications of the production function attempt to account for the quality of human capital – education, training, and health of workers – in the measure of L. But human capital is more frequently captured in TFP.

Business environment and governance: The business environment is deeply interlinked with a country's governance. The World Bank's annual *Doing Business* publication[1] implicitly asks this question: what are the obstacles to starting a small business in a country? It then ranks 190 countries on 12 metrics that are important to starting or running a business. The metrics used in that exercise are:

- Getting electricity
- Dealing with construction permits
- Trading across borders
- Paying taxes
- Protecting minority investors
- Registering property

(continued)

Box 2.3 (*continued*)

- Getting credit
- Resolving insolvency
- Enforcing contracts
- Labor market regulation
- Starting a business
- Selling to government

While not exhaustive, these considerations capture many critical aspects of the business environment and governance.

Political and economic stability – including both security issues (war or civil strife being a serious impediment to efficient production) and macroeconomic stability (low and stable inflation, sensible fiscal policies, manageable government, and external debt) – are also essential to a productive business environment.

¹ World Bank, *Doing Business* (2017), www.doingbusiness.org/

INCOME CATCH-UP IN COUNTRIES OPEN TO CAPITAL INFLOWS

The processes behind catchup elaborated in the previous section – raising domestic saving, raising TFP through technology transfer and institutional reform, and increasing labor force participation – can be slow. Once we admit international capital and labor flows, the transitional dynamics (that is, the rate at which relatively low per capita GDP countries catch up to relatively high per capita GDP countries) should speed up.

Consider the effects of labor and capital flows between two countries with *potentially* identical levels of A – one country starting with a higher capital–labor ratio and therefore higher GDP per capita than the other. We know that diminishing returns to capital mean that the marginal product of capital (or the rate of return on capital) is higher, the lower the capital–labor ratio. Thus, in search of higher returns, capital should flow from richer (high K/L) countries to poorer (low K/L) countries. Conversely, labor will flow from poorer to richer countries.[16]

The incentives for labor and capital mobility from differing marginal returns to factors of production can be stunningly large. Lipschitz et al., for

---

[16] Later in this chapter we will see that remittances from workers employed abroad feed into a country's GNP, a more inclusive measure of output than GDP.

example, find that for identical levels of TFP, the marginal return on capital in a number of Central and Eastern European countries in 2002 would have been some 5–8 times that of advanced countries in Western Europe.[17] In theory, significant flows of capital (from west to east) and labor (from east to west) between two countries with differing initial capital–labor ratios could, in the extreme, completely offset underlying differences in saving rates and working population growth rates, leading to rapid and full convergence of per capita GDP across countries.

In practice, the incentives for capital flows to capital-scarce countries are much reduced (and at times even disappear) because TFP is typically substantially lower in the poorer (capital-scarce) countries. Moreover, in cases where TFP is high enough to elicit very large inflows, the lower K/L countries will be hard pressed to absorb these inflows without severe disruptions. (Developments in the Baltic countries – exemplified by the case study on Latvia in the online companion volume illustrate this point.) But, as discussed in Chapters 6 and 7, in many cases sizable inflows will occur and will be an important influence on developments and at times vulnerability to financial crises in recipient countries.

SO DOES INCOME CONVERGENCE ACTUALLY OCCUR?

Ultimately, whether or not convergence actually occurs is an empirical question. Do historical data support the conclusions of the simple economic model: that, barring identifiable impediments to technology transfer and/or significant differences in saving rates (in a closed economy) or barriers to capital flows, income convergence should take place, even if slowly? There has been a large amount of empirical work on what is called "the convergence hypothesis." On the whole, these studies broadly suggest that although the last decade has seen remarkably rapid increases in per capita GDP in many developing countries, longer-term data are far less consistent with the convergence hypothesis.

- First, on the basis of highly comprehensive data (on per capita GDP covering 118 countries during 1960–1985), Barro and Sala-i-Martin find countries' 25-year growth rates to be essentially uncorrelated with initial (1960) levels of per capita GDP.[18] In other words,

[17] Lipschitz, Leslie, Lane, Timothy, and Mourmouras, Alex, Real Convergence, Capital Flows and Monetary Policy: Notes on the European Transition Countries, in Susan Schadler (ed.), *Euro Adoption in Central and Eastern Europe: Opportunities and Challenges*, IMF, Washington, DC (April 2005), 61–69.

[18] Barro, Robert, and Sala-i-Martin, Xavier, *Economic Growth*, MIT Press, Cambridge, MA, 2004.

a country that starts out with a low per capita GDP does not grow faster over a 25-year period than a country with a higher initial level of per capita GDP. The gap between rich and poor does not systematically tend to fall simply because of the diminishing return to capital and the chain of influences it produces.

- Second, however, narrowing the sample to a more homogeneous group of countries or regions – e.g., 20 OECD countries during 1960–1985 or the 50 states of the United States during 1980–2000 – produces a clear pattern of income convergence. Among these more homogeneous samples of countries – that is, among countries with similar institutions, legal frameworks, and other attributes that affect decisions on investment and production – convergence is observed. In these more narrowly defined samples, lower per capita GDP countries or (within the United States) states systematically grow faster than higher per capita GDP countries or states.

These empirical regularities have led to a fairly widespread view that income convergence across countries is not "absolute" but rather is "conditional." It will only occur if "structural" conditions in the lower per capita GDP countries support growth to approximately the same extent as those in the most advanced countries. Such influences are likely to work mainly through factors and policies that we have identified in TFP.

Not surprisingly, therefore, much importance has been placed on institutional differences across countries. Countries where the rule of law, the costs of doing business, or macroeconomic stability are distinctly inferior to practices in richer countries are not likely to be able to achieve the same TFP or K/L as rich countries, so they will remain permanently poorer. This type of assessment is the basis for a number of multilateral institutions (the IMF, the World Bank, and the OECD, for example) to place substantial emphasis on "structural" reform in their policy recommendations to all countries, but particularly those that lag behind per capita output levels of major industrial countries.

2 The Demand Side

Aggregate demand does not always equal supply potential. When consumers cut their spending (perhaps because of insecurity about prospects for employment or asset market valuations) or investors reduce their acquisition of machinery or structures (perhaps because the cost of borrowing or uncertainty about the strength of future final demand rises), producers and retailers typically experience an unintended accumulation of inventories that is costly to finance. This, in turn, may lead companies to cut employment and the utilization of production capacity as they try to adjust to the lower than expected level of demand and the excessive level of inventories. This behavior is prudent at the level of the individual company, but when aggregated across the whole economy it raises job insecurity and further reduces consumption. A recessionary vicious circle can therefore be set off.

The duration of any such downturn depends on its specific circumstances and on how quickly prices and wages adjust. It is also influenced by whether governments pursue countercyclical fiscal policies (automatic or discretionary changes in taxes and spending), central banks pursue countercyclical monetary policies (changes in interest rates or quantitative measures), and such policies are effective. Private sector expectations also play a role, and they may be influenced (whether deliberately or inadvertently) by government policies. Therefore a sound framework for analyzing the demand side of an economy separately from the supply side is critical for judging the causes of a specific cycle, the need for countercyclical policies, and the likely economic response to them.

Our understanding of aggregate demand and the analytic focus on demand-side fluctuations is due to the work of John Maynard Keynes in response to the Great Depression of the 1930s when demand persistently fell far short of potential supply.[19] The decade-long slump forced economists to widen their view of influences that drove activity from a rather narrow focus on supply-side conditions to demand-side conditions as well.

The Keynesian revolution elicited a change in focus as well as an enormous amount of work on macroeconomic data catchment systems – initially in advanced countries but subsequently in almost all countries, albeit at different degrees of reliability. To understand the sources of the depression and decide on policy responses it was necessary to have aggregate data not only on output and employment, but also on income and demand and their principal components. The data collection was driven by the need to inform policy decisions in a world where macroeconomic policy had come to be seen as a key governmental responsibility.

The objective of this section is to use this data catchment system – principally the National Accounts data on demand and its components – to understand the channels through which various shocks feed through the

---

[19] Great Britain's depression got a head start on other countries with the return to the gold standard in 1925. Keynes's innovative thinking about macroeconomics was already in evidence in his opposition to this policy.

economy.[20] A surprising amount of information can emerge from an analysis of the identities that comprise the National Accounts.

One caveat is important. Much of this section has to do with static ex post algebraic identities – that is, how the components of GDP measured in different ways must add up. These identities are useful because they discipline macroeconomic analysis. But there is always more to the story. Any independent ("exogenous" in the jargon) change in a category of spending will elicit a number of "endogenous" behavioral changes in other variables (prices, wages, interest rates, and expectations), which in turn cause changes in other categories of spending. A full analysis has to trace all of the dynamic effects of the initial change. For example, for a given level of GDP, an increase in government expenditure may crowd out private expenditure or widen the current account deficit, and this is what we would find in the identities. But if GDP is far below potential, the additional expenditure may elicit increases in output and employment to meet the additional demand, so that no (or smaller) crowding out or balance of payments effects occur. The behavioral transmission channels will be implicit (and, at times, explicit) later in this chapter and in subsequent chapters.

a Expenditure and GDP

There are a number of ways to build the measure of GDP but we want to focus here on the demand or aggregate expenditure approach. (Box 2.4 explains how to build the same measure of GDP through production- and income-based approaches.)

The aggregate expenditure approach starts from the observation that everything produced leads to expenditure. If a company produces goods and doesn't sell them they are added to inventories and are part of inventory investment. Even though this may be unintended investment, it is included as part of expenditure.

---

[20] The term National Accounts refers to the set of data collected and published by the government on a country's aggregate economic activity – its output, income, and expenditure. These data are subject to internationally agreed definitions and a systematized set of consistency tests. They include aggregate measures of activity – GDP being the most frequently cited – and their components – e.g., consumption and investment as components of aggregate expenditure, wages, and profits as components of aggregate income, and agricultural output and industrial production as components of aggregate output. In this chapter we are concerned chiefly with real flow variables (those that are measured over a specified period of time and adjusted to eliminate the effects of price changes), but in subsequent chapters we will deal with nominal flows (measured at current prices) and stocks like wealth that are measured at a point in time.

Measuring real GDP (by expenditure, output, or income) raises a slew of practical difficulties. For example, how do we measure services that are traded on the black market (e.g., a plumber who works for unrecorded cash payments in order to evade taxes) or services for which we do not have a price (e.g., many government services)? Some services that add to

---

Box 2.4 Other Ways of Measuring GDP

GDP is the sum of all output of goods and services in the economy. It can be measured from three perspectives: expenditure (as discussed in the text), output or production, and income. We explain the latter two approaches in this box.

GDP from the vantage point of *output or production* is measured by summing the value-added of each producer in the economy at constant market prices. Because one sector's output can be input for another sector and part of the latter's gross output, we have to avoid double counting and measure only the *value-added* (measured at constant market prices) of each sector.

$$GDP = \Sigma(O_i - Intermediate\ consumption_i) \qquad (2.6)$$

O_i = gross output of sector i (often measured as total sales of the sector)

Intermediate consumption$_i$ = raw materials, goods, and services purchased by enterprises in sector i and consumed or used up as inputs in production

In practice, data for this approach are more often used for micro- than macroeconomic analysis.

The income-based measure of GDP recognizes that all output sold produces income for someone – broadly, wages, company operating surpluses, and other production expenses. Thus we can measure GDP at what is called basic prices by summing all income from production activity and indirect taxes attached to factors of production (such as payroll taxes and property taxes) less subsidies on factors of production.

$$GDP = \Sigma\,W_i + \Sigma\,Profilts_i + \Sigma\,Indirect\ taxes\ on\ factors_i$$
$$- \Sigma\,Subsidies\ on\ factors_i \qquad (2.7)$$

W = wage income
i includes all productive sectors of the economy

(continued)

Box 2.4 (*continued*)

This measure of GDP will differ from measures at market prices by the amount of indirect taxes on products (e.g., sales taxes) less product-specific subsidies. We will see in Chapter 3 that this offers a view of GDP that is central to macroeconomic analysis.

By way of illustration, data for Canada are shown in Table 2.1.

TABLE 2.1 *Canada:* 2013 *GDP*
(billions of 2013 Canadian dollars)

GDP by incomes		GDP by production	
Gross value-added at basic prices	1777.2	Gross value-added at basic prices	1777.2
Subsidies on production	−5.4	Gross output	3353.2
Taxes on production	86.7	Intermediate consumption	1576.0
Wages and salaries	828.7		
Employers' social contributions	132.4		
Gross mixed income	216.4		
Gross operating surplus	518.4		

Source: Government of Canada, Statistics Canada, Supply and Use Tables (15–602-x) 2013 SUT – Canada – S Level.xlsx

measured GDP (e.g., pollution abatement) do not add to output in a true sense because they simply reverse the (unrecorded) negative value-added of another industry. Separating pure price increases (which should not add to real GDP) from quality improvements (which should) can be difficult. For example, increases in prices of computers may reflect more sophisticated computers and should not be fully included in the GDP deflator. Methods for dealing with these sources of inaccuracy in measuring true GDP exist – some satisfactory, others less so – but we will not go into them. Suffice to say, GDP is a useful, if imperfect, measure of productive economic activity.

GDP, the most common measure of activity, is equal to all expenditure by residents (consumption, fixed investment, and inventory investment), minus that part of spending that is satisfied by nonresident producers (imports of goods and services), plus spending by nonresidents on goods and services produced domestically (exports). The following is the National Accounts identity for GDP.

$$GDP = C + IF + IN + X - M \tag{2.8}$$

C = consumption by the private sector and the government

IF = fixed investment by the private sector and the government

IN = inventory investment

X = exports (spending by nonresidents on domestic output)

M = imports (consumption and investment satisfied by nonresident production)

This definition of GDP can be disaggregated in various ways to help understand and assess questions about the demand side of the economy, the nature of macroeconomic shocks, and likely effects of policy responses to shocks.

b Sources of Demand

The identity represented in equation (2.8) sets the stage for many different ways of slicing up GDP. Analysis of components is often in terms of growth rates (percentage changes) rather than levels. But percentage change calculations are precluded for components that may switch from positive to negative (such as inventory accumulation and the foreign balance [X – M]), so percentage point contributions to GDP growth are often shown for these items.[21]

Often, in assessing the robustness of near-term activity, analysts are interested in the strength of domestic demand (over which domestic countercyclical policies have some degree of influence) as opposed to nonresident or foreign demand for domestic production. We therefore see references to domestic demand or total domestic demand – i.e., the sum of all consumption and all investment by residents. It is GDP excluding the part that is exported and without subtracting the part satisfied by imports. GDP therefore consists of total domestic demand plus net exports, sometimes called the foreign balance.[22]

---

[21] The percentage point contribution is calculated as the absolute change in the variable from the previous period, divided by the level of GDP in the previous period, multiplied by 100. A smaller positive foreign balance (or reduced, but still positive, inventory investment) would show a negative contribution to growth. If we showed contributions for all demand components, they would sum to the growth rate.

[22] Frequently a weakening of the foreign balance is called a negative contribution to GDP but this is not always correct. A fall in FB does reduce GDP if a larger *proportion* of a *given* level of TDD is satisfied through imports. But if C + IF + IN rise by the same amount as M and there is no change in X, the fall in the FB neither raises nor lowers GDP. The GDP

$$GDP = TDD + FB \qquad\qquad (2.9)$$

TDD = total domestic demand
FB = foreign balance = X – M

The sources of domestic demand are also important for assessing the cyclical strength of an economy. An important consideration here is the division between final domestic demand and inventory accumulation – that part of investment that is production stockpiled by producers or retailers. Inventory investment tends to fluctuate around a low amount relative to the size of the economy and often is negative (when producers and retailers draw down inventories, for example, in response to unexpectedly strong final demand or a structural change that reduces the efficient level of inventories). Insofar as inventory accumulation (or decumulation) is unintended (i.e., it results from a gap between what producers expected to sell when they made their production decisions and what they actually sell in a given period), significant inventory accumulation often presages a cyclical downturn in GDP, and, conversely, a significant drop in inventories may signal a cyclical upswing.

$$TDD = FDD + IN \qquad\qquad (2.10)$$

FDD = final domestic demand

Consumption can be divided into nondurable consumption (such as food or services) and durable consumption (such as household appliances), which may have some investment-like attributes. Investment can be disaggregated into spending on machinery and equipment, spending on building structures or plant, and spending on inventories (as discussed above). The first and second of these are called fixed investment as opposed to inventory investment. The composition of spending as between consumption and investment has obvious implications for the future. For example, a consumption boom especially on durables might be expected to be temporary as many durable consumption expenditures are one-off. A bulge in investment spending on plant and equipment, in contrast, is likely to presage greater capacity and higher output in the future.

Yet another window on the robustness of economic activity is the strength of private demand. Final domestic demand comprises private consumption and fixed investment and government consumption and

identity – which measures domestic production – includes imports in C and I, and imports must therefore be subtracted through the larger negative FB term.

investment.[23] In well-designed countercyclical fiscal policy, softness in C_p and I_p would raise concerns about cyclical weakness and may prompt consideration of raising C_g and I_g.

$$FDD = C_p + IF_p + C_g + IF_g \qquad (2.11)$$

C_p = private consumption
IF_p = private fixed investment
C_g = government investment
IF_g = government fixed investment

The discussion in the previous few paragraphs should not be taken to suggest that domestic demand is more important than exports or imports. Increasing exports is frequently a central part of a country's growth strategy in the long run (a small or poor country can vastly expand its growth opportunities by capturing export market share), and the foreign balance can be a critical shock absorber in the short run (producers facing cyclical weakness at home can try to export more abroad or increase penetration of domestic markets previously dominated by imports). Also, the foreign balance can help to smooth domestic consumption over time. For example, a crop failure that reduces the available domestic supply of rice can elicit an increase in rice imports (a drop in FB) to cushion domestic consumers against a sharp drop in rice consumption.

Most analysis of exports and imports focuses on the balance of payments accounts (discussed in Chapter 7) rather than on the National Accounts framework. There is a strict correspondence between the two, but it requires looking beyond GDP, for while GDP covers trade in goods and services, it does not include other sources of income from abroad or income paid to nonresidents. These flows are included in the external accounts and in a broader National Accounts definition of economic activity gross national income (GNI).

Gross national income (which is sometimes called gross national product or GNP) is GDP plus net factor income from abroad:

$$GNI = GDP + NFI \qquad (2.12)$$

GNI = gross national income
NFI = net factor income from abroad

---

[23] Government spending in the GDP accounts includes only spending on goods and services. It does not include the parts of government spending (covered in the fiscal accounts in Chapter 5) on transfers. These categories of fiscal expenditure are not government purchases of goods or services, but rather a mechanism whereby the government finances private spending on goods and services.

NFI comprises net income from labor services (i.e., earnings from domestic residents working abroad minus payments to foreign residents working domestically) and net income from capital services (e.g., interest on loans made to foreigners minus interest paid on foreign borrowing). Depending on the structure of a country's economy, the difference between GNI and GDP can be trivial or significant in assessing a country's economic performance. There are countries where remittances by residents working abroad are a significant part of income, and where fluctuations in this source of income are important for domestic living standards, for the financing of investment, and thus for growth. Box 2.5 provides examples of countries where net labor or capital income is important.

Gross national disposable income is GNI augmented by net transfers from or to abroad (TR) that are unrelated to factor earnings. Usually these are public foreign aid or private philanthropy.

$$GNDI = GNI + TR \qquad (2.13)$$

or

$$GNDI = C_p + IF_p + C_g + IF_g + IN + X - M + NFI + TR \quad (2.14)$$

$GNDI$ = gross national disposable income
TR = net transfers from or to abroad

Box 2.5 Are Differences between GDP and GNI Important?

For many countries NFI is rather stable and small so levels of and even movements in GNI and GDP are similar. But some countries have structural characteristics that make the difference large, and usually once a gap opens up it tends to persist. If the gap is volatile, not only levels but also growth rates of GDP and GNI differ significantly over time.

To know when it is important to look beyond GDP as a measure of income, we must consider the situation of each country. For example, in 2015 Thailand (shown in Table 2.2) had a gap between GDP and GNI of only 5 percent of the level of GNI. In sharp contrast, in Ireland GDP has for several decades been substantially higher than GNI. This is at least in part because Ireland has a large amount of investment from nonresidents that gives rise to substantial profit remittances to foreign entities (that is, negative NFI). In another set of circumstances, an oil exporter like Kuwait has huge reserves of accumulated financial wealth (much of it invested abroad) and thus large interest earnings from foreign investments (positive NFI). And Lesotho, which

Box 2.5 (*continued*)

has had large remittances from nationals employed in mining in neighboring South Africa, also has high positive NFI so that GDP was about 80 percent of GNI in 2015.

TABLE 2.2 *Ireland, Kuwait, Lesotho, and Thailand: GDP and GNI Measures, 2015*
(billions of US dollars, and ratios)

	GDP	NFI	GNI	GDP/GNI
Ireland	283.7	−57.6	226.1	1.25
Kuwait	114.0	14.8	128.9	0.88
Lesotho	2.3	0.3	2.6	0.88
Thailand	399.2	−20.7	378.5	1.05

Sources: World Bank National Accounts data, drawing on OECD National Accounts data files. http://databank.worldbank.org/data/reports.aspx? source=&country=KWT

The last four terms of equation (2.14) are identical (or closely related) to the current account balance in the balance of payments accounts.

$$GNDI = C_p + IF_p + C_g + IF_g + IN + CAB = TDD + CAB \quad (2.15)$$

$CAB = X - M + NFI + TR$ = current account balance of the balance of payments

Box 2.6 provides a summary example of the National Accounts from the demand side.

c The Real Resource Constraint

Now that we have reviewed the basic definitions of activity as seen from the demand side, we can parse various arrangements of the National Accounts identity. The aim is to isolate the origin of shocks to demand and consider subsequent effects from the shock within the constraint that the identity, in whatever precise form it is expressed, must always hold. The starting point will be a rearrangement of the GNDI identity called the real resource constraint.

Essentially, as presaged in the supply part of this chapter, this identity shows that domestic investment, which builds the capital stock for future production, is constrained by resources available from domestic saving and

Box 2.6 National Accounts Measures of Economic Activity –
Schematic Summary of Expenditure Components

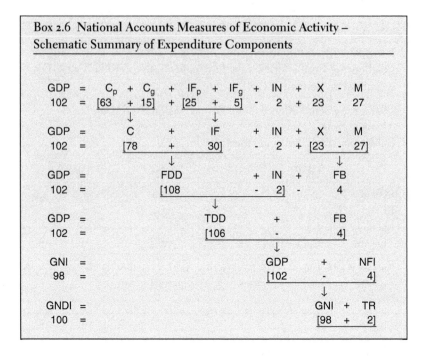

from foreign saving channeled to the domestic economy. The real resource constraint is the summary expression for the total amount of resources available for domestic investment.

We start from the definition for GNDI and aggregate private and public consumption and private, inventory, and public investment. This gives us

$$GNDI = C + I + CAB \qquad (2.16)$$

$$I = IF + IN$$

Gross national saving is GNDI minus aggregate consumption (GNDI – C), so rearranging terms we get the real resource constraint

$$I = S - CAB \qquad (2.17)$$

S = gross national saving

or, expressing the current account position as a deficit,

$$I = S + CAD \qquad (2.18)$$

CAD = –CAB = current account deficit

Thus domestic investment is constrained by the resources available to accommodate it – the sum of domestic saving (due to abstaining from consumption) and the resource transfer from abroad (through the current account deficit).

If we want to focus more on fiscal policy – perhaps to think about how government consumption and taxes might influence domestic saving, investment, and the current account – we can disaggregate saving into its private and government components so that

$$I = S_p + S_g + CAD \qquad (2.19)$$

S_p = private saving
S_g = government saving = government revenue – government current
  spending

If we want to focus on private investment (I_p, as against total investment) we can rearrange the equation by subtracting government investment from both sides and noting that the overall government surplus is equal (by definition) to government saving (government revenue less government current spending) minus government investment. This tells us that, at the end of the day, a drop in the government's budget surplus (or an increase in the deficit) must, by definition, be matched by either a reduction in private investment or an increase in the external current account deficit unless it is offset by higher private savings.

$$I_p = S_p + GS + CAD \qquad (2.20)$$

I_p = total private investment (fixed and inventory)
GS = government surplus = $S_g - I_g$

If we want to focus on total domestic demand (TDD is typically called absorption in the context of analyzing the real resource constraint) and the current account of the balance of payments, we can define absorption as total consumption plus investment and, rearranging equation (2.16), write

$$CAD = GDA - GNDI \qquad (2.21)$$

$GDA = TDD$ = domestic absorption

That is, the current account deficit is the difference between expenditure (or "absorption") and income.

Each of these arrangements of the National Accounts identity or the real resource constraint facilitates analysis, providing a disciplined framework for considering the nature of shocks to the economy, the cyclical position of the economy, and the likely effects of countercyclical policies. Box 2.7 illustrates these formulations with data for the United States.

We started the discussion of the real resource constraint with the statement that the identities must always hold. This is true. However, there are myriad adjustments to prices and activity that take place in the process of equilibrating saving (domestic and foreign) with investment. These are important to policy decisions at any point in time, but are not always obvious from looking at the identities alone.

For example, consider a sudden spike in global uncertainty because of some geopolitical tension that frightens consumers. Domestic saving suddenly rises but domestic investment does not. Imports fall, but assuming this chain of reactions was happening in all countries, export markets would also contract. In such circumstances, the real resource constraint might be brought into balance by price and wage adjustments but more likely there would be an involuntary increase in inventory investment and in subsequent periods lower output and employment which would curtail saving. In such circumstances, and

---

Box 2.7 Expenditure, Saving, Investment, and the Current Account in the United States

Here we show key National Accounts concepts with data from the US Bureau of Economic Analysis.[1] The data are in current (rather than constant) prices, anticipating topics in Chapter 3.

In first panel of Figure 2.5, the top line shows GDA (or, equivalently, total domestic demand). This aggregate comprises four components: private consumption, private investment, government consumption, and government investment. Private investment here includes inventory accumulation. Notably, GDA exceeds GNDI with the difference made up by the current account balance (CAB) (see equation [2.21] and Box 2.6). CAB (or GNDI–GDA) is shown in the bottom line of the panel and is negative, indicating a resource transfer from abroad.

The second panel of Figure 2.5 partitions the CAB into the saving–investment (S–I) components of the government and the private sector (as in equation [2.20]).[2] (Note the difference between the scales of the two panels.) The top line shows private S–I. In 2005–2007 it is negative, thus driving the CAB (the bottom line in the figure) lower (i.e., into larger deficit). But in 2008–2016 it is

Box 2.7 (*continued*)

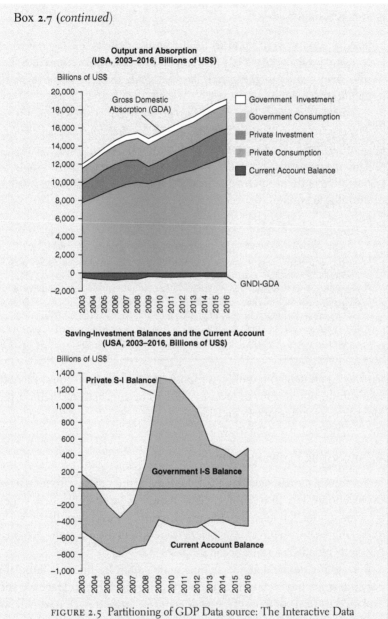

FIGURE 2.5 Partitioning of GDP Data source: The Interactive Data Application of the US Department of Commerce, Bureau of Economic Analysis (https://www.bea.gov/itable/index.cfm)

(*continued*)

Box 2.7 (*continued*)

positive, thus driving up CAB (reducing the deficit). But even after 2007 the positive private S–I is swamped by negative government S–I (the shaded area in the panel), so that CAB remains negative (in deficit) throughout.

The data presage the discussion of fiscal policy in Chapter 5. The 2008 financial crisis and the recession that followed led to a drop in private investment and a jump in private saving. The government deficit (its I–S balance), however, rose sharply, reflecting both the automatic fiscal stabilizers and discretionary fiscal stimulus to counter the recession.

[1] Thanks are due to Robert Kornfeld of the Bureau of Economic Analysis of the US Department of Commerce for clarifying our understanding of the data.

[2] Saving is measured from the income side of the data catchment system and investment from the expenditure side, and a statistical discrepancy (SD) between the two measurement systems exists. It reflects the use of different data sources and sampling errors. Thus, in fact, CAB = Private S–I + SD + Government S–I. For simplicity of graphical exposition, we include SD in private S–I. For example, in 2010, CAB (–446) = Private S–I (1264.6) + SD (49.2) + Government S–I (–1759.8), but we have shown Private S–I as 1313.8.

---

barring a counteracting policy response, the saving–investment identity would hold but at a lower level of GDP. The mechanisms behind the identities are important to consider.

d Forecasting Economic Activity

Policy formulation proceeds not only from a diagnosis of the current state of the economy but also from a view about where it is headed – i.e., a projection for the next few quarters or years. This section, therefore, is a brief digression on forecasting before we return to the use of the National Accounts identities for diagnostic purposes.[24]

Forecasting demand and its components – both for the near term (1–2 years) and for the medium term (3–5 years) – is difficult. Here we will explain the broad contours of methodologies for forecasting, but we will not

---

[24] An aside on terminology: a more pernickety writer would shun the word "forecast" in favor of "projection," but we will follow common usage in a less stringent use of terms, so that the terms "forecast" and "projection" are used interchangeably. The objection to "forecast" (or "prediction") is that it smacks of soothsaying. Mostly what economic forecasters produce are *projections* – i.e., forecasts that are explicitly contingent on a given set of assumptions.

go into the precise mechanics of how to make forecasts. The purpose is to characterize the underlying calculations that have gone into forecasts that are publicly available from national governments and institutions such as the IMF, the OECD, and the World Bank.

Most near-term forecasts of economic activity are concerned with GDP and work up from forecasts of the individual components of demand. Recall

$$GDP = C_p + IF_p + C_g + IF_g + IN + X - M \qquad (2.22)$$

Typically, forecasts for the government consumption and investment components are taken from information on the government's intentions as outlined in forward-looking budget plans. If the forecaster considers some elements of the budget implausible, the expenditure projections will usually be adapted accordingly (see Chapter 5). Forecasts for exports and imports are typically made in the context of the balance of payments analysis (see Chapter 7) and depend mainly on current international competitiveness (some measure of the real exchange rate – see Chapter 3) and forecasts of demand at home (for imports) and abroad (for exports).

For projections of private domestic demand – consumption and investment – two (complementary) approaches are used. First, forecasters estimate past relationships between leading indicators and subsequent developments in consumption and investment or simply assess qualitatively the direction of change of leading indicators. The precise leading indicators differ from country to country: typical leading indicators for consumption are consumer confidence surveys, weekly hours worked, wage developments, and applications for unemployment benefits; and for investment, surveys of business confidence, new orders of capital goods for future delivery, capacity utilization, and building permits issued.

Second, the substantial literature on theories of household consumption behavior and firm investment decisions yields structural relationships that can be used together with econometrically estimated parameters to make forecasts. Consumption spending is typically determined by variables such as current income, expected future income, and wealth (as in the Permanent Income hypothesis and the Life Cycle Saving hypothesis).[25] Projections of fixed investment are commonly based on an accelerator model where they depend on expected future output growth. Also, as we saw in the supply-side section, the cost of capital should have an influence. Inventory investment is

---

[25] It is usually assumed that the marginal propensity to consume out of income is reasonably stable on average over the cycle at around 0.70–0.75 in advanced countries, substantially lower in some Asian countries, and perhaps much higher in poor countries supported by aid.

obviously exceptionally difficult to forecast because it absorbs unexpected developments in final demand. Unless the starting point is a cyclical peak or trough (so that a correction seems inevitable), a stable accumulation of inventories in line with economic activity is typically assumed.

Any good set of projections will be carefully checked for internal consistency. For example, consumption should be consistent with the best estimates of household income; if it is not, there would be a sharp change in household saving behavior that will need to be explained. Household income cannot be inconsistent with projections or assumptions about employment, average weekly working hours, and wage developments.

Two main drawbacks of relying on econometric relationships militate toward greater reliance on judgment and the checking of initial estimates against leading indicators. Most importantly, estimated relationships frequently are not stable over time, especially if there are discontinuities (e.g., changes in the structure of taxes) in the environment, so the exercise of judgment outside a structural model is impossible to avoid.[26] In addition, the more sophisticated the structural modeling approach used, the more exacting the data requirements and the less likely that such data will be available on a reliable basis.

Forecasts of the components of GDP are summed to reach an aggregate. At the aggregate level, again, consistency checks with other information are important. Projections of GDP built up from components are tested against those based on leading indicators – which, at least for advanced countries, are typically composites of variables such as surveys of purchasing managers, shipping data, and speed of delivery of orders from suppliers to vendors – and adjusted for seeming inconsistencies. A good deal of qualitative judgment is inevitable and sensible.

Medium- to long-term forecasts are made from the supply-side framework explained earlier. These serve as an important consistency check on the short-term forecasts. Specifically, any output gap should close over a period of 3–5 years. If the forecasts do not produce this alignment of

---

[26] Macroeconomic relationships – like that between consumption and income – are an aggregation of myriad optimizing decisions by individual agents. It is plausible that the parameters of these optimizing decisions are stable so that each agent will respond predictably to various changes in the environment for consumption (such as actual or anticipated shifts in taxation). But estimates of the broad relationship between consumption and income are generally crude aggregations that omit the underlying parameters that enter into the individual microeconomic optimization. If, alternatively, we base our estimates on the optimization process of some postulated (but invisible) "representative agent," we will have to assume parameters rather than estimating them. We will probably also miss significant differences across the diverse universe of individual consumers.

demand- and supply-side approaches, it is necessary to reassess (a) whether the estimate of potential output is plausible and, if so, (b) what is preventing or delaying a closing of the gap between actual and potential output. To the extent that there is some structural rigidity in the economy that is preventing a return to "potential" output the notion of "potential" would need to be revised contingent on this rigidity.

3 Playing with the Concepts: Macroeconomic Shocks and Policy Responses

In this section we will consider two different shocks – a new aid transfer and a deterioration in the current account balance – to illustrate the thought process of tracing the effects of a shock or determining the best macroeconomic policy response. In these thought experiments, we will see how different configurations of the real resource constraint help pinpoint the problem, its effects, and the constraints on policy responses.

a A New Aid Transfer

Let's consider first how we would trace the impact of a foreign inflow shock on the macroeconomy. Let's consider the specific case of a low-income developing country receiving a large increase in official aid in the form of a current transfer. Obviously the intent of the aid-giver is to finance a process that raises the recipient country's per capita GDP. Considering the aid inflow in the context of the National Accounts identities helps determine whether the conditions are in place for that result to occur.

In the first instance, the aid inflow reduces the current account deficit and raises government revenue (as aid takes the form of a transfer to the government).

$$I_p = S_p + GS \uparrow + CAD \downarrow \qquad (2.23)$$

Suppose the aid is spent on imported goods – e.g., medication or tanks. Both GS and CAD go back to their initial levels because of increased government spending on the one hand and the inflow of imports on the other. In this case, in economics jargon, "the transfer is fully effected" – i.e., the financial transfer has resulted in a real resource flow insofar as the additional government spending has elicited an inflow of imports. The low-income country is probably better off.

But suppose, alternatively, that the government decides to spend the aid funds on nontraded goods – that is, the sorts of goods that can only be supplied domestically and cannot be imported.[27] Let's take the case of road construction. GS rises with the inflow and falls back as in the previous case, but there is no immediate offsetting increase in imports (and thus CAD). How will the terms in the identity be changed so as to ensure that the equation will balance? We know that it will have to balance in the recorded data. But how it gets to balance and at what level of GDP depends on the amount of spare capacity in the economy (the output gap) and various other factors.

Let's say actual output is below potential so there is an abundance of unemployed labor. When the government spends the aid on road construction, new workers are hired, income and output go up, and some mix of higher saving, private investment, and imports serve to balance the equation. This scenario gives rise to a happy story about how the transfer is effected.

Or it may be that there is no output gap or abundance of qualified labor so that the spending on road construction bids up wages across the economy and then prices. This reduces the competitiveness of the export sector so that nontraded goods production effectively crowds out export production (CAD↑), effecting the transfer in a less benign fashion. Indeed, if competitiveness and export growth are critical to the development of the economy, this mechanism for effecting the transfer may be quite disruptive.

Having a sense of the existing output gap is critical to the policies of both the aid donor and the aid recipient. If the aid is going to finance traded goods, problems are unlikely, and aid is likely to improve the circumstances of the recipient. If, however, aid is financing nontraded production and the availability of qualified labor is scant, sequencing (providing training or workers from abroad before providing aid devoted to road construction) or more gradual disbursement of aid needs to be considered. For example, some research finds that aid is most effective at raising living standards if accompanied by a program of structural reform that prepares a country for efficient absorption of aid.

[27] The concept of nontraded goods (which implicitly also includes services) is important and will be used repeatedly throughout this book. It is not straightforward. Economists tend to think of nontraded goods chiefly as services provided by doctors, lawyers, or hairdressers, or by domestic real estate, as opposed to manufactures or commodities that can easily be imported. For a small country with the financial resources to pay for imports, certain goods (e.g., wheat and tractors) are available (effectively without limit) in global markets at global market prices. But the domestic availability of other components of demand, like road construction or services, cannot be increased quickly or without significant price changes. These are in effect nontraded goods.

These are just the starting considerations. More broadly, one must look at other data – prices, wages, the real exchange rate, fiscal and monetary accounts, and the balance of payments – to flesh out the story. Subsequent chapters will provide ideas on how to go about this task.

b A Shock to a Country's Current Account Position

The second shock to consider is a large increase in a country's current account deficit. It may be that the country is still able to borrow on international markets to finance the larger deficit so the problem may not be immediately dire. Also, as we will see in later chapters, if a country has a fully flexible exchange rate, the increase in the deficit will start a self-correcting process. The following analysis, however, will consider the frequently encountered case where foreign debt is already high and a country does not let its exchange rate respond fully to market forces. Then financing the deficit through foreign borrowing in the first instance, but adopting policies to reduce the deficit relatively quickly is important. The National Accounts identities are key to determining the source of the current account shock and how to best correct it.

Consider the definitions of a current account deficit that we get by rearranging the national accounts identities:

$$CAD = M - X - NFI - TR \qquad (2.24)$$

a balance of payments approach: focused on trade and income flows

$$CAD = ABS - GNDI \qquad (2.25)$$

an absorption approach: focused on the gap between output and absorption

$$CAD = \left(I_p - S_p\right) + \left(I_g - S_g\right) = \left(I_p - S_p\right) - GS \qquad (2.26)$$

a resource constraint identity: focused on private and government I–S balances

The identities point to several influences that could be at play and to questions that policymakers must answer to fashion a policy response. Is the widening current account deficit broad-based in trade or caused by a specific event? Is it occurring in a cyclically strong or weak economy? Is the cause domestic or foreign in origin? On the domestic side, have the changes been in income or absorption, in saving or investment? Are such changes concentrated in the government's accounts or in the private sector? Typically, a mix of influences is at work so the task is to identify which are the most important and how they might interact. The example below – graphically illustrated in Figure 2.6 – sketches a chain of considerations.[28]

From the balance of payments approach, we would identify which component(s) of the deficit had moved sharply. A sudden drop in exports or rise in imports may be transitory or permanent; a judgment on its longevity would determine how vigorous a policy response is required. A broad-based rise in imports and fall in exports would prompt an analysis of whether competitiveness had worsened (this process will be discussed in Chapter 3). It would also push us to scrutinize the income-absorption and investment–savings conditions to determine whether the problem arose more from accelerating domestic absorption or weakness in output growth.

Let's start with the case where the current account deficit has a clear counterpart in rising absorption. It must be determined whether this was driven by discretionary changes in government policies or by cyclical conditions in the private sector. If it is related to a fiscal expansion, an obvious response would be to reverse the expansion (GS↑) – by raising taxes or cutting government expenditure. The composition of the fiscal response would need to be considered. Was the fiscal expansion the result of higher government investment or a current spending binge (i.e., lower saving)? If the former, and additional investment was viewed as essential to future growth, the onus would be on raising taxes or cutting government con- sumption while sparing investment cuts.

The absorption approach would focus on the source of the increase in absorption. Suppose the increase in absorption came from a cyclical boom (due to rising domestic demand) in the private sector? An example would be a housing bubble that elicited sharply higher spending on home pur- chases and furnishing and a surge in real-estate investment. In such cir- cumstances, a direct tool for addressing the problem would be a tightening of monetary policy – raising the cost of borrowing to finance consumption and investment. But a tightening of fiscal policy (either by allowing auto- matic fiscal stabilizers to work or discretionary policy changes) might also be considered. Until the current account shock is corrected (by endogen- ous changes or countercyclical policies becoming fully effective) the larger current account deficit would be financed either by funding from abroad or by drawing on the foreign exchange reserves of the central bank (insofar as

---

[28] The decision tree is crude and only illustrative. It is simpler, less iterative, and less nuanced than any real-world analysis would be. Fiscal, monetary, and exchange rate policies alluded to are fleshed out in subsequent chapters.

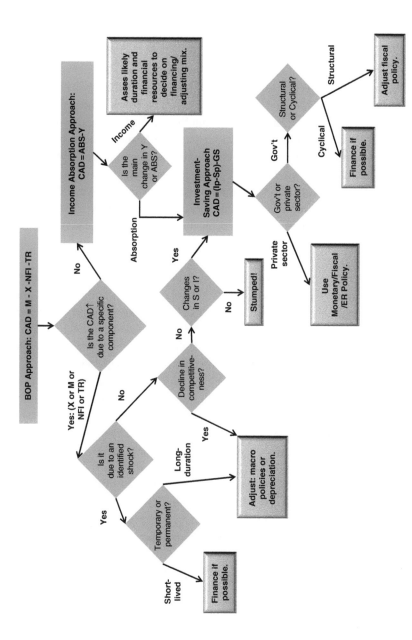

FIGURE 2.6 Widening current account deficit: diagnosis and prescription

the central bank views the shock as a temporary aberration and wants to resist a depreciation of the currency).[29]

If the increase in the current account deficit appears to be related to falling (or decelerating) GNDI, a different set of questions would come into play. Is there an identifiable transitory shock, such as a poor harvest or a major industrial strike? In other words, is the trajectory of potential output unchanged by the shock so that output should recover to its pre-shock trend within a year or two? In this case, a depreciation might be seen as unnecessarily disruptive and a better option could be waiting out the shock, tolerating the larger current account deficit, and financing it either by borrowing abroad (possibly from the IMF) or drawing down the central bank's foreign exchange reserves.

More complicated considerations arise if the increase in the current account deficit occurs against the backdrop of cyclical weakness in the domestic economy.[30] This could be the case, for example, if a global economic slowdown caused a drop in exports while home demand for imports was relatively inelastic to income (e.g., because imports were concentrated on necessities such as food and fuel). The cyclical weakness would probably have caused a reduction in tax revenues and an increase in government spending on entitlements ($GS\downarrow$). The government deficit would therefore have increased and this would have been another influence raising the current account deficit. But should the government try to reduce its deficit in circumstances of very weak economic activity?

The investment–saving approach requires some analytic subtlety in these circumstances. Determining the appropriate fiscal policy requires going beyond the resource constraint identity to consider the level of GNDI at which the identity balances. There are two broad views about the effects of government austerity during a recession. Some assert that given (a) exports constrained by weak demand abroad and (b) private investment and consumption undermined by uncertainty about prospects for a global recovery, a government retrenchment (i.e., $[Ig - Sg]\downarrow$ or, equivalently, $GS\uparrow$) will lead only to the identity being balanced at a level of output well below potential (which will reduce imports and CAD).

The opposite viewpoint is that fiscal austerity (by reducing government borrowing) will lower domestic interest rates, put downward pressure on

---

[29] Chapter 4 discusses monetary policy in this context and elucidates the relationship between monetary policy and using central bank foreign exchange reserves to cover external payments imbalances.

[30] This is an unusual case. Usually cyclical weakness in domestic demand will reduce the current account deficit. But the case here would be realistic if the domestic slowdown occurs in the context of a global recession.

price and wage inflation, and reduce private saving (because of a lowering of the expected future tax burden). Few economists would argue that a fiscal retrenchment will increase GNDI in the short run. But some would argue that, over time, these changes will elicit increases in private consumption ($C_p\uparrow$ and $S_p\downarrow$), in private investment ($I_p\uparrow$), or in export supply ($X\uparrow$) that will lead to higher output, thereby balancing the resource constraint identity at a higher level of output.

Understanding this debate requires thinking through the basic identities. But both sides go beyond the identities to make implicit or (sometimes) explicit assertions about behavior – i.e., how (through the intermediation of prices, wages, interest rates, exchange rates, or confidence about the future) private market participants respond to the stance of policy. The identities discipline the argument; the plausibility of the behavioral assumptions determines whether or not we buy it.

A somewhat easier set of circumstances to diagnose (though designing policy responses can be difficult) would be a fundamental deterioration in supply-side conditions. This would cause actual and potential output to decelerate and therefore the current account deficit to rise. Attention would need to shift to underlying problems that are usually structural in nature or entail worsening competitiveness and profitability of domestic production. Because output is constrained in this case by supply-side conditions rather than by deficient demand, policy responses must focus on structural measures. Fortunately, such policies typically do not have negative second-round effects. However, they are not easy to devise and implement. If supply-side policies were readily identifiable and implementable, why were they not adopted before? The reason is that supply-side policies often entail removing barriers or structural impediments to growth that are part of the political fabric of the country and are protected by powerful lobbies or ideologies. But sometimes these forces weaken in the face of imminent crisis.

These simple examples will be examined again and again as we use basic relationships for macroeconomic diagnostics in the rest of this book.

4 Exercises

1 Suppose an economy is stifled by burdensome institutional constraints on private economic activity – a corrupt and inefficient bureaucracy that requires bribes and costly lobbying before permits are issued for undertaking any new business activity – and disincentives that militate against foreign direct investment and the adoption of new technology. A new

government is elected. It alleviates the constraints on activity and new technology. Explain how this development will likely influence (i) wages, (ii) employment, (iii) profits, (iv) investment, and (v) capital flows. Will it raise output? Will it increase the rate of growth?

2 Consider a country with substantial natural resource wealth. As a result of its abundant resources it has a history of large current account surpluses matched by purchases of foreign assets. The domestic labor force is fully employed, but participation of the working-age population is low and skills are in short supply. These labor force characteristics reflect traditional and religious restrictions on women in the workforce that limit women to a relatively menial subset of jobs (often well below their education and skill levels) and discourage participation.

  (i) Discuss the difference between GDP and GNI in this economy. What does each really measure?

  (ii) If these restrictions in the labor market are immovable, what policies could the government adopt to raise the growth of GDP? Discuss how these policies would affect the difference between GDP and GNI.

  (iii) If these gender restrictions in the labor market can be ameliorated and eventually removed, how will the economy respond? Will anyone be hurt by the change and if so what is the likely reaction?

3 Suppose a country is at full employment of capital (i.e., a high capacity utilization rate) and labor. A new government comes to power on a populist platform and embarks on a program of substantial increases in government current expenditure. Trace the likely effects through the national accounts aggregates. How, if at all, will developments differ if the country is initially in a recession – actual output well below potential – and hence with ample spare production capacity?

4 A dire drought destroys the maize crop in a developing country where maize is the most important domestic food crop. Such droughts are very rare occurrences. Prior to any policy action, what is likely to happen to the private and government saving – investment balances and the current account? How should the government respond and what considerations should be adduced in deciding on the appropriate policy response?

CHAPTER 3

Inflation, Relative Prices, and Expectations

This chapter covers prices very broadly construed. Five topics are examined:

1 *Different ways of measuring the aggregate price level.*
2 *Changes in the aggregate price level – inflation and deflation, though we will focus on inflation, which over most of the past century has been the predominant policy concern.*
3 *The critical relative prices for macroeconomic analysis:*
   a *unit labor costs and value-added deflators – their relevance to profitability and income distribution,*
   b *traded and nontraded components of the CPI – what drives them and how they influence resource allocation,*
   c *various measures of a country's international competitiveness.*
4 *Real and nominal interest rates and inflation expectations.*
5 *Interest arbitrage and international financial linkages.*

Chapter 2 focused on output, income, and expenditure in real terms, that is, in the prices and costs of a particular base year. But nominal values (i.e., current money values), which reflect both aggregate inflation and changes in relative prices, are equally important.[1] Price and cost changes add several additional dimensions to macroeconomic analysis. Not only can we account for output, income, and expenditure in easy-to-measure nominal terms, but we also get the tools to assess inflationary or deflationary conditions and the influences of relative prices on the allocation of resources, the

[1] We often approximate nominal growth as the sum of real growth and inflation (measured in terms of the GDP deflator). If rates of change are all measured as first differences of logarithms, this relationship is correct; if rates of change are measured in conventional percentage changes, the approximation errors can get quite large if the component changes are large. Suppose the deflator rises by 15 percent and real growth by 5 percent, then we might approximate nominal growth at 20 percent. But, more accurately measured, nominal growth is: $100[(1.15 \times 1.05) - 1] = 20.75$ percent.

international competitiveness of a country, and the distribution of income. In this chapter, we will start by considering aggregate inflation and then put the mechanics of several relative prices that are critical to macroeconomic analysis under the microscope.

From a macroeconomic perspective, we think about prices in four main ways:

- Inflation, or sustained increases in the aggregate price index (i.e., a weighted measure of all output prices or all consumption goods prices), responds to macroeconomic imbalances.[2] As intimated, but not fleshed out in Chapter 2, any actual or expected gap between domestic demand and supply elicits some combination of rising or falling inflation and changes in the current account balance. These developments can be either a signal of disequilibrium (due perhaps to excessively expansionary policies) or an equilibrating response to a demand or supply shock.

- Changes in relative prices, that is, in the prices of one category of goods or services relative to those of another, are a key driver of all consumption and production decisions. As such, they are the central nervous system of a market economy. The multitude of relative price and cost signals emanating from every sector of the economy determine profitability, resource allocation, income distribution, and international competitiveness.

- Interest rates are also a type of price: they measure the payment earned for delaying consumption from the current period until some future time, or the payment incurred for spending now against future income, and are thus also critical to decisions about consumption and investment. They embody the time dimension of economic decision-making insofar as they link the rate of return an investment must generate and the time preference of consumption of domestic or foreign savers. Expectations about future developments affect the formation of all prices, but nowhere is the role of expectations more obvious and important than in the determination of interest rates. We therefore discuss the role of expectations most thoroughly in the part of the chapter dealing with interest rates.

---

[2]   We will use the term "macroeconomic imbalances" in many different contexts in this book to refer to differences between large aggregates of activity or entries on balance sheets which over time must come into balance in order for economic developments to be sustainable.

- Exchange rates, that is, prices of one currency in terms of others, connect all other prices and costs across countries and currencies. They are thus central to macroeconomic analysis: to the analysis of price and cost competiveness across countries and, together with expectations, to the relationship between interest rates and financial markets across countries.

1   The Price Level, Inflation, and Deflation

Economists need a simple way of linking imbalances in the real economy to inflation (as opposed to either a one-off change in the price level, or a relative price change that increases the price of a good, such as food or fuel, with a large weight in the price index). This link to inflation is often through the rate of unemployment via the so-called Phillips curve, and this explains, in part, why central banks, charged with keeping inflation within targeted bounds, are so focused on the rate of unemployment.

The Phillips curve assumes (based on historical data) that a negative relationship exists between the unemployment rate and wage inflation (and usually price inflation). The expectations-augmented Phillips curve, however, adds some behavioral elaboration:

- First, it posits a "natural rate of unemployment" – often called a non-accelerating inflation rate of unemployment (NAIRU). At the NAIRU most willing workers are employed, and the residual unemployment is either frictional (i.e., reflecting only workers in transition between jobs) or structural (i.e., due to an institutional impediment to higher employment).
- Second, it takes account of shifts in the Phillips curve as price expectations are incorporated into wage negotiations. When expansionary tendencies in the economy, emanating from either government policies or an overly ebullient private sector, push unemployment below the NAIRU, wages have to increase to induce more workers into the labor force. But these wage developments increase prices, and as these price increases are incorporated into expectations and wage negotiations, wages have to rise even further to induce reluctant workers to accept employment. Thus an attempt to hold the unemployment rate below the NAIRU puts in place an accelerating process of wage and price inflation.

Potential GDP is often associated with an unemployment rate at the NAIRU.[3]

When we talk about inflation, or changes in the general price level, we are, in principle, envisaging a uniform percentage increase in prices and wages across the economy that amounts to a reduction in the purchasing power of money. Governments (and especially central banks) are concerned about this pure form of inflation (and its converse, deflation) for several reasons. By itself, inflation reduces economic efficiency by imposing so-called menu costs on suppliers – i.e., the cost of repeatedly changing price tags. More dramatically, when inflation gets high it can tend toward accelerating inflation: when moderately high inflation diminishes the purchasing power of money, people rush to swap their cash or cashlike assets for goods, thereby aggravating inflation.[4] Very high (or hyper) inflation entails a breakdown of public confidence in the currency and undermines the role of money as a store of value, means of transaction, and unit of account. The currency depreciates rapidly on open foreign exchange markets or black markets, and the inflation swamps the signaling role of relative price changes.

But the notion of steady uniform changes in all prices (and costs and other nominal variables) is a theoretical construct. In practice inflation always entails relative price changes. If demand exceeds potential output, the equilibrating role of inflation relies entirely on some other nominal variable being sticky. Thus if excess demand elicits inflation and nominal wages are sticky, then real wages decline, reducing demand for goods, increasing employment and output, and thus helping to restore equilibrium. This equilibrating change would not occur if wages and inflation increased at the same rate.

The changes in relative prices induced by inflation can be capricious, and they affect income distribution and resource allocation. For example, inflation reduces real incomes of people with fixed nominal incomes (often the pensions of the elderly) by much more than those who can renegotiate wages at short intervals. Another example: when loans have fixed interest rates or rates that fail to anticipate inflation, the process will benefit debtors at the expense of creditors as the real value of loans (i.e., the command of the nominal amount

----

[3] The NAIRU is a useful construct. But for an open economy, as we will see later in this chapter, the inflationary response to demand that exceeds potential output will also be influenced by global supply conditions and the willingness of nonresidents to finance excess domestic demand.

[4] Cash and cashlike assets are those that do not pay an interest rate that reflects expectations of inflation.

over goods and services) is eroded. And yet another example: depending on how the nominal exchange rate anticipates or responds to inflation, there will likely be changes in competitiveness (i.e., the profitability of producing goods that are traded internationally) that will influence investment, the allocation of resources more generally, and production.

Deflation – a generalized and persistent drop in prices – also entails arbitrary shifts in distribution and allocation; it is as problematic as (and sometimes more problematic than) inflation. For example, if most interest rates cannot go below zero, deflation (usually in circumstances of very weak economic activity) will likely lead to higher real interest rates (nominal interest rates plus the rate of deflation) than are warranted by demand conditions. This will make it difficult to adopt monetary policies to help the country exit a recession. Deflation will usually favor creditors over debtors (as the real value of nominal debt increases) and will exacerbate fiscal problems for countries with outstanding debt.

Ideally inflation would be steady and in no more than single digits. In a world where downward nominal price and wage changes are sticky, this should be high enough to facilitate the small changes in relative prices that are warranted by developments in the real economy. But it should not be so high as to create significant economic distortions or to induce a vicious circle of acceleration as people rush to escape from money. Most econometric work finds negligible real costs from inflation rates in this range. In general, we see stable and problem-free rates of inflation that are in the 3–8 percent range in emerging and developing economies where structural changes are likely to require significant changes in relative prices. Advanced countries almost all aim for inflation of about 2 percent.

No one measure of inflation can summarize the information needed to assess the incidence and effects of inflation. Therefore numerous indices of inflation exist. It is useful to understand what the most commonly used ones measure.[5]

The GDP deflator, the initial focus of the next section, is a value-added price index for the whole economy. Real GDP is the sum of production (value-added) in each part of the economy measured at prices in some base year. Nominal GDP is the sum of value-added measured at current prices. Thus the ratio of nominal to real GDP gives the GDP deflator, which is usually shown as an index with the base year set at 100. Box 3.1 provides more detail on separating out changes in real GDP from those in nominal GDP.

---

[5] We do not define or discuss all frequently cited indices (e.g., the producer price index) because they are not relevant to the subsequent analytics in the chapter.

Box 3.1 Relative Price Changes and the Measurement of Real GDP

(Adapted, with permission, from notes by Donogh McDonald)

Measuring GDP requires aggregating hundreds of raw data series. But how does one add up tons of steel and gallons of wine? The standard approach is to use prices in a base year:

$$Y^{2008}(2006 \ prices) = \sum_{i=1}^{n} P_i^{2006} Q_i^{2008} \qquad (3.1)$$

But the problem comes when relative prices change. For example, prices of computers have been falling substantially while demand for these computers (and thus the volume of production and consumption) has been rising. In these circumstances GDP growth rates based on old base year prices will be much higher than those based on more recent prices.[1]

Thus the rate of growth of real GDP in 1998 was:[2]

- 4.4 percent using 1995 as the base year
- 6.5 percent using 1990 prices
- 18.8 percent using 1980 prices
- 37.4 percent using 1970 prices

Government statistical agencies address the problem by regularly rebasing national accounts. While this provides more accurate estimates of recent growth rates, updated weights will distort growth rates in the distant past as the weights for goods that have seen relative price declines will be too low.

Chained volume indices address the problem. A chained Laspeyres Index (LI) calculates growth in year t using the prices of the previous period $(t-1)$ – the numerator has current output volumes and the denominator last year's volumes. The base year is advanced each year so that quantities are always valued with the previous year's prices.

$LI = L\{Y(t)/Y(t-1)\}$

$$= \left[\sum_{i=1}^{n} P_i(t-1)Q_i(t)\right] / \left[\sum_{i=1}^{n} P_i(t-1)Q_i(t-1)\right] \qquad (3.2)$$

(More precisely, the rate of growth here is $100 \times (L{-}1)$.)

The chained Paasche Index (PI) does the same calculation using prices of the current year (t) to evaluate volumes in both year t and year $t-1$.

Box 3.1 (*continued*)

$$PI = P\{Y(t)/(Y(t-1)\} = \left[\sum_{i=1}^{n} P_i(t)Q_i(t)\right]/\left[\sum_{i=1}^{n} P_i(t)Q_i(t-1)\right]$$
(3.3)

Again, the base year is advanced each year.

The Fisher Volume Index is constructed using a geometric mean of the two above indices – i.e., the square root of their product.

$$Y(t)/Y(t-1) = \sqrt{PI \times LI}$$
(3.4)

Thus, the percentage change in real GDP is $100[Y(t)/Y(t-1)-1]$.

While many advanced countries use chained-weighted indices, and these do effectively address measurement problems in circumstances of changing relative prices, they complicate other arithmetic calculations – e.g., conventional contribution-to-growth calculations for the components of GDP do not add up to the GDP growth rate.

[1] In fast-growing emerging market economies, one might expect growth of both demand and prices for nontraded goods and services to rise more quickly than for traded manufactures. Old weights would then understate growth.

[2] See Whalen, Karl, A Guide to U.S. Chain Aggregated NIPA Data, *The Review of Income and Wealth*, 48 (2) (June 2002), 217–233. Also Steindl, Charles, Chain Weighting: The New Approach to Measuring GDP, *Current Issues in Economics and Finance*, 1(9) (1995), 1–6.

On the expenditure side, the GDP deflator is made up of price changes for each component of domestic expenditure – consumption and investment. But by adding the deflator for exports and subtracting that for imports, it measures the aggregate price of only domestic value-added.

The Consumer Price Index (CPI) is the most frequently cited index of prices and is widely used in inflation targeting by central banks.[6] It is a weighted average of prices paid by households for consumer goods, a gross rather than value-added measure. Therefore, a drop in prices of imported consumer goods reduces the CPI (though not the GDP deflator). The weights in the CPI reflect the shares of different categories of goods and services – food, fuel, medical services, etc. – in consumption. These

[6] Some central banks target also, or primarily, a "core" CPI – i.e., a CPI index that excludes particularly volatile elements such as energy and food. Some also pay careful attention to the consumption deflator component of the GDP deflator.

weights change over time, raising issues related to revisions and comparability similar to those noted in Box 3.1 in connection with the GDP deflator. The weights also differ over space and income levels – between urban and rural families and between rich families and poor families. So, in fact, there are many CPIs. However, when press reports cite the CPI they are usually referring to some broadly representative index.

The CPI may move differently from the GDP deflator. Changes in the external terms of trade – the index of export prices divided by that of import prices – are one important source of differences between movements in the CPI and the deflator. If increases in export prices outpace those of import prices (a terms-of-trade gain), the GDP deflator will rise more quickly than the CPI. If import prices rise more rapidly than those of exports (a terms-of-trade loss), the reverse occurs. Box 3.2 illustrates how changes in the terms of trade create a gap between the two indices. Besides exports, the CPI also excludes domestically produced investment and intermediate goods. We focus on the CPI in the second part of the next section.

Box 3.2 Price Indices and the External Terms of Trade

The GDP deflator captures the prices of the goods and services that the country produces. The CPI captures the prices of goods and services that are consumed. The former includes prices of exports but not those of imports; the latter excludes exports but includes imports of consumer goods. Thus changes in the terms of trade will drive a wedge between the two indices. Consider Figure 3.1 showing the two indices for Israel for the period 2006–2014 from the IMF's 2015 (Article IV) Consultation Report on Israel.

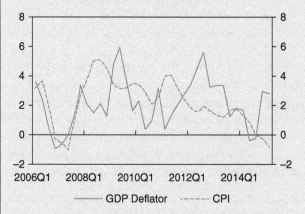

FIGURE 3.1 Israel: GDP deflator and CPI (Y/y percentage changes)
Source: Haver Analytics.

Box 3.2 (*continued*)

Figure 3.1 elicits an obvious question: why, at times, do the indices diverge? Figure 3.2 provides the answer: appreciable changes in the external terms of trade explain the divergences.

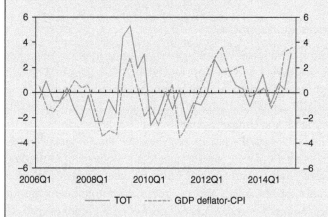

FIGURE 3.2 Israel: terms of trade and GDP deflator – CPI differences (Y/Y percentage changes)

Thus, for instance, the terms-of-trade gain for oil-importing countries when the global price of oil drops drives a wedge between the CPI and the GDP deflator. Such divergences raise questions for policy. For example: (i) Which index should policy target? (ii) If wages are indexed to a price index, which of these two indices is the most appropriate. The answers to these questions can be highly significant for the effects of policy.

2 Macroeconomic Aspects of Relative Prices

Shifts in relative prices are the nerve impulses of market economies. In practice, changes in narrowly designated categories of prices (e.g., copper versus aluminum or steel versus nickel) influence production and consumption decisions for these goods. Both producers and users seek to anticipate such relative price changes so as to minimize costs and maximize profits. In macroeconomics, however, we zoom out and consider broader, more aggregated, categories of relative prices and costs. In this section we focus on two central relativities – input versus output prices and prices of traded versus nontraded goods and services. The first is at the core of production decisions, while the second influences both production and consumption decisions. Both are critical to assessing a country's competitiveness and the sustainability of a country's international balance of payments position.

a Output Prices and Input Costs

Let's go back to the National Accounts, but now bring in prices of output and of inputs (i.e., wages and the cost of capital). This gives us a simple framework for understanding and representing the distribution of income between labor and capital and what it may mean for investment, profitability, employment, and competitiveness.

Total nominal income is the sum of wage income (the product of hourly wage rates and labor employed, measured as total employment multiplied by average weekly hours worked) and other income (capital employed times the rental cost of capital, and the return to entrepreneurship, or profit).[7] Total income from wages and salaries $(W.L)$ is the lion's share of income and, for simplicity, we will assume that all other income is subsumed under capital income $(R.K)$.

So, nominal income equals wage income and capital income

$$Y_n = W.L + R.K \tag{3.5}$$

Y = total income (subscripts n and r denote, respectively, nominal and real)

W = hourly wage rate

L = labor input

R = rental cost of capital

K = capital input

Dividing through by Y_n yields labor's share and capital's share of total income on the right side and unity (to which they sum) on the left side. Alternatively, dividing through by Y_r gives us the GDP deflator on the left side and its components – the cost of labor and the cost of capital per unit of output – on the right side. The concepts of unit labor cost and unit capital cost are important to the discussion.

---

[7]   Recall from Box 2.1 how inputs are measured. For simplicity, in the sections that follow, we will ignore the differences between various income/output measures – GDP, GNI, GNDI – and simply designate nominal income Y_n and real income Y_r.

$$P_y = ULC + UKC \qquad (3.6)$$

P_y = GDP deflator
ULC = unit labor cost
UKC = unit capital cost

For good reason, economists pay a great deal of attention to unit labor costs. Labor costs are the major share of income, and ULCs are an important determinant of profitability and competitiveness.[8]

Let's delve into what unit labor costs represent. By construction

$$ULC = W.L/Y_r \qquad (3.7)$$

Y_r/L is labor productivity or the amount of output that each worker produces in some specified period of time (here an hour). So we can write

$$ULC = W/PROD \qquad (3.8)$$

$PROD$ = Y_r/L = labor productivity

Or in terms of rates of change (first differences of logarithms, designated by lower-case italicized letters)

$$ulc = w\text{--}prod \qquad (3.9)$$

It is clear from these expressions that one should never identify ULCs crudely with wage rates. There are cases where low wages are associated with relatively high ULCs because productivity is very low (or vice versa). As we saw in Chapter 2, this may reflect a relative dearth of physical capital, or poorly trained workers (a dearth of human capital), or an economic environment that is not conducive to economic activity – low total factor productivity. The latter would be the case, for instance, if there were some combination of primitive technology, inefficient financial intermediation, arbitrary regulatory and fiscal systems, confiscatory taxes, corruption, and/or other aspects of poor governance that lower TFP.

Developments in ULCs are often a key to understanding much of what is going on in the macroeconomy, but the analysis can be complex. Some particularly important implications of developments in ULCs concern prospects for inflation, the distribution of income between labor and capital, profitability, and international competitiveness.

---

[8] In this section we look at ULCs in the whole economy, but often discussions of ULCs focus on the manufacturing sector because (a) they may be easier to measure in this sector so that the data are more reliable, and (b) for many countries the manufacturing sector is *the* traded goods sector and as such most affected by international competitiveness.

(i) Unit Labor Costs and Inflation

Let's look at inflation first. It may be tempting to interpret wage increases as inflationary. And an increase in inflation may indeed start with an autonomous increase in wages (e.g., resulting from a push by unions to raise wages and their share in overall income). But rising wages are not always inflationary. Specifically, when they are not reflected in rising ULCs the implication is that they are merely compensating labor for higher productivity. In this case, they have no direct bearing on the GDP deflator. If, on the other hand, wage increases outpace increases in productivity, ULCs rise and put upward pressure on the GDP deflator as producers resist a compression of profit margins.

But even this latter case requires careful analysis. First, the ULC is a nominal variable, and nominal variables generally rise with inflation. If, therefore, increases in ULCs are consistent with the targeted rate of inflation, then labor is merely maintaining its share of income rather than putting upward pressure on inflation. Second, while ULC increases that outstrip targeted inflation may well be an early warning of inflationary pressures, this is not always the case. In these circumstances, an assessment of the inflationary impetus of the rising ULC index depends upon whether the ULC increases are changes away from equilibrium or equilibrating corrections of distortions in the previous period or in the index base year.[9] An increase in ULCs that pushes swollen (disequilibrium) profit margins back toward more normal levels is not necessarily inflationary.

(ii) Unit Labor Costs, Profits, and Income Distribution

Definitionally, if ULCs rise more rapidly than the aggregate GDP deflator, labor's share of aggregate income increases. The rest of income is made up of a combination of contractual capital costs and residual profits (or returns to entrepreneurship). A squeeze on the latter component – due to ULC inflation in excess of aggregate deflator inflation – may be a disincentive to investment, to entrepreneurial activity, and ultimately to firms' use of labor. This would be the case for any sharp profit squeeze; but even a continuous slow erosion of profitability may be detrimental to production, employment, investment, and international competitiveness.

The dangers of slow long-term or large short-term increases in profit's share also merit attention. Because most household income is from wages,

---

[9] This point – that inferences from movements in the index are contingent on an assessment of conditions prevailing in the previous period or in the base year of the index – will be reiterated; it applies to all of the diagnostic inferences from price and cost indices in this chapter.

and the propensity to consume from wage income is higher than that from capital income, a rising share of capital can have a negative effect on consumption. General concerns about fairness (in this case, income distribution between the more and less wealthy segments of the population) can also arise.[10]

For an open economy, a distributional shift away from capital may render macroeconomic conditions less supportive of growth. This is because capital is far more mobile internationally than is labor: if returns to capital shrink, capital is more likely to be redirected to other, lower-ULC countries, thereby depriving the home country of future investment and employment growth. We will come back to this when we discuss competitiveness.

A rapid rise in ULCs may be undesirable even if the overall rate of inflation ex post is such that it is not squeezing profits. Suppose a country's central bank has a twin mandate to control inflation and to seek full employment. If a strong labor union movement is successful in pushing up ULCs and the scope for cutting profit margins is limited, the options for employers generally boil down to either raising prices or cutting employment. If tight monetary conditions militate against the former, wage push could lead to higher unemployment. The central bank, therefore, may be pressured into easing monetary conditions and tolerating higher prices (and higher inflation if the process repeats itself) so as to forestall a rise in unemployment. Not surprisingly, policymakers keep a careful watch on ULCs.

(iii) Unit Labor Costs and International Competitiveness

Measuring ULC inflation against inflation in the overall GDP deflator (or ULC inflation in the manufacturing sector against inflation in the manufacturing value-added deflator) can inform inferences about competitiveness and profitability. The most basic intuition here is that any increase in ULCs that significantly exceeds increases in value-added deflators raises questions about whether the profit share is adequate to keep the country competitive for potential or actual investors.

This use of ULCs – in effect focusing on factor shares – does not necessarily provide definitive answers. There are plausible economic models that allow for gradual and secular shifts in factor shares – e.g., from capital income to labor income – without any diminution in competitiveness. Nevertheless, rich insights are gained from a ULC analysis of

---

[10] In many successful developing countries profit shares are very high at an early stage of development. We would not be alarmed, therefore, to see a slow erosion of the profit share over time. A sudden large shift, however, would ring alarm bells.

competitiveness, as we shall see below. Before turning to this, however, we introduce another relative price critical to assessing competitiveness.

b Traded and Nontraded Goods in the CPI

A second take on relative price mechanics that is central to analyses of both the demand and supply sides of the economy focuses on the CPI.

For analytic purposes, we partition the CPI into prices of traded goods and services (P_w) and nontraded goods and services (P_n) – i.e., goods and services that are not and, given current logistical constraints, cannot be exported or imported.[11] No definitive classification of goods into these two categories exists, but standard practice is to put many services (such as real-estate and rental services, utilities, and medical, legal, and retail services) into the nontraded category and to classify the rest as traded goods.

In principle, traded goods are priced at the international price $(P_w$ measured in an international currency such as US dollars) multiplied by the exchange rate (E) defined as the number of domestic currency units per dollar. In practice, exchange rate changes do not pass through immediately into domestic prices of traded goods: wholesalers or retailers absorb part of the price change initially, perhaps because they hold sizable inventories acquired at the old price or because it may be optimal to ignore potentially reversible exchange rate fluctuations for some time rather than changing all prices, reprinting catalogues, and so on. But considering traded goods prices as equivalent to $P_w.E$ is a simple and reasonably accurate approximation over time.

The partition into traded and nontraded goods is useful because it distinguishes prices subject only (or predominantly) to domestic demand pressures from those set in international markets for all but the largest countries. Consider, for instance, a country that discovers vast oil wealth or is the recipient of large international transfers or capital inflows so that its financial capacity and thus its spending rises very rapidly. Such an increase in income or wealth will almost certainly raise the prices of nontraded goods such as housing (because the price increases are the mechanism that pulls resources into the sector to increase supply). But

---

[11] In fact goods and services span a spectrum from fully traded (e.g., homogeneous commodities with large international markets) to fully nontraded (e.g., domestic utility services). Some goods and services (e.g., medical services) may be largely nontraded, but become traded at the margin when quality differentials across countries are large. Also, some traded goods become nontraded when the government imposes effective barriers to trade.

the additional spending will have little or no influence on the prices of traded goods insofar as these are available in almost unlimited supply in international markets. This latter point – generalized to state that small countries face an infinitely elastic supply of imports and demand for exports at global market prices – is known as the "small country assumption." It applies to most countries (see Box 3.3). Thus a country in these circumstances will see a rise in the price of nontraded goods relative to the price of traded goods.[12]

For simplicity, let us write the CPI as a log linear index of traded and nontraded goods with weights, respectively, of β and $(1-\beta)$.[13] We can then take differences of the logarithms of all variables (shown as lower-case acronyms) and write consumer price inflation as

$$cpi = \beta(e + p_w) + (1 - \beta)p_n \qquad (3.10)$$

cpi = the rate of change of the consumer price index

β, $1 - \beta$ are respectively the shares of traded and nontraded goods in the CPI

e = rate of change of the exchange rate vis-à-vis the US dollar (an increase is a depreciation)

p_w = rate of change of the world price of traded goods (measured in dollars)

p_n = rate of change of the price of nontraded goods (and services)

As noted, the rate of inflation of nontraded goods will be determined by excess demand and that of traded goods largely by the exchange rate and foreign inflation – i.e., global supply and demand conditions. Any sudden upward shift in domestic aggregate demand will elicit an increase in the relative price of nontraded goods. This relative price change, in turn, will increase profits in the nontraded sector and induce a shift in factors of production (labor and capital) out of the traded goods sector and into the production of nontraded goods.

---

[12] If the exchange rate is fixed, the price of traded goods will not change appreciably while that of nontraded goods will rise. If the exchange rate is flexible, the discovery of oil may lead to an appreciation of the currency so that the relative price change may entail a fall in prices of traded goods.

[13] This CPI index is $CPI = (EP_w)^\beta P_n^{(1-\beta)}$. We can linearize this equation by taking logarithms of all variables. Then, recalling that the first difference of a logarithm is a rate of change, we can get the percentage change in the CPI by taking changes in the variables of the log-linear equation.

Box 3.3 Traded Goods and the Small Country Assumption

The small country assumption, often adduced for analytic purposes, posits that traded goods are relatively homogeneous and traded in a global market. Countries are assumed not to have sufficient monopoly power to influence prices and are consequently price takers for imports and exports. Each country therefore faces an infinitely elastic (i.e., flat) global demand curve for its exports and supply curve for its imports. Thus prices are given and exports are determined by the domestic supply curve and imports by the domestic demand curve.

If traded goods prices are set in euros (or some other global currency) and we analyze demand and supply conditions in terms of domestic currency ("crowns"), a depreciation of the domestic currency (an increase in the number of crowns per euro from E_0 to E_1) constitutes an upward shift in the demand curve for exports and the supply curve for imports. This upward shift increases the supply of exports and reduces the demand for imports by moving along the export supply curve and the import demand curve as depicted in Figure 3.3. In the case of exports, therefore, the price is given and analysis requires information only about the supply curve (and, for imports, the demand curve).

It is not necessary that goods are homogeneous for this small country assumption to hold; it will apply as long as they are similar enough for the market to establish an equilibrium relative price between them. Consider a bicycle manufacturer in Eastern Europe. Before the fall of the Berlin wall and the opening up to trade with the West, the manufacturer produced heavy, cheap, steel bicycles with squeaky brakes. Domestic consumers bought them because they lacked alternative options. After trade opened up, consumers had a choice between state-of-the-art titanium German or French bicycles for €1,000 or heavy and clumsy steel bicycles for €400. If almost all consumers think that this price differential is too small – i.e., it is worth saving for an extra six months to buy the better bike – then the domestic manufacturer is in trouble. The company is trying to set the price even though it has no monopoly power; unless it lowers the price it will eventually go out of business.

If, however, the domestic producer of a good is a major supplier, with sufficient monopoly power to influence the global price, it sets the price in local currency. In this case, a depreciation lowers the price (in euros or any other global currency) in international markets and increases global demand and exports. Analysis then requires information about both the supply curve and the demand curve and a real exchange rate index using export unit values may be meaningful. In circumstances of monopsony power, analogous reasoning applies to imports. In this case

Box 3.3 (*continued*)

one needs to analyze both supply and demand, and there may be useful information in a real exchange rate index using import unit values.

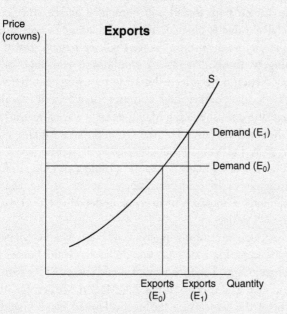

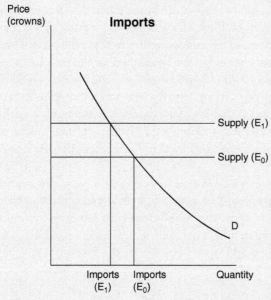

FIGURE 3.3 Exports, imports, and the exchange rate for a small country

c Relative Prices and Competitiveness

A starting point for thinking about competitiveness is the notion of purchasing power parity (PPP) – i.e., that the exchange rate is in equilibrium when a basket of goods costs the same in different currencies when converted at that exchange rate. Given both traded and nontraded goods, and good reasons for their relative price to change, this may be a bit of a stretch for the level of prices at any point in time (as we shall see below). But it is intuitively appealing to think that, at an equilibrium exchange rate, a homogeneous good should be priced the same in a single numeraire currency regardless of the country and currency in which it is sold. *The Economist* magazine publishes a Big Mac Index as a way of measuring purchasing power between currencies on the grounds that a McDonald's Big Mac hamburger is the same product whether it is purchased at McDonald's in New York or Moscow or Madrid (Table 3.1). Using differences in purchasing power of each currency in terms of Big Macs, *The Economist* calculates a measure of over- or undervaluation of each currency against the US dollar.

Let's consider the mechanics of this measure. If a Big Mac in Mexico costs 19 pesos and the same Big Mac costs one dollar across the border in Texas, the PPP exchange rate – i.e., the rate that would ensure PPP – would be 19 pesos to the dollar. If the price of the Big Mac in Mexico rises by 10 percent and that of the same Big Mac in the United States rises by 2 percent, then the peso should depreciate by the difference (8 percent) to maintain PPP in hamburgers. If the Mexican peso depreciates by less than 8 percent the Big Mac would be more expensive in Mexico than in Texas (in terms of either dollars or pesos). We could then say the peso had seen a real appreciation; thus PPP would no longer hold and Mexico would be less competitive. At any point in time the Big Mac index shows the level of the imputed over- or undervaluation of the domestic currency vis-à-vis the US dollar compared with the corresponding PPP exchange rate (insofar as the latter can be based on one good even if it is an exceptionally homogeneous good).

In analyzing exchange rates, we generally consider a broad price index rather than a single good, and we generally look at changes rather than levels because we don't know the equilibrium ratio between countries' price indices at any point in time. Therefore, if inflation in a particular year is 10 percent in Mexico and only 2 percent in the United States, any

TABLE 3.1 The Economist's *Big Mac index and imputed currency misalignments*

Country	Price of a Big Mac converted at market exchange rate on July 12, 2017 to US dollars	Imputed over(+), under(−) valuation relative to US dollar (in percent)
Switzerland	6.74	27
Norway	5.91	12
Sweden	5.82	10
United States	5.3	−
Brazil	5.1	−4
Canada	4.66	−12
Australia	4.53	−15
Euro Area	4.47	−16
Argentina	4.13	−22
United Kingdom	4.11	−22
Japan	3.36	−37
Turkey	3.01	−43
China	2.92	−45
Mexico	2.75	−48
Russia	2.28	−57
Taiwan	2.26	−57
South Africa	2.26	−57
Egypt	1.75	−67

Source: The Economist, July 13, 2017

depreciation of the peso of less than 8 percent will constitute a real appreciation of the peso and a loss of competitiveness for Mexico.

This idea of macro-level PPP is like the notion of pure inflation: it ignores real economic changes and equilibrating changes in relative prices.[14] While our discussion of competitiveness will be much more

[14] Given integrated global markets, PPP seems sensible for traded goods, but less so for a basket that includes both traded and nontraded goods. If, however, one thinks in terms of changes in prices from one equilibrium to another, it is easier to understand. Assume that, initially, traded goods are priced the same in two countries (adjusted for the exchange rate) and that in both countries the relative price between traded and nontraded goods is in equilibrium. Then any purely nominal shock to prices in one country (e.g., an increase in the money supply) should change the exchange rate so that in the new equilibrium the initial relative price between traded and nontraded goods is unchanged and thus the initial

granular, the idea of PPP will, nevertheless, be a useful conceptual building block to bear in mind.

Almost everyone thinks a country's competitiveness is important and that it has something to do with prices, productivity, costs, and exchange rates. But there are different concepts of competitiveness, and without careful consideration of these differences concepts used in a particular analysis may be unclear or inappropriate. The sections below draw on the concepts of unit labor costs and on the partition of the CPI into traded and nontraded goods to discuss two measures of competitiveness and when each is the appropriate concept.

(i) ULC Measures of Competitiveness

Start by reverting to the discussion of ULCs. If a global company is looking for a location for a particular manufacturing plant – a platform for production to be exported globally or regionally – what kind of competitiveness indicator is relevant to its choice? The cost of capital is probably not very important because the company can raise capital in the most cost-effective global markets. The cost of land may be relevant, although usually this does not bulk large in overall costs. But labor costs are highly relevant – they usually amount to more than half of value-added in manufacturing. So wage rates are important.

Other factors are also critical – those (described in Chapter 2 and, especially, in Box 2.3) that comprise the technological, institutional, legal, and infrastructural environment that determines total factor productivity. But total factor productivity influences labor productivity, and ULCs are defined as wage rates divided by labor productivity.[15] ULCs, therefore, cover much of what enters into the decision of where to locate the manufacturing plant.

The global company will make its location decision based largely on where it expects to make the greatest profit. But given that profits (or markups over cost) can be proxied by value-added prices minus ULCs, companies compare ULCs across countries as a reasonable measure of the relative competitiveness of those countries as a location for investment. The relevant price (or cost) index to use in a calculation of the real

purchasing power relationship for a basket of goods priced in the two currencies is restored. However, as we shall see, a real (as opposed to nominal) shock to an economy will likely elicit an equilibrating change in the relative price between traded and nontraded goods and a departure from PPP.

[15] Recall that for a production function of the form $Y = AK^{\alpha}L^{1-\alpha}$, labor productivity is represented as $Y/L = A(K/L)^{\alpha}$.

exchange rate (RER) is thus a ULC index. This ULC-based index of the RER focuses on how price and cost signals influence the allocation of resources across countries.

If the choice were simply between two locations – the company is deciding whether to locate its new plant in Texas or Mexico – only one real exchange rate is involved:

$$RER = ULC(mex)/[ULC(tex).E] \qquad (3.11)$$

RER = the real exchange rate
E = the local currency price of dollars

By dividing an index of Mexico's ULC (in pesos) by an index of its exchange rate, we are translating it into dollar terms so that we can compare it with the Texan ULC.[16] The RER shown above for Mexico is negatively correlated with Mexico's competitiveness – i.e., if ULCs increase in Mexico, Mexico's competitiveness deteriorates. If either ULCs rise in Texas or the peso depreciates against the US dollar (i.e., E rises), Mexico's RER goes down, and Mexico becomes more competitive.

More often, when a company is trying to judge a country's competitiveness, it assesses it against a group of countries, not just one competitor. The real exchange rate measure needs to weight the countries in this group. We may think it appropriate to weight them by their share in global manufacturing trade or their share in global production of manufactures. No weighting scheme is ideal and various schemes – some simple, others more complicated as they take into account the economic responsiveness of the country to relative price changes – have been proposed. Such weighted-average RERs are usually referred to as real effective exchange rates (REERs). It is important to understand the particular construction of the REER and to be clear on how closely it relates to the question at hand.

Assume we are assessing Mexico's competitiveness against a group of three other emerging market (EM) economies with weights (ω_i such that $\sum \omega_i = 1$).

---

[16] Because we usually measure ULCs, exchange rates, and real exchange rates in index form, some juggling is necessary to ensure that dimensions are correct unless the index base is 1. If the numerator is an index with a base of 100 and the denominator is the product of two indices each with the same base of 100, then we would have to multiply the crude arithmetic result by 10,000 to get it in the form of a real exchange rate index with a base of 100.

We need to use the exchange rate for each currency to measure its ULC in US dollars.[17]

$$REER\,mex = \left[ULC(mex)/\sum \omega_i ULC_i\right] \times$$
$$\left[\sum\left\{\omega_i\left(E_i/E(mex)\right)\right\}\right]$$

REER = the real effective (i.e., weighted) exchange rate
E_i = units of the currency of country (i) per US dollar (often in index form)

When the term on the left side – Mexico's real effective exchange rate – rises, Mexico's competitiveness deteriorates. The first bracketed term on the right-hand side is Mexico's ULC index relative to a weighted average of those of its competitors. The second term is Mexico's nominal effective exchange rate (i.e., a weighted average of bilateral exchange rates). It transforms all of the ULC data into a common currency and is defined here such that an increase in the nominal effective exchange rate means a loss of competitiveness for Mexico.

Generally, we look at indices of ULCs for each country based on a range of goods, so we use a ULC index for each country.[18] Similarly, we use an exchange rate index. Given that baskets of manufactures differ across countries by content, quality, and brand reputation, sensible inferences from REER levels are usually not possible. Instead we look at changes. While real attributes of a country's exports may change over time, validating changes in real exchange rates, a significant and rapid real appreciation is usually at least

---

[17] Sometimes REERs refer to real effective exchange rates using a price index and the term RULCs is used for real effective exchange rates using ULCs. We will use REERs for all measures of competitiveness while specifying the particular component price or cost index.

[18] We may be analyzing all goods and services using an economy-wide ULC index, or (more often the case) only the manufacturing or industrial sector using a ULC index for manufacturing or for all industry. The European Commission has data on ULC-based real exchange rates for both the manufacturing sector and the whole economy at https://ec .europa.eu/info/business-economy-euro/indicators-statistics/economic-databases/price- and-cost-competitiveness/price-and-cost-competitiveness-data-section-2016_en. It also pro- vides data on nominal exchange rates and price-based real exchange rates; the latter are relevant to the following section. The Federal Reserve Bank of St. Louis provides OECD real exchange rates for many countries based on ULCs in manufacturing at https://fred .stlouisfed.org/tags/series?t=exchange%20rate%3Boecd%3Breal%3Bunit%20labor% 20cost&ob=pv&od=desc. Its publicly available data bank also has real exchange rates based on price indices. The US Bureau of Labor Statistics used to provide really informative data on ULC-based real exchange rates and the components of the calculation for major trading countries at www.bls.gov/web/prod4.supp.toc.htm. These data are no longer published but reviewing the available data from 1950 to 2011 is informative on how they are derived.

a prima facie indication that the country's industries are losing competitiveness. Such an indication should prompt an investigation of other data to look for supporting evidence or contradictory evidence. For example, if a real appreciation is coupled with a diminution in direct foreign investment, a loss of export market shares, or increased foreign import penetration of domestic markets, then the case for interpreting it as reduced competitiveness is stronger. Chapter 7 elaborates on these points.

(ii) Price Index or Traded–Nontraded Measures of Competitiveness

A second central measure of competitiveness focuses on how price signals influence the domestic allocation of resources between production of traded and nontraded goods. Suppose a country's domestic demand $(C + I)$ suddenly increases because the government has embarked on a large multiyear spending program. If sufficient spare production capacity exists – i.e., output is below potential – this additional spending may elicit primarily a quantity response, so that output rises. But if there are supply constraints then satisfying the extra demand requires increasing net imports (i.e., fewer exports and/or more imports). If part of the additional demand falls on nontraded goods, a reallocation of factors of production from traded goods industries to nontraded goods industries will be necessary. The traded–nontraded price measure of the real exchange rate summarizes conditions that will lead to this internal resource flow in the economy.

Consider Figure 3.4 in traded–nontraded goods space.

The curved line on which A and B lie is the production possibility frontier (PPF) of the economy. It shows all the combinations of traded and nontraded goods that the country can produce in conditions of full employment given its current capital stock and the current state of technology and institutions. Let's assume that these supply conditions (implicit in the PPF) are constant while we examine a change in other variables between two periods – the initial period (with a zero subscript) and the next period (with a subscript of 1).

Point C is GDP measured in terms of nontraded goods (Y_n/P_n) at their initial price. Point D is GDP measured in terms of traded goods $(Y_n/E.P_w)$ at their initial price. Thus the slope of CD – $[(Y_n/P_n)/(Y_n/E.P_w)]$ or, more simply, $E.P_w/P_n$ – is the ratio of traded to nontraded goods prices – the relative price – in the initial period.[19] The relative price line is tangential to the PPF at point A, the initial equilibrium position. At this point, the

---

[19] This is sometimes referred to as the *internal* terms of trade as opposed to the more commonly used *external* terms of trade, which is the relative price of exports to imports.

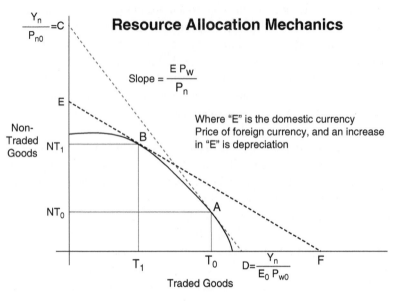

FIGURE 3.4 Relative prices and resource allocation

production of traded and nontraded goods, shown respectively on the horizontal and vertical axes, is T_o and NT_o.

What happens when an increase in demand occurs in an economy that is producing at its potential? To the extent that the demand is for traded goods, it can be accommodated through trade at a given global (foreign-exchange-denominated) price. But to the extent that the demand is for nontraded goods, by definition it can only be met by increasing domestic production – moving northwest on the PPF from initial equilibrium A to new equilibrium B. At this point the output of traded goods has dropped from T_o to T_1 and the output of nontraded goods has risen from NT_o to NT_1. Note that the drop in output of traded goods does not mean that effective demand for these goods is lower. In fact, the difference between output (T_1) and demand (which exceeds T_o) is reflected in a larger trade deficit or a smaller trade surplus.

The shift in production is elicited by a change in relative prices and profitability.[20] The increase in demand raises the price of nontraded goods (relative to traded goods), flattening the relative price line. As the relative price of nontraded goods rises, the relative equilibrium wage in this sector

---

[20] Note that the relative price change could be effected with a fixed exchange rate and a rise in the prices of nontraded goods, or by an appreciation of the exchange rate that would reduce the domestic price (and the profitability in production) of traded goods. In a flexible exchange rate regime, some combination of the two would be most likely.

increases, pulling labor out of traded goods production into nontraded goods production. Similarly, increased profitability in this sector pulls capital (or at least reorients new investment) into nontraded goods production. Thus the relative profitability (or internal competitiveness) of the traded goods sector declines. Unless the initial increase in spending is prompted by changes that raise net current account inflows – such as a gain in inward transfers or higher income from exports of a natural resource – this deterioration in competitiveness will likely produce a larger current account deficit or a smaller surplus.

The difficulty in actually using traded–nontraded price measures for analyses of competitiveness is coming up with a proxy for both types of prices. Sometimes this is done by disaggregating the CPI, using its services component as a proxy for nontraded goods and its goods component as a proxy for traded goods. Another much-used approach is to compare some broad price index – the CPI or the GDP deflator – across countries, adjusting the measures by exchange rates. This entails simply using CPIs or GDP deflators (rather than ULCs) in our REER measure. The intuition here is that such broad indices include both traded and nontraded goods and that traded goods prices (expressed in the same currency) are more or less arbitraged across borders. Therefore, differences between countries in a broad index of inflation (expressed in a common currency) are driven by (and thus reflect) differences in changes in nontraded goods prices. On this logic, higher CPI inflation in Mexico relative to the United States (when both are measured in a common currency) probably reflects an increase in nontraded relative to traded goods prices in Mexico.

Careful analysis is required to determine whether an apparent real appreciation due to such a relative price shift is problematic for the sustainability of balance of payments financing and growth, or simply a benign equilibrating change. A jump in government spending in circumstances of full employment may bump up inflation and cause a problematic deterioration in competitiveness. But there are numerous real-world circumstances where analysis of internal relative price mechanics is relevant and conclusions are more nuanced.

One example is so-called Dutch Disease – i.e., when domestic spending increases substantially and rapidly following the discovery of large deposits of a natural resource. The substantial spending and relative price changes that typically follow the discovery of natural resources can be destructive of other traded sectors of the economy, possibly damaging to governance, and ultimately detrimental to achieving economic growth that is diversified in its sources and thus less vulnerable to shocks. Box 3.4 discusses Dutch Disease and policies aimed at avoiding the so-called resource curse.

Another example is related to the Balassa–Samuelson effect (named for the economists who first focused attention on it). Consider circumstances where an EM economy is growing fast owing to increases in technology transfers from more advanced countries primarily into its traded goods sector (related, perhaps, to foreign direct investment). Productivity gains in traded goods substantially outpace those in nontraded goods and this intersectoral disparity will also be larger than that in trading partners.

Box 3.4 Resource Discoveries and Relative Prices – Dutch Disease

One issue for which assessing internal relative prices and costs is central is Dutch Disease – a major consideration in countries that discover large deposits of natural resources.

The name comes from the experience of the Netherlands after the discovery of large natural gas resources in the 1960s. The increase in wealth and subsequent spending pushed up nontraded goods inflation, pulling resources into nontraded goods production and depressing the non-gas, traded goods (largely manufacturing) sector. The term Dutch Disease is now applied to the relative price shifts that follow resource discoveries (or a surge in the price of a natural resource export) and resulting changes in the structure of production.

Dutch Disease can be seen as benign: an equilibrating change in relative prices that reflects the transition to a new structure of production and composition of exports. But the perils of Dutch Disease are important. Countries often wish to constrain its progress so as to avoid excessive dependence of domestic income on the natural resource sector (and the volatility in natural resource prices) and any slowing of employment growth as less labor-intensive resource extraction displaces more labor-intensive manufacturing. Also, Dutch Disease can be exacerbated by political economy developments (governance can suffer and government spending sprees can be hard to contain when revenues are seemingly abundant). Policymakers in countries with large resource discoveries therefore keep a close eye on the relative price of nontraded goods.

The broad effect of a natural resource discovery on the relative price of nontraded goods is robust. A recent study of over 150 countries during 1970–2013 finds that a resource discovery with the sample's median value of 10 percent of GDP led on average to an increase in the relative price of nontraded goods of 2 percent over 10 years.[1] But the variation in this price effect is large. To illustrate, Figure 3.5 shows an index of the price of domestic nontraded goods

Box 3.4 (*continued*)

relative to the price of nontraded goods in the United States (both expressed in US dollars) in the 10 years surrounding natural resources discoveries in Norway (1979) and Ghana (2007).[2] The present values of the discoveries relative to prediscovery GDP were roughly comparable.

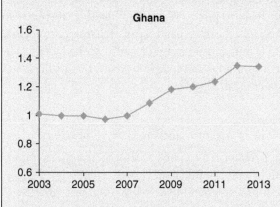

FIGURE 3.5 Ratio of domestic price of nontraded goods to US price of nontraded goods (each expressed in US$)
(index = 1 in year of resource discovery)

In both countries relative nontraded prices rose, but the size and persistence of the rise differed substantially. A key influence was differences in policy mitigations in the two countries, to which we return in later chapters.

[1] Harding, T., Stefanski, R., and Toews, G., *Boom goes the Price: Giant Resource Discoveries and Real Exchange Rate Appreciation* (May 2017), manuscript. We thank the authors for providing the data.

[2] This measure differs from the relative price of nontraded goods used elsewhere in this section. It compares the average nontraded goods price at home to that in the United States, not the average nontraded goods price to the traded goods price at home. If traded goods prices are arbitraged, this measure should move similarly to a broad real exchange rate index.

In the traded goods sector higher productivity will lead to higher wages without raising ULCs or prices. But as growth also increases the demand for nontraded goods where productivity is not increasing rapidly, retaining labor in that sector will push wages up by more than productivity and thus raise prices. A real exchange rate measure based on a broad index – say the CPI – will show an apparent loss of competitiveness, even though the shift in internal relative prices is an equilibrating response to a beneficial development. On the other hand, a real exchange rate measure based on unit labor costs in manufacturing (or traded goods more generally) may well show an improvement in competitiveness. Box 3.5 illustrates the Balassa–Samuelson effect in Slovakia.

Box 3.5 Balassa–Samuelson Effects and the Case of Slovakia

Consider the case of Slovakia in the period 2000–2010, using data from the 2010 IMF (Article IV) Consultation Report. Figure 3.6 shows export shares and three different measures of the real effective exchange rate. One REER measure is based on CPIs, one on the ULCs for the whole economy, and one on ULCs only in manufactures (i.e., the bulk of traded goods). An increase in these REER indices might be taken to reflect a worsening of competitiveness.

Both whole-economy measures show real appreciation, i.e., worsening competitiveness, but the manufacturing sector seems to be gaining competitiveness on average in terms of a ULC-based index. This is a puzzle for any simple inference about competitiveness.

One reasonable inference would be the so-called Balassa–Samuelson effect: Slovakia may be experiencing a catchup in manufacturing technology with more advanced competitors, leading to rapidly rising productivity (TFP). Therefore, even though wages may be rising, ULCs in manufacturing are falling relative to other countries. But because income is rising rapidly, demand is also increasing and putting upward pressure on wages overall and prices of nontraded goods (where productivity gains are less rapid). Increased demand and prices are forcing a shift into the production of nontraded goods where prices can rise to offset higher ULCs. This internal resource shift is reflected in the CPI-based measure and is not inconsistent with the whole-economy ULC-based measure. The shift of labor out of manufacturing does not necessarily mean a reduction in

Box 3.5 (*continued*)

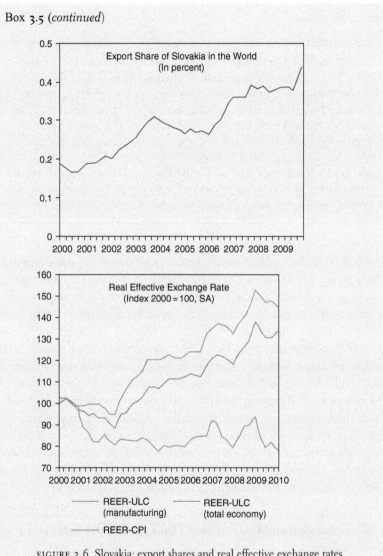

FIGURE 3.6 Slovakia: export shares and real effective exchange rates

output: higher productivity may well offset – or more than offset – lower employment.

If this story is correct we would probably expect to see Slovakia growing relatively rapidly with little or no loss in export market share

(*continued*)

Box 3.5 (*continued*)

despite the CPI-based measure of "loss" in competitiveness. (And, indeed, real GDP and exports in real – volume – terms grew respectively by 5 percent and 11 percent per year on average over the 10-year period; the figures are even more impressive – 6 percent and 14 percent – if one excludes the drop in output and exports in 2009 when the global economy entered the great recession.) This situation would be consistent with a benign reallocation of resources from traded to nontraded goods to match the changing structure of demand. The potential danger would come from excessive inflation and bubbles in nontraded sectors (most obviously real estate – see Chapter 6), but there would be nothing to suggest such a danger in the data discussed thus far.

We have considered two concepts of competitiveness at some length.[21] Often these go in the same direction: a boom in demand for nontradables may raise input costs and reduce the profitability of producing tradables relative both to domestic nontradables and to tradables produced in competitor countries. But sometimes they go in opposite directions – as in our Balassa–Samuelson example. Glib cookbook inferences from standardized indices of competitiveness are often wrong. A competent economist will look at all available REER measures, assess conditions in the base year of the index (or in the period prior to the particular change being considered), think through the appropriateness of the weighting scheme where the measures involve multiple countries, and adduce other data – on inflation and trade and demand – before coming to any definitive conclusion about the underlying forces driving developments. These issues will be explored further in the context of the balance of payments in Chapter 7.

3 Intertemporal and International Linkages: Interest Rates and Expectations

Insofar as we have been discussing prices at a point in time and inflation over a period of time, the idea of time has been implicit. But we have not considered time explicitly. While relative prices in any period are the nerve

---

[21] Other RER indices may be equally important. For example, as touched on in Box 3.3, an index using export prices ("export unit values") may be very useful for assessing competitiveness in circumstances where countries have a degree of monopoly power and thus some influence on the prices of their goods in global markets.

system that determines allocation and distribution, interest rates are the prices that constitute the link between time periods.

Interest rates are complicated. They balance investment and saving in any period and thus reflect all of the intertemporal influences on investment and saving: expectations of price changes, expectations of future demand, the gain from postponing consumption, the real return on investment, the riskiness of loans, and the risk appetite of lenders. Because domestic spending may be financed by foreign saving and foreign investment by domestic saving, interest rates also influence and are influenced by international financial linkages: exchange rate expectations and circumstances in global capital markets.

This section elucidates some of these connections.

a Interest Rates and Expectations about Inflation

At least superficially, everyone knows what interest rates are: they are what one has to pay for borrowing money to buy a house or a car, or they determine the earnings we get on savings placed in a bank or bond. There are many interest rates – depending, among other factors, on the length of time of the loan (higher interest rates usually compensate for the illiquidity entailed in longer-term loan commitments) and the security offered (a mortgage secured on the equity of a house will generally be at a higher rate if it amounts to 80 percent of the equity than if it amounts to only 20 percent).

But at a more conceptual level, the interest rate is the intertemporal terms of trade – the price of shifting spending between periods. Consider a world with only two periods (t and $t + 1$) and no inflation. If one has a wealth endowment of $10,000 at the start of period t, one can choose between spending it all in period t, or earning interest (at a rate i_t) in period t and then spending a greater amount, $10,000(1 + i_t)$, in period $t + 1$, or some combination of the two.[22] The utility of spending now is usually greater than that of spending in the future. The interest rate is the compensation offered for waiting. On the other side of the transaction is an

---

[22] One could draw a graph depicting this intertemporal choice (it would be similar to Figure 3.4, albeit without the production possibility frontier and with an intertemporal spending indifference curve): the vertical axis would show spending in period $t + 1$, the horizontal axis spending in period t, and the relative price slope would be $1 + r_t$ (where r is the *real* interest rate defined in the text). Changes in the real interest rate would shift spending between periods.

investor who will pay interest for borrowing the money in period t if the return on the investment exceeds the cost of borrowing.

Expectations of inflation change the calculation. I may postpone buying a new car this year for $10,000 if I can buy a better car next year for $10,000(1 + i_t). But if I expect the price of the car to rise, then the calculation depends on the difference between the nominal interest rate (i_t) and the expected rate of inflation (π_t^e). (Note that we will use π to designate inflation when we are abstracting from the particular index used.) There is no sense in waiting unless the real interest rate ($r_t = i_t - \pi_t^e$) is positive and high enough to compensate my austerity. Thus any discussion of interest rates needs to distinguish between real and nominal rates; it is the former that are critical to most saving and investment decisions, and to macro-economic analysis.

Because real interest rates depend on expectations of inflation that are not directly observable, their measurement is complicated.

Economists usually account for expectations in one of four ways:

- Static – i.e., inflation is not expected to change at all, which may be appropriate if policies affecting inflation are very stable.
- Adaptive – i.e., based on the view that people adapt expectations to recent historical experience. For example, if inflation has been fluctuating in a range of 3–6 percent per year for some years, adaptive expectations would posit that economic agents will expect inflation next year to be some weighted average of recent rates within this range. More recent experience is usually more heavily weighted than that which is more remote in time.
- Rational – i.e., consistent with their model of how the economy works. For example, if one has a model of inflation that depends on the difference between the rate of money expansion in the previous year and the rate of growth of potential output in the economy, then a change in either of these variables will change inflation expectations in a way consistent with the model.
- Data-based – i.e., either derived from surveys of economic agents or inferred from financial market data. Inferences may be made from relationships between long- and short-term interest rates, from relationships with exchange rates, or from interest rate data directly, such as the difference between yields on inflation-indexed bonds and conventional bonds.

Whatever the approach to estimating inflation expectations, these expectations are seen as affecting consumption and investment decisions, partly by feeding into perceptions of the real interest rate.

While interest rates are critical market-clearing prices, central banks influence these prices – i.e., they use interest rate policy – to affect demand.[23] The massive weight of central banks in overnight (or very short-term) money markets allows them to set very short-term nominal interest rates, to influence short-term real interest rates, and thus to affect demand and in turn inflation or deflation. For example, the central bank can restrict the money supply and raise the (nominal and real) short-term interest rate to reduce demand and inflation. But as inflation and inflation expectations decline, nominal interest rates across the maturity spectrum will also fall to establish a real rate equilibrium that balances the demand and supply of investible resources.[24]

It is important to understand that real interest rates across the maturity spectrum depend, ultimately, on real circumstances (see Box 3.6) and that the efficacy of monetary policy has limits. If, in a recession, the dearth of investment is due to some real structural phenomenon, monetary stimulus may not be effective. If the scope for real increases in output is not as large as envisaged, an expansionary monetary stance could well elicit a price–wage inflationary spiral and a widening current account deficit. These effects will have further ramifications for expectations, interest rates (especially those beyond the very short term), and exchange rates. Thus real interest rates can be influenced (at least at the short end of the maturity spectrum and for some time) by monetary policy, but they cannot be controlled by the monetary authorities.

Box 3.6 Real Interest Rates and the Real Economy

It is important to understand that the real interest rate is a real – as opposed to a monetary – variable. It is instructive to consider the equilibrating role of the real interest rate from two perspectives.

(continued)

---

[23] Some sectors of the economy – most obviously, housing, automobiles, and consumer durables – are particularly interest-rate sensitive.

[24] Similarly, in a recession where saving is plentiful, fixed investment is anemic, and inventories are rising because of weak sales, a central-bank-induced negative real interest rate shock may well exert the intended countercyclical increase in demand to get the economy back up to potential. But as deflationary expectations ebb (or expectations of inflation rise) nominal interest rates across the spectrum will rise back to a real equilibrium rate.

Box 3.6 (*continued*)

First, suppose the economy is in equilibrium, inflation is low and steady, and the real interest rate is properly anticipating inflation and balancing the demand and supply of investible savings. Now assume that an overly dovish central bank lowers the short-term nominal interest rate (its "policy rate") below the initial equilibrium because it believes (erroneously) that growth is below potential. In the short run, real interest rates may fall along the maturity spectrum, increasing demand and putting upward pressure on inflation. Saving will drop and investment will rise (in response to the lower real interest rates) and inflation expectations will adjust (upward) to the new reality. These developments will lead to a rise in all freely determined nominal interest rates (due to higher inflation expectations) and, indeed, higher real rates (reflecting the dearth of saving) and thus a steepening of the yield curve. Important interest rates (like the medium- to long-term rates that influence decisions on investments and purchases of homes and cars) will rise. These higher rates will last until the initial equilibrium is reestablished. The speed at which these adjustments occur is uncertain, so that central bank errors can add considerable volatility to the real economy. In most cases, however, the central bank will realize its error as inflationary forces emerge, and it will reverse its initial lowering of the policy rate to hasten a return to equilibrium.

Second, consider the same scenario in the context of the Cobb–Douglas production function analysis of Chapter 2, where Y_r is real output, K the capital input, and L the labor input.

$$Y_r = AK^\alpha L^{1-\alpha} \tag{3.13}$$

If we differentiate this function with respect to capital, we get the marginal product of capital – the incremental output produced by the addition of a unit of capital.

$$\delta Yr/\delta K = \alpha A(K/L)^{-(1-\alpha)} \tag{3.14}$$

This is a real relationship that depends negatively on the capital–labor ratio and positively on total factor productivity (A). But real interest rates cannot be unrelated to this. In the initial equilibrium the real interest rate balances the return on investment (the marginal product of capital) with the supply of savings available for investment. If the real interest rate is reduced below the marginal

(*continued*)

Box 3.6 (*continued*)

product of capital, investors will borrow and invest as much as possible – presumably up to the point where the increase in the K/L ratio renders the return on the last investment equal to the real cost of borrowing. If (following from the assumption that the initial real interest rate was an equilibrium) there are not sufficient savings to finance this additional investment, interest rates will rise back up to the point where the real interest rate balances investment with savings.

In the first perspective above we implicitly assumed that the real relationship prevails and that prices and nominal interest rates adjust to restore the initial equilibrium. But if monetary policy is determined and persistent in forcing down real interest rates, and if sufficient foreign saving (ignored in our examples) is forthcoming to finance the additional investment elicited, then adjustment may occur through a higher K/L ratio and a reduced real return on capital. This could have many and various longer-term effects – on investment, the capital–output ratio, the balance of payments and international investment position, and growth. And the new equilibrium real interest rate may well be different from the initial equilibrium level.

b Interest Rates, Expectations, and International Financial Linkages

This section deals explicitly with the international linkages in financial markets through interest rates and exchange rates that, thus far, have only been alluded to. For countries open to external financial flows, interest rates and exchange rates are determined simultaneously and interdependently, they link domestic developments with those in global financial markets, and these linkages are a significant constraint on domestic monetary policy. Chapter 4 expands on the implications for monetary policy, Chapter 6 on the implications for domestic financial markets, and Chapter 7 on the implications for the balance of payments.

Interest rates and expectations, besides being the critical link between the present and the future in all macroeconomic analysis, also link financial markets between countries and currencies.

Consider a numerical example. Suppose you have $100 and the nominal interest rate on a one-year government bond in the United States is i_{us}. You can invest this money for a year and at the end will have $100(1 + i_{us})$. Alternatively you can buy Mexican pesos at the exchange rate E_t (the price of dollars in pesos at time t) and invest in a one-year Mexican government bond at interest rate i_{mex}. In this latter case, at the end of the year you will have $100.E_t (1 + i_{mex\ t})$ in pesos, which you can convert back into dollars (by dividing by E_{t+1}). If the rate of interest on pesos is much higher than that on dollars this might seem like a preferable strategy. But this will only be true if the value of the peso against the dollar does not fall by more than enough to offset the interest rate differential. So, clearly, the investment decision depends not only on interest rates but also on your expectation of the dollar–peso exchange rate at the end of the year (E^e_{t+1}). The breakeven equilibrium position can be written as

$$1 + i_{us.t} = (E_t/E^e_{t+1})(1 + i_{mex.t}) \qquad (3.15)$$

i = nominal interest rate (with subscripts showing the United States and Mexico)

Subscripts on the exchange rate E show the transaction date and superscript (e) denotes an expectation at time t for the value at time $t + 1$.

This equation is referred to as uncovered interest parity. If the left side is larger you stay in dollars, if the right side is larger you move into pesos. But, of course, you don't know what the peso exchange rate will be at the end of the year, so making a guess about the future peso rate involves a risk. If your preferred habitat is the US dollar rather than the peso, and given that there is risk attached to E^e_{t+1}, it makes sense to add a risk premium (rp) to the equation to compensate for the risk of an error in expectations.[25]

$$1 + i_{us.t} = (E_t/E^e_{t+1})(1 + i_{mex.t})/(1 + rp) \qquad (3.16)$$

rp = the risk premium (measured in the same dimension as the interest rate – i.e., if the US interest rate is 4 percent, the risk premium is 2 percentage points, and no change is expected in the exchange rate, then $i_{mex} = (1.04 \times 1.02) - 1 = 6.08$ percent)·

In financial markets, it is not necessary to take the risk on exchange rate expectations because there is a forward market for pesos against dollars.

[25] "Preferred habitat" is the numeraire currency in which an investor measures the rate of return. This will differ between investors and is likely to be the investor's home currency. But, for our purposes, it is easiest to think of it as the currency in which the largest weight of investors measures returns. A "risk premium" is the additional return that is required to compensate for risk – in this case the exchange rate risk. If the expected future exchange rate were the same as the current rate, there would still be a probability distribution around this expected value and some risk attached to it. Therefore, the interest rate on the peso would probably still need to be a couple of percentage points higher than that on equivalent dollar assets to compensate for the risk of a depreciation of the peso.

If you make the investment in pesos and you know that at time $t + 1$ you will have $100.E_t(1+i_{mex\ t})$ in pesos, you can sell that many pesos forward at time t at the forward exchange rate F_t^{t+1} – i.e., the price of dollars in pesos quoted at time t for a transaction that will be consummated at time $t + 1$. This means we can write an arbitrage equilibrium equation by simply substituting the forward exchange rate for the expected future spot rate.

$$1 + i_{us.t} = (E_t/F_t^{t+1})(1 + i_{mex.t}) \qquad (3.17)$$

F_t^{t+1} = the forward exchange rate for $t + 1$ quoted at time t

In principle this equilibrium should always hold unless there is counterparty risk – i.e., some perceived probability that the Mexican government will renege on its repayment or that the counterparty to the forward exchange rate transaction will fail to deliver. In practice, the difference between the two sides of the equation is usually very close to zero.[26]

Reverting to (3.16), ignoring counterparty risk, and rearranging yields

$$[(1 + i_{mex.t})/(1 + i_{us.t})] = (E_{t+1}^e/E_t)(1 + rp) \qquad (3.18)$$

If the risk premium is zero, this equation can be simplified to show that the expected depreciation of the Mexican peso over any period is equal to the difference in nominal interest rate yields between risk-equivalent bonds that mature at the end of the period. This means that, because of an expected depreciation of the peso, the Mexican government has to pay a higher rate than the US government to borrow. If the risk premium is positive, the required rate differential is even higher.

This is an important equation. Suppose there was a sudden exogenous jump in the risk premium on pesos, perhaps because of increased uncertainty about developments in the price of oil or political uncertainties in Mexico (either of which would increase the volatility of the exchange rate of the peso). Then one of two things would have to happen: either the spot value of the peso would have to drop proportionally ($E_t\uparrow$) to keep the right side of the equation unchanged; or the Mexican interest rate would have to jump so that the left side of the equation increased to match the right side (or some combination of the two). These changes in E_t and/or $i_{mex\ t}$ would need to be even larger if, at the same time, the expected future exchange rate of the peso were to drop ($E_{t+1}^e\uparrow$).

---

[26] We often see this relationship as an approximation showing that the equilibrium spot-forward exchange rate differential ("forward discount or premium") is equal to the interest rate differential.

Thus a jump in the risk premium related to some future event has an immediate effect: the interest rate has to rise to reflect the higher risk premium, and/or the peso has to depreciate immediately to the point where an appreciation (or a smaller depreciation) is expected. If the government or central bank resists a rise in the interest rate, the exchange rate will react. Thus the interest rate and the exchange rate are determined simultaneously and are interdependent. A country (or its central bank) cannot control both interest rates and exchange rates unless it limits international financial transactions.[27]

Every economy is buffeted by real developments and price signals emanating both from domestic markets and from abroad. Price signals from abroad can be particularly difficult to interpret correctly; the ways in which they impose constraints on the domestic policy and influence domestic developments can be subtle, but nevertheless important. The message from this section is that changes in exchange rates (real and nominal) are determined interdependently with changes in interest rates (real and nominal), price and exchange rate expectations, and risk premia. Box 3.7 will be useful for those interested in synthesizing the various international price considerations covered in this chapter. It develops the full relationship between real interest rates, inflation expectations, and expectations of exchange rate developments taking into account trade in goods and services and in financial instruments.

Box 3.7 Real Interest Rates, Real Exchange Rates, and Interest Arbitrage

Over anything but the shortest run, where the central bank can exercise substantial control, the nominal interest rate reflects a summation of expected interest rates for shorter periods within the longer period. These in turn reflect expectations about both future central bank policy and inflation and myriad risks ranging from changes in a government's borrowing to private borrowing patterns. We can write the nominal interest rate (i) in terms of the real interest rate (r) and the inflation expectation (π^e) at time t for the period until the contract matures. (The duration of the contract is arbitrary, so this may be an inflation expectation for a 2-year or a 10-year period.) Thus

(continued)

---

[27] This is often referred to as the impossible (or unholy) trinity: an exchange rate objective requires relinquishing influence over domestic interest rates or restricting international financial transactions; an interest rate objective requires relinquishing either control of the exchange rate or restricting financial transactions. These ideas are developed further in Chapter 4.

Box 3.7 (*continued*)

$$1 + i_t = (1 + r_t)(1 + \pi_t^e) \tag{3.19}$$

Continuing the Mexico–US analysis of uncovered interest parity from the text, we know that

$$(1 + i_{us.t}) = (E_t/E_{t+1}^e)(1 + i_{mex.t})/(1 + rp) \tag{3.20}$$

The inclusion of a risk premium (rp) reflects the assumption that most investors have a preferred habitat in US dollars and the expected exchange rate (pesos per dollar) at maturity is subject to risk. Substituting (3.19) into (3.20) and rearranging puts inflation expectations explicitly into the international arbitrage between the United States and Mexico.

$$(1 + r_{mex.t})(1 + \pi_{mex.t}^e) = (E_{t+1}^e/E_t)[(1 + r_{us.t})(1 + \pi_{us.t}^e)(1 + rp)] \tag{3.21}$$

If we set the risk premium initially at zero and rearrange we get

$$[(1 + r_{mex.t})/(1 + r_{us.t})] = [E_{t+1}^e/E_t][(1 + \pi_{us.t}^e)/(1 + \pi_{mex.t}^e)] \tag{3.22}$$

This tells us that if purchasing power parity held for aggregate price indices – i.e., if changes in the exchange rate were expected to perfectly offset the aggregate inflation differential – the right-hand side of the equation would equal unity and real interest rates would be equalized between the two countries.[1]

This is an awkward result insofar as underlying real returns on capital (and thus equilibrium real interest rates) are likely to be higher in capital-scarce Mexico (unless TFP is substantially lower), but we might well expect to see a real appreciation (rather than a depreciation) of the peso from Balassa–Samuelson effects (discussed in Box 3.5). The conundrum is usually resolved by assuming that the risk premium is not zero, so that

$$[(1 + r_{mex.t})/(1 + r_{us.t})] = [E_{t+1}^e/E_t][(1 + \pi_{us.t}^e)(1 + rp)/(1 + \pi_{mex.t}^e)] \tag{3.23}$$

As an aside, it is worth noting that the forward peso/dollar rate (F_t^{t+1}) at time t for time $t+1$ is likely to differ from the expected future spot rate insofar as the forward discount is usually identical to the nominal interest rate differential and thus includes the risk premium. If $E_t = 20$, $E_{t+1}^e = 21$, $i_{us\ t} = 5\%$, and $rp = 2$ percentage points, then

(*continued*)

Box 3.7 (*continued*)

$$i_{mex.t} = 100[(E^e_{t+1}/E_t)(1+i_{us.t})(1+rp)-1] = 12.455\% \quad (3.24)$$

and

$$F^{t+1}_t = E_t[(1+i_{mex.t})/(1+i_{us.t})] = 21.42 \quad (3.24)$$

[1] Recalling that $1+\pi^e = P^e_{t+1}/P_t$, we can show that if purchasing power holds then
$[E^e_{t+1}/E_t][(1+\pi^e_{us\ t})/(1+\pi^e_{mex\ t})] = 1$

4 Exercises

1 Ignore for simplicity the differences between measures of aggregate output and expenditure and just designate aggregate output (GNP or GDP) as Y. Suppose nominal Y in 2017 is €1,000 billion and this comprises €1,000 billion in total domestic demand plus €300 in exports of goods and services minus €300 billion in imports of goods and services. All wages are indexed to the CPI and wages account for 65 percent of income while capital and entrepreneurial income (hereafter "profits") amount together to 35 percent of the aggregate. At the beginning of year t the country, an oil importer, suffers a substantial terms-of-trade loss: import prices rise by 20 percent owing to a jump in oil prices in global markets while, at the immediate time of the price jump, exchange rates and all prices and volumes of domestic output are completely unchanged. Assume that in the short run, with which we are concerned here, the real volume of demand for higher-priced imports remains unchanged.

In answering the questions below do not be concerned about second-order effects; the objective is simply to get quick rule-of-thumb results for the immediate impact.

  (i)   What (in qualitative terms) will happen to (a) the GDP deflator and (b) the CPI?
  (ii) Can you suggest how one might calculate the effective loss of real income as a percentage of aggregate income?
  (iii) What happens to "profits" in year t and what will likely be the ramifications of this?

2 You are charged with the task of assessing the competitiveness of an economy but your client is not entirely clear on what this means and exactly what your assessment will be used for. The country in question is a rapidly developing country with a recent history of high growth in both absolute and per capita terms. You look at two different measures of competitiveness: (a) a real effective exchange rate (REER) using CPIs for the home country and an appropriately weighted average of its trading partners and competitors to convert the similarly weighted nominal effective exchange rate into real terms, and (b) a REER rate with the same weights but using ULCs in the manufacturing sector rather than CPIs. You find that the CPI-based REER shows a substantial real appreciation of the home currency and thus a seeming erosion of competitiveness, but the manufacturing ULC-based rate shows a depreciation and thus a seeming gain in competitiveness.

(i) Suggest a plausible scenario that would explain your REER observations.

(ii) What additional data would you want to look at before coming to any conclusions about competitiveness?

(iii) What would you advise a client who was thinking about investing in the country?

Note: Readers will be capable of more complete answers to these questions after absorbing the material on the balance of payments in Chapter 7. It may, therefore, be worth returning to this question at that stage.

3 You are part of a team of consultants to the government of a small island economy. The country in question produces three goods: construction (which is nontraded), textiles (largely for export), and gold (all for export). Gold ore reserves are very large and are not expected to be depleted in the foreseeable future. The central bank allows the exchange rate to be flexible but it intervenes to reduce rapid changes in the rate. The global markets for textiles and gold have been fairly stable and boring for the last few years, and the economy has seen steady if unspectacular growth, full employment, and a balanced external current account. But this year the dollar price of gold has doubled.

(i) What will be the likely effects of this sharp price change on resource allocation in the economy?

(ii) What, if any, problems does this present, what policies would you prescribe, and what judgments would they depend upon?

Note: readers should be able to provide a partial response to this exercise after this chapter, but will be capable of a much more complete answer after working through the fiscal, monetary, and balance-of-payments material in the following chapters. It may, therefore, be worth returning to this exercise again at a later stage.

4 A presidential election is about to be held in the United States, and the two candidates differ starkly on trade policies. One wants to expand a free trade agreement between the United States and Mexico. The other wants to change or end the agreement and impose barriers on imports from Mexico to protect US businesses from Mexican competition. Mexico has prospered under the free trade agreement with the United States: its growth has been sustained and its small current account deficit has been easily financed without concerns about an excessive buildup of foreign debt. As the US presidential campaign progresses, polling results raise the probability of a win for the protectionist candidate. This may change the perceived exchange rate risk for the peso, but it is generally accepted that default risk remains negligible. The Mexican central bank targets inflation and allows the peso to float; but it intervenes to offset excessive volatility and exchange rate movements that it sees as unwarranted and likely to be reversed.

(a) As the polls move in favor of the protectionist candidate, describe and explain (verbally, i.e., without equations) the likely effects on (i) the exchange rate of the peso against the dollar, and (ii) interest rates on peso debt.

(b) Suppose the initial one-year interest rate on pesos is 10 percent and that on dollars is 5 percent. The initial spot value of the peso is 20 to the dollar, and the initial risk premium is 2 percent. What is the expected future value of the peso one year hence consistent with these numbers?

(c) Now suppose that with the increased probability of the protectionist candidate winning, the US interest rate is unchanged and the Mexican authorities somehow manage to keep the one-year peso interest rate unchanged. But the expected future peso exchange rate is depreciated by 4 percent relative to that derived above, and the risk premium has risen to 5 percent. What is the new equilibrium spot exchange rate of the peso?

CHAPTER 4

Monetary Policy and Accounts

This chapter on the role and conduct of monetary policy covers four broad topics:

1 *The monetary framework and how it constrains policy options.*
2 *Countercyclical monetary policy and its limits.*
3 *How to read central bank and banking sector balance sheets.*
4 *How to use these balance sheets for policy analysis.*

Money is the source of much confusion in economic thinking. Many people do not differentiate clearly between monetary holdings and command over real resources, between money and real wealth. Casual discussion about money and wealth brings to mind the story of a central bank governor of a high-inflation country who tells his dictatorial president-for-life that the country is running out of money. The governor has in mind hard currency holdings (foreign exchange reserves) that can be used to buy goods, as opposed to local currency that can be produced at will but has become almost worthless over years of high inflation. The dictator executes his governor when, on inspection of the central bank vaults, he finds a large stock of local currency notes adorned with his handsome visage. The story is probably apocryphal, but it illustrates a confusion about money that can be costly – especially for brave (or foolhardy) central bank governors.

It also illustrates, in the extreme, the constant need to recognize the limits of a policy that works through a nominal instrument (i.e., money or nominal interest rates) but often seeks to have real effects. These limits become critical especially when political influences come into play – e.g., a government that wants a central bank to print money to finance a higher deficit or to ease private credit conditions excessively. They also define the balancing act that central banks face in, on the one hand, preserving the value of the domestic currency (as a store of value, a means of exchange, and a reliable numeraire), while, on the other hand, using monetary policy as an instrument of countercyclical macroeconomic policy.

Another feature of monetary policy is that the choices available to a central bank and the effectiveness of any policy depend on the framework in which it operates. "Framework" in this context refers to a country's financial arrangements and the commitments that constrain the actions of its central bank. The exchange rate regime and the openness of the country to international financial flows are critical components of this framework. A small open economy with a fixed exchange rate does not have the same options for policy as a large country with a floating exchange rate. Understanding monetary policy choices and their effects requires first knowing the country's monetary framework.

This chapter, therefore, starts with a discussion of monetary policy frameworks and then turns to a description of the scope for countercyclical monetary policy within the most commonly used framework at present. Next the chapter explains how to read the monetary accounts. The last section focuses on how to use the monetary accounts as a diagnostic device and for policy analysis; it uses a number of thought experiments and real-world illustrations to elucidate these uses.

1 Monetary Policy Frameworks

"Inflation is always and everywhere a monetary phenomenon."[1] Milton Friedman wrote these words in 1970, and they remain a well-respected description of the medium to long run. Shocks and other pressures on prices can start inflationary processes and even sustain them for a while, but monetary accommodation is necessary for persistent inflation above moderate levels. A country's monetary policy framework is the formal statement of how a central bank's decisions on the nominal variables under its purview (its policy interest rate, the exchange rate, and/or the domestic money supply) are constrained.

Illustrations of the importance of a monetary policy framework abound. Take a government with a widening deficit but not wishing to raise taxes or cut spending. An obvious temptation is to press the central bank into excessive monetary expansion. Such money creation increases the government's command over resources ("seigniorage"), and inflation surprises (increases in inflation not anticipated in nominal interest rates) reduce

---

[1]   Friedman, Milton, The Counter-Revolution in Monetary Theory, IEA Occasional Paper, No. 33, Institute of Economic Affairs, London 1970, 11, https://miltonfriedman.hoover.org/friedman_images/Collections/2016c21/IEA_1970.pdf.

the real cost of servicing its debt. Inflation, therefore, is a type of tax that shifts resources from the private sector to the government (see Box 4.1). A strong monetary framework is a constraint on the central bank's succumbing to such pressure.

Box 4.1 Seigniorage and the Inflation Tax[1]

When the central bank increases the outstanding stock of non-interest-bearing base money, it transfers real resources to (increases the purchasing power of) the government. It usually does this by buying outstanding bonds (private or government) from the private sector. On the asset side of the central bank balance sheet there is an increase in interest-bearing bonds; on the liability side, an increase in cash or other base money that is either unremunerated or remunerated at a very low rate. So the profits of the central bank rise, and much of this is transferred to the government.

We can define real resources from seigniorage as the change in the money base divided by the price level

$$SEI = \frac{dMB}{dt} \frac{1}{P_t} \qquad (4.1)$$

Assume (following Cagan) that the demand for monetary base in real terms is a function of real GDP (Y_r) and inflation (π)

$$MB = P \cdot F(Y_r, \pi) = P \cdot e^{(\lambda - a\pi)} Y_r \qquad (4.2)$$

From (4.2) we can write

$$\frac{dMB}{dt} = P \cdot \frac{dF}{dY_r} \frac{dY_r}{dt} + \frac{dP}{dt} F(\ldots) + P \cdot \frac{dF}{d\pi} \frac{d\pi}{dt} \qquad (4.3)$$

substituting (4.3) into (4.1) yields

$$SEI = \frac{dF}{dY_r} \frac{dY_r}{dt} + \pi \cdot F(\ldots) + \frac{dF}{d\pi} \frac{d\pi}{dt}$$

If there is no inflation, the second and third terms on the right drop out, and the first term shows that the government can earn seigniorage by satisfying the higher demand for monetary services due to real growth. If there is inflation, the second and third terms show a tradeoff.

(*continued*)

Box 4.1 (*continued*)

From the second term, the higher the inflation rate, the higher the seigniorage from the inflation tax, *for any given demand for money base*. The money base is the tax base, and inflation is the tax rate. From the third term, however, the higher the inflation rate, the lower the demand for money so that the base for the inflation tax declines.

Given stable coefficients (λ and α) in the money demand function of equation (4.2), it is easy to show that the steady-state inflation rate that maximizes the inflation tax is $\pi = \frac{1}{\alpha}$; therefore, if the absolute value of the inflation elasticity of demand for real base money (α) is ½ then the optimizing rate of inflation is 200 percent. But in reality α is unlikely to be stable. It is more likely that the demand for money will simply collapse as inflation becomes more punitive. Countries that have relied excessively on the inflation tax have usually ended up in hyperinflation.

[1]   Cagan, P., *The Monetary Dynamics of Hyperinflation in Studies in the Quantity Theory of Money* (ed. Milton Friedman), University of Chicago Press, Chicago, 1956

A monetary policy framework consists, broadly, of three parts: it spells out the objectives that are to guide monetary policy decisions, the tools that are to be used to meet those objectives, and strategies for informing the public of the central bank's views and outlook. Because monetary policy decisions operate through financial markets that are highly sensitive to new information, small changes in actual policy or in market expectations of what policy will be can elicit rapid and substantial flows of funds, both domestically and internationally. The framework seeks to avoid disruptive policy surprises by giving market participants a reasonable degree of predictability on policy responses to new developments. This transparency also bolsters confidence in the commitment to an objective and thus helps to anchor market expectations.

A useful lens through which to view the evolution of monetary policy frameworks is the impossible (or unholy) trinity mentioned in Chapter 3. It characterizes the choice central banks must make about the constraints under which they will operate. To repeat the definition of this key concept, it holds that a central bank cannot over time simultaneously fix the exchange rate, maintain openness to external financial markets, and pursue an independent monetary policy (i.e., set interest rates that are different from the structure of interest rates in global markets). Of the three pillars of the trinity, a central bank can choose only two. Any central bank that ignores this constraint will sooner or later need to choose which part of the trinity to jettison. For example, in an economy open to global financial markets, a central bank that cuts its interest rate to stimulate demand when a negative output gap occurs will set off financial outflows. All else being equal, this increase in demand for foreign currency puts pressure on the domestic currency to depreciate. So if the central bank wanted to maintain a fixed exchange rate, it would have to sell its foreign exchange reserves into the market. If the exchange market pressure were sustained, reserves would eventually be depleted. The central bank would need to decide whether to stop the financial outflows by imposing controls, to realign its interest rate with the dominant global interest rate, or to let its currency depreciate. We will explore the manifestations of the impossible trinity in section 5.

Before developing the tools to do this, however, we review how actual choices on monetary frameworks have evolved.

a The Bretton Woods Period: A Reserve Currency Anchor

The Bretton Woods period ran from the end of World War II until 1973. The monetary policy framework for the vast majority of countries was actually a set of rules governing the international monetary system.[2] It essentially consisted of a commitment by every participating country to fix a par value for the exchange rate of its currency against the US dollar and to conduct foreign exchange market intervention (unlimited purchases or sales of foreign exchange) to keep the actual exchange rate at, or very close to, the par value. De facto, international financial flows were rather limited during most of this period – less by outright controls or restrictions than by the as yet underdeveloped linkages among financial institutions.

In fact, even with limited financial mobility, it proved difficult for many countries to sustain both an independent monetary policy and a fixed exchange rate. Monetary easing in one country that inflated costs and prices

---

[2] The Bretton Woods System was established at a global conference, held at Bretton Woods, New Hampshire in 1944, which set up the rules and institutions for the postwar monetary system. The Bretton Woods System ended with the advent of generalized floating among most advanced countries in 1973.

(relative to those of trading partners) would weaken competitiveness and the current account of the balance of payments. Although the current account response to monetary easing is slower than that of an open financial account, if current account deficits are sustained then the same pressures for depreciation (and need for sales of central bank reserves) would occur. The Bretton Woods framework was therefore disciplining for all countries (except the United States).

The United States' exception was due to its currency, the US dollar, being the reserve currency (the currency in which most other countries kept foreign exchange holdings). The United States could create dollars and therefore could not be forced into more stringent monetary conditions by a loss of reserves. However, until August 1971 the United States was committed to exchanging gold for foreign holdings of dollars at the fixed price of $35 per fine ounce. Therefore, too rapid an expansion of the dollar money supply would have reduced the feasibility and credibility of this commitment.

Several sources of strain on the Bretton Woods system emerged in the late 1960s. Expansionary policies in the United States pushed up inflation, accelerating outflows to other large countries. In some countries, fixed parities made equilibrating real appreciations (due to substantial productivity gains and Belassa–Samuelson effects) impossible to achieve without unwanted inflation.[3] And, for many countries, the constraint on monetary policy autonomy became increasingly unacceptable. When, in 1971, the United States revoked its pledge to exchange dollars for gold at a fixed rate, the effective nominal anchor in the system became simply the self-imposed restraint of the US Federal Reserve System (the central bank of the United States, often called "the Fed"). In 1973, many large countries took the final step of abandoning their commitment to fixing their exchange rates. They were then free to conduct independent money policies, consistent with their growth and inflation objectives, while leaving the level of their exchange rates to market forces.

With the demise of the fixed exchange rate system, countries had to find a new monetary policy framework that would constitute a nominal anchor to contain inflation and inflationary expectations.

---

[3] Even under a fixed exchange rate system changes in real exchange rates can take place through differences in inflation. If underlying real conditions (perhaps technology and productivity) improve in one country relative to others, that country's competitive position improves, it experiences balance of payments surpluses, foreign exchange gains, increases in its money supply, and, eventually, an equilibrating real appreciation through higher inflation. Difficulties emerge, however, if the country is resistant to an increase in inflation.

b Money Supply Targeting

After the Bretton Woods era, money supply targeting with exchange rate flexibility came into vogue for central banks in large economies. (Many smaller countries continued to fix their exchange rates to the dollar or to another major trading partner, and thus to forgo independent monetary policy.) Money supply targeting was an organizing framework for central banks' independent monetary policy decisions. It was based on the view that there is an econometrically robust, stable, long-run money demand function – i.e., a parametric relationship between the amount of money the public wished to hold and the influences affecting that demand (chiefly the price level, real GDP, and the short-term nominal interest rate). True, it was acknowledged that the money demand function might exhibit short-run instability. But insofar as real GDP was taken to be determined by real supply conditions over time and nominal GDP by the money supply, an appropriate target for the money supply would allow the central bank to achieve its inflation objective.[4]

Money supply targeting was exemplified by the policy of the German Bundesbank in the 20 years after 1974. For most of this time the Bundesbank would announce an annual money target based on a calculation of *potential* real GDP one year ahead and an acceptable rate of inflation.[5] There was a small automatic countercyclical element in this calculation insofar as monetary conditions would be somewhat less stringent if real GDP fell below calculated potential and more stringent if GDP was above the calculated potential. If one plays around with the equations, the similarities between this framework and a nominal GDP targeting regime or an inflation targeting regime become apparent – but *only* if one really believes in the stability of a relatively parsimonious money demand function.[6]

---

[4] The conventional long-run money demand equation of the time looked like this:

$$Ln(M/P)_t = \alpha + \beta \cdot Ln(Y_{r,t}) + \gamma \cdot i_t$$

with M being the relevant monetary aggregate and variables (other than i) in logs. Parameters α, β, and γ were thought to be well-determined and stable over time. Short-run dynamics were usually introduced when estimating the parameters.

[5] The actual monetary aggregate targeted was a weighted average of various conventional aggregates.

[6] The Bundesbank missed its money targets about as often as it hit them. But the press conference at the end of each month, on monetary conditions and where the money supply was relative to target, was an effective device for communicating the Bundesbank's views on the economy and influencing expectations about inflation and thus, most importantly, wage negotiations.

The demand for any given monetary aggregate, however, is sensitive to financial innovation (e.g., the growth of near-money savings options and new credit instruments). Therefore, as innovation accelerated in the 1980s, confidence in a stable relationship between money and the conventional variables in the money demand equation eroded. Countries (usually large ones) not fixing to the dollar or another major currency started to move to a more discretionary (less mechanical) regime of reviewing a broad array of economic data and then setting a short-term official interest rate in order to affect monetary conditions and, ultimately, inflation. Objectives for growth and employment also started to take on greater weight. The result was a relatively nontransparent process that was seen as providing an insufficient anchor to expectations about how central banks would respond to shocks and what inflation would be.

c Inflation Targeting

By the early 1990s, support started to grow for so-called *inflation targeting* (IT). This reflected diminishing confidence in the stability of estimated money demand functions, a move toward flexible exchange rates in more countries, and a desire for a more formal constraint on monetary policy discretion. Central banks in New Zealand, Canada, the United Kingdom, and Sweden, as the earliest inflation targeters, contributed to developing the practical aspects of this policy framework.

In practice, IT amounts to the central bank having a target (or target range) for inflation, and then setting some short-term official or "policy" interest rate to achieve that target. At periodic meetings, the central bank's monetary policy committee (MPC) – the group that in most countries makes interest rate decisions – reviews the multiyear outlook for inflation and decides whether to raise the policy interest rate, lower it, or keep it unchanged in order to meet its inflation target.[7] Lags between changes in monetary conditions and changes in inflation mean that, in fact, IT entails setting monetary conditions today to achieve the targeted inflation rate in the future, perhaps two years hence.

The central bank then uses its policy instruments – generically, the short-term interest rate (or rates) under its purview, purchases and sales of securities, and, perhaps, changes in the reserves that banks (often called depository institutions, or DIs) are required to hold at the central

---

[7]   Not all central banks have MPCs: interest rate decisions in some are made by the senior management of the central bank. In the United States, the equivalent of the MPC is called the "Open Market Committee (OMC)."

bank -to affect inflation and inflation expectations..[8] The traditional view has been that through its control of the short-term policy rate and its effect on expectations, the central bank can influence the whole structure of interest rates (including longer-term segments of financial markets), although it is recognized that the structure almost never moves in lockstep.

IT is consistent, in principle, with the impossible trinity. Most IT countries are broadly open to financial flows from and to other countries (what we will call an open external financial account [EFA]) and yet can exercise monetary policy independence because they permit at least some flexibility of their exchange rate. (Box 4.2 elaborates on the meaning of an open EFA.) IT thus represents a fundamental choice about the tradeoffs in the impossible trinity: while countries typically value a degree of stability – or, at least reduced volatility – in the exchange rate (which occupies such a central role in most economies), most value even more (i) the ability to set domestic interest rates at the level appropriate for the country's cyclical position and inflation objective, and (ii) the opportunity to use foreign savings to finance investment (or the opportunity to place domestic savings in excess of domestic investment needs abroad) through unrestricted financial flows.

Box 4.2 What Is an "Open" or "Closed" External Financial Account?

The terms "open" or "closed" external financial account (EFA, often called the "capital account" based on now out-of-date terminology) are used as an approximation for what are actually not black and white designations. While most large advanced countries can unambiguously be labeled open, many countries fall on a spectrum between fully open and fully closed. Determining where they fall (and thus how the mechanisms described in the text actually work) can be tricky for several reasons.

Many emerging market countries have partial and often not very effective restrictions on EFA flows. They want to be open to inflows of FDI or other stable long-term inflows. They may also want to finance government deficits by bond issues in major financial centers or

(continued)

---

[8]   DIs are often also called "deposit money banks" (DMBs) or commercial banks.

Box 4.2 (*continued*)

nonresident purchases of domestic currency bonds. But once a country opens to such flows, it can be hard to screen out speculative short-term flows, and these are seen as complicating macroeconomic management. Volatile short-term flows are the main drivers of the limits on policy independence in a fixed exchange rate system and exchange rate volatility in a floating system. Many emerging markets therefore have restrictions that seek to limit short-term, more speculative financial flows, but permit longer-term, more stable inflows. The effectiveness of such measures is never perfect.

Another problem in classification stems from the difference between de jure (legal) and de facto (what we shall call effective) openness. In short, countries may have few legal restrictions on EFA flows but small actual flows, perhaps because of illiquid domestic financial markets, low domestic savings, or risk premia so high that foreign investors are not interested in their assets. Other countries may have substantial legal restrictions but these are porous and unenforceable, so that there are sizable flows especially in times of distress. Several Latin American countries had such a combination during the 1980s and 1990s when deteriorating economic conditions sparked large outflows that slipped through the legal restrictions. The IMF keeps a compendium of members' EFA restrictions, but the correlation between these and actual flows is not strong.

Characterizations of a country's openness might rely on the size of a country's actual EFA flows. The problem here is that low current flows are not a reliable indication of future flows. For example, a country facing a surge in inflows that are feared to be potentially volatile may employ measures to try to contain them. Such active EFA management, increasingly supported by the IMF, then becomes an adjunct to monetary policy in managing the policy response to shocks. However, it means that the country, viewed as open, may in fact become effectively more closed.

In the end, we use "effective openness" for countries that have some combination of low or ineffective legal restrictions on EFA flows, adequate sophistication of domestic financial markets to accommodate foreign inflows, and low enough risk premia to make it plausible that nonresidents would consider holding the country's assets. This is not a watertight designation of a country's openness.

The advantages of IT as a framework for domestic monetary policy decisions are accountability, transparency, an anchoring of expectations, and breadth. The senior officials in the central bank – the governor and the members of the MPC – are accountable for meeting the target, and both the target and the decisions of the committee are open to critical scrutiny. Insofar as the inflation target is credible, it helps anchor expectations of price and wage setters; these expectations feed back through wage and price developments to actual inflation in later periods. And in assessing the inflation outlook and making policy the central bank can have a perspective that is broader than that summarized in the money demand function. It can consider any influences included in the most encompassing model of inflation: the output gap, wage and productivity developments, changes in exchange rates, the terms of trade, the government budget, or anything else that is likely to affect inflation.

The weakness of IT stems from the notion that central bankers focus solely on inflation measured by an index of prices of goods and services. In fact, they would be remiss if they didn't pay close attention to myriad other considerations, not just for their effect on inflation but also as threats in their own right to economic stability. Such considerations might include large financial inflows or outflows through the EFA, rapid credit growth, asset price bubbles, unsustainable changes in external competitiveness, changes in fiscal policy, and cyclical swings in activity. Formally, some countries have a "dual mandate" – i.e., a mandate to target both the inflation rate and output or the unemployment rate. But insofar as most central banks would adjust policy if some development not included in the formal mandate were to run awry, IT leaves some scope for murkiness in the predictability of policy.

d Radical Frameworks for Specific Circumstances: Currency Boards and Dollarization

The disciplining features of fixed exchange rates are imposed even more rigidly in a currency board regime or in a dollarized regime. The former involves a commitment to a fixed parity vis-à-vis a reserve currency, but with an added feature: when a central bank operates as a currency board, it issues domestic currency only in exchange for the reserve currency. Therefore, the currency board's monetary liabilities are 100 percent backed by reserve currency holdings – a feature meant to secure credibility either after a period of extreme money expansion and instability or in circumstances where currency unification is in prospect (e.g., Estonia and Lithuania leading up to euro adoption). Except for transfers of profits, largely from foreign interest earnings on reserve holdings, currency boards do not extend financing to the government. There is absolutely no scope for independent monetary policy. Box 4.3 describes Bulgaria's adoption of a currency board to break a hyperinflation in 1997.[9]

Box 4.3 Bulgaria: The Anatomy of a Decision to Adopt a Currency Board

Bulgaria's simmering economic crisis during 1994–1996 exploded in late 1996 (see Box 4.8 below). The problems underpinning the crisis were deep in the fabric of society (especially weak governance over loss-making public enterprises and ensuing fiscal and monetary support for them after central planning ended in the early 1990s). From a macroeconomic viewpoint three aspects of the crisis stood out.

First, after years of poor supervision and prudential control of both state- and privately-owned banks (which were major conduits for supporting loss-making enterprises), growing awareness of pervasive insolvency set off bank runs in 1996. Not only did the ensuing loss of the deposit base further worsened banks' balance sheets but many of the deposits were in foreign currency. The central bank supported banks faced with these deposit outflows by supplying local currency and foreign exchange.

Second, government finances were unsustainable. Despite surpluses on the general government primary account (revenue – expenditure + interest costs) almost continuously since 1993, other cascading factors kept public debt above 100 percent of GDP. Critical among these were debt inherited from the central planning era, lending to and direct purchases of equity in banks, and extreme debt servicing costs as effective interest rates far exceeded nominal GDP growth. (Fiscal sustainability is covered in Chapter 5.)

Third, massive excess money creation fed a rise in inflation to a peak of over 2,000 percent in March 1997. Money creation reflected direct central bank financing of banks and the government. The latter

---

[9] The adoption of a currency board typically succeeds in bringing inflation down rapidly. But insofar as the rate of inflation under the currency board may initially still exceed that of trading partners for some time, substantial real appreciation often occurs in the early stages of a currency board. Often some real appreciation persists and eventually strains the sustainability of the currency board.

Box 4.3 (*continued*)

was constrained by an annual legal limit, but the government did an end-run around the ceiling by borrowing from commercial banks, which in turn received support from the central bank. With high inflation and depreciation, the demand for domestic currency dropped precipitously. Distrust of banks also prompted residents to withdraw foreign currency deposits from September 1995 onward. Nevertheless, valuation effects raised the share of these foreign currency deposits to 55 percent of total deposits by the end of 1996.

Two failed stabilization attempts during 1995–1996 had destroyed public trust in any government action to address the problems. A complete break from the past was essential, and a new government in early 1997 provided the needed political setting.

A rigid rules-based system – in the form of a currency board – was seen as the only way to credibly halt monetary accommodation of banks and the government. Other parts of the stabilization program were critical to the success of the currency board:

- The public debt stock/GDP had to be reduced, and, for banks that could be made solvent, balance sheets strengthened. This was largely accomplished through the extreme inflation and depreciation during the program discussions in early 1997. Those influences slashed the real value of domestic currency debt and raised the value of foreign-currency assets of banks (foreign exchange liabilities having been drawn down with the outflow of FX deposits). The IMF and other sources of official support helped the government service debt as public confidence was restored and risk premia on the debt fell.
- Reforms to the banking system (closing banks, privatization, prudential reforms, and improved supervision) and to the government's tax and spending authority were put in place to support the system after the initial stabilization.
- Broader economic reforms – in tax, public spending, and regulatory policies – were adopted to create an environment favorable for investment and growth.

Stabilization began soon after plans for the currency board were announced in early 1997 (before implementation on July 1, 1997). Annualized inflation for July–December fell to 35 percent, while the annualized commercial bank lending rate fell from 727 percent in March to 14 percent in December. The currency board remains in effect as the monetary anchor.

Dollarization is an even more extreme approach to disciplining monetary policy. It entails eliminating a domestic currency and using the US dollar in its place. (Other major currencies can serve this purpose, but the issuing country must be large enough that demand in the user country is a small part of total money outstanding.) Obviously, dollarization leaves no possibility for monetary financing of the government or any form of monetary policy independence. But dollarizing also involves forgoing seigniorage (there is no central bank). It offers the highest possible credibility that domestic inflation will be very close to that in the reserve currency country. Dollarization is infrequent and mainly adopted in very small economies with minimal nontraded goods sectors and very close ties to the issuing country (e.g., Panama has used the US dollar as its currency since 1904) or in countries that have had to tackle hyperinflation (e.g., Zimbabwe in 2008 after inflation hit 231 million percent).

2 Policymaking under IT

IT has come to be seen as the most robust framework compatible with open capital markets, a reasonable degree of monetary discipline, and sufficient scope for countercyclical monetary policy.[10] For most countries, monetary policy is seen as a (if not the) key instrument of countercyclical policy under flexible exchange rates. Models of macroeconomic policy in an open economy – the canonical model being the Mundell–Fleming (MF) model described in Box 4.4 – support these views. IT has thus become the most widely used monetary framework.[11]

IT makes sense only for countries committed to exchange rate flexibility and independence of the central bank from political interference. The first of these prerequisites reflects the impossible trinity principle. In practice most inflation-targeting central banks do not have fully flexible exchange rates (i.e., a commitment to abstaining from all foreign exchange intervention and no consideration of the level of the exchange rate in policy decisions). But such central banks can at most smooth sudden or large changes in market-determined exchange rates; any effort to prevent an equilibrium change in the exchange rate will put the inflation target at risk (when efforts are made to resist a nominal appreciation) or exhaust official reserves (when efforts are made to resist a nominal depreciation).[12]

---

[10] Most countries that have not adopted IT are very small, highly open economies with small nontraded goods sector.

[11] Although some central banks continue to fix their exchange rates or control them within a narrow band, these are mainly in small countries that have very large traded goods sectors.

[12] A frequent quandary for IT central banks is whether and to what extent a sizable exchange rate change is equilibrating or a market overshoot imparting needless and possibly costly volatility.

Box 4.4 The Mundell–Fleming Model of Internal and External Equilibrium[1]

Macroeconomic policy aims to establish and maintain internal and external equilibrium. Full internal equilibrium means GDP at potential, unemployment at the NAIRU, and inflation at the target rate. External equilibrium means the balance of payments is in a sustainable position – i.e., autonomous external financing flows match the current account position at existing exchange rates.

One of the early, simple, but powerfully insightful models of the dual equilibrium in an economy open to capital flows is the Mundell–Fleming (MF) model. It starts from the classic closed-economy, Keynesian IS–LM framework – in interest rate and income space – which has an equilibrium locus for the goods market (IS, where investment equals saving, albeit not necessarily at full employment) and an equilibrium locus for the money market (LM, where the demand for money equals the supply). There are two policy instruments – control over the money supply (monetary policy) and over government spending (fiscal policy). The IS–LM model determines the combination of fiscal and monetary policy that will achieve simultaneous equilibria in the two markets at the full-employment level.

MF widens this model to an open economy – where external disequilibrium elicits feedback through either financial flows or exchange rates, depending on the policy regime. This leads to two possible ways of viewing the domestic money market: as part of the broad international money or capital market because the country has fixed its exchange rate to the currency of a large global player; or as a market cleared by interest rate and exchange rate changes because the country has a floating exchange rate.

The key insight from the MF model is that the relative efficacy of a country's monetary and fiscal policies depends on its exchange rate regime – i.e., whether the country has a fixed or flexible exchange rate. With fixed exchange rates, fiscal policy is very powerful and monetary policy ineffective. An increase in government spending in a country with a fixed exchange rate creates an incipient increase in interest rates that immediately attracts foreign financial inflows to cover any external current account imbalance. Foreign capital is attracted to even tiny gaps between global and domestic interest rates – in effect,

(continued)

Box 4.4 (*continued*)

interest rates cannot change so there is no financial crowding out. The fiscal action raises income, and the money supply increases endogenously to accommodate demand.[2] In contrast, an attempt at monetary expansion is doomed to failure: a lower interest rate leads to financial (balance of payments) outflows, reducing the money supply until market interest rates are back at international levels. With floating exchange rates, the efficacy of fiscal and monetary policy is reversed. Fiscal policy becomes powerless – an expansion elicits higher interest rates and a contractionary currency appreciation – and monetary policy becomes *the* powerful countercyclical instrument – lower interest rates both boost domestic demand directly and elicit an expansionary currency depreciation.

These conclusions come from cases of pure floating or fixed exchange rates. In reality, most countries now allow some degree of flexibility in exchange rates, although they often seek to limit their range and volatility. The MF insights remain relevant: the more a country's exchange rate is determined by market forces, the greater its ability to use monetary policy independently and the less effective its fiscal policy.

[1]   Fleming, Marcus J., Domestic Financial Policies under Fixed and Floating Exchange Rates, *IMF Staff Papers*, 9 (1962), 369–379; Mundell, Robert A., Capital Mobility and Stabilization Policy under Fixed and Flexible Exchange Rates, *Canadian Journal of Economic and Political Science*, 29 (4) (1963), 475–485. The description here is brief, aimed at stating the main insights.

[2]   Among numerous other limiting assumptions – e.g., elastic output, static exchange rate expectations, perfect substitutability between domestic and foreign assets – the analysis is short run in that it ignores any possible deterioration in the country's international investment position (see Chapter 7) and possible repercussions for risk premia.

The second of these prerequisites reflects the need to prevent political influences from subverting the policy instruments needed to achieve the inflation target. Countries differ in their approach to setting the inflation target, which almost always is with reference to consumer prices.[13] For

[13] Most central banks target the CPI, but in the United States the target is the consumption component of the GDP deflator. Most also closely watch the "core" index (CPI or consumption deflator) which strips out volatile food and fuel prices, so as to avoid chasing frequent one-off shocks. There are good reasons also to monitor the broad GDP deflator which, as noted in Chapter 3, responds differently to terms-of-trade changes.

example, in the United Kingdom the government sets the target, while in the euro area the European Central Bank sets the quantitative definition of price stability. But both are consistent with *instrument independence* – i.e., the central bank is free to employ its policy instruments as it judges necessary to achieve the inflation target. The latter is the critical aspect of independence for IT.

IT begs the question of how a central bank should respond to developments apart from inflationary impulses. Strictly speaking, a central bank can have only as many policy goals as it has independent instruments (in most circumstances this is only one). Most countries therefore have what is called a single mandate: in reaching their policy decisions they may consider a range of developments in the economy, but they are formally charged only with minimizing deviations from an inflation target. The Fed, however, has a dual mandate – a formal objective for minimizing deviations from an inflation target and maximizing employment.[14] A dual mandate means that circumstances will arise when, with its one instrument, the Fed cannot target both inflation and full employment. Thus, one goal must temporarily be assigned a lower priority.[15]

For most IT countries, the so-called Taylor rule provides a summary of how monetary policy works. It is more a descriptive device than a prescriptive rule – it would be folly to think that central banks' policy-making committees follow anything like a mechanical rule. But it is a useful shorthand method of viewing decision-making and, at times, has tracked actual policy quite well.[16] It is characterized by equation (4.5):

$$i_t = \pi_t + r_t^* + a(\pi_t - \pi_t^*) + b(Y_{rt} - Y_{rt}^*) \tag{4.5}$$

[14] This is the common characterization of the Fed. In fact, the Fed formally has a triple mandate, which includes conducting monetary policy to promote "moderate long-term interest rates." The latter is frequently seen as encompassed by the mandates on stable inflation and maximum employment.

[15] The following statement of the decision-making body of the Fed is an example of how multiple objectives are handled. "In setting monetary policy, the [Open Market] Committee seeks to mitigate deviations of inflation from its longer-run goal and deviations of employment from the Committee's assessments of its maximum level. These objectives are generally complementary. However, under circumstances in which the Committee judges that the objectives are not complementary, it follows a balanced approach in promoting them, taking into account the magnitude of the deviations and the potentially different time horizons over which employment and inflation are projected to return to levels judged consistent with its mandate." www.federalreserve.gov /faqs/money_12848.htm

[16] It is named for its originator John Taylor of Stanford University.

The monetary authorities set their policy interest rate in period t according to a rule that takes into account the inflation rate (π), the equilibrium cyclically neutral real interest rate (r^*), the target inflation rate (π^*), real GDP (Y_r), and potential GDP (Y_r^*). If output were at potential and inflation at target – i.e., the two terms in parentheses were zero – the nominal interest rate would be set at the equilibrium real rate plus inflation (at target by assumption). But if inflation is above target or output above potential, the central bank would raise the official interest rate to tighten monetary conditions.

The Taylor rule is obviously appropriate for dual mandate IT. But is the inclusion of both the deviation of inflation from the target and output from potential appropriate for a single-mandate country? Even the strictest single-mandate advocate would answer in the affirmative insofar as the output gap term captures an important signal of whether future inflation is likely to deviate from the target. Also, in practice, even single-mandate central banks are never impervious to developments in the real economy whether or not they are reliable predictors of future inflation.

One could estimate the coefficients (a and b) to get an indication of the philosophy of the central bank during any period; a change in central bank thinking would change these coefficients. For example, in a single-mandate country, if the central bank were exclusively focused on targeting inflation, a would be large and b would depend on the perceived influence of the output gap on future inflation. Indeed, b might be zero if the output gap were seen as irrelevant to future inflation. A large b would indicate greater attention to countercyclical considerations however justified. The critical point in the rule (the "Taylor Principle"), however, is that on average when inflation goes up the *real* interest rate has to increase to tighten conditions. Thus a has to be positive so that the sum of the two coefficients on π (i.e., $1 + a$) is greater than 1.[17]

Beyond the seeming simplicity of the Taylor rule, central bank policy-makers need to consider many issues. One important consideration is that today's interest rate policy affects inflation only after a lag of a year or two. Therefore, the π_t in the central bank's decision rule is really π_{t+n} – i.e., the central bank is adjusting its policy interest rate based on its projection of inflation over the relevant future period. This is license to ignore ("see through") transitory influences insofar as they can be distinguished from more permanent changes.

---

[17] It is not unusual for a central bank to characterize a bout of above-target inflation as temporary, due to some short-lived phenomenon, and thus to ignore it (as irrelevant to the medium-term inflation projection) in setting the official interest rate.

A second consideration that has received much attention in recent years is the level of the cyclically neutral real interest rate – a critical variable that economists theorize about but cannot observe – and whether it has changed. This is important because MPCs need a compass to help them consider whether the level of the policy rate – as opposed to any change they decide on – is in a range of easy or tight monetary conditions.

A third difficulty, discussed in Chapter 2, is that of pinning down a common (and ideally correct) view of potential output and thus the output gap.

Finally, policymakers are concerned about not only the current setting of their policy instrument but also its future path. This means that central banks are always engaged in forecasting. Future inflation will be affected by an array of factors – both policy variables and developments in the economic environment – and by the reactions and responses of economic agents to these developments. MPCs, therefore, use both judgment and models to project inflation and to understand developments more broadly.

MPCs use both old-style estimated macroeconomic models and more technically sophisticated dynamic stochastic general equilibrium (DSGE) models. The difficulty with the former is that they lack microeconomic foundations and thus cannot deal with the responses of agents to changes in circumstances or policies (the so-called Lucas critique). DSGEs rectify this shortcoming by modeling a representative agent optimizing subject to technological and institutional constraints. DSGEs are stochastic insofar as the agents modeled are beset by random shocks. But DSGEs are still subject to criticism, especially related to the realism of transitional dynamics: one class of these models assumes unrealistically frictionless changes in endogenous variables, and the other imposes somewhat arbitrary frictions in an effort to mimic the real world. Both types require heroic aggregation: treating diverse agents as homogeneous. The state of modeling in central banks, therefore, is far from settled.[18]

This discussion has been largely about inflation, but concern about deflation has taken center stage in Japan for some time and in other advanced economies since the 2008 financial crisis. As noted in Chapter 3, if demand is weak and nominal interest rates cannot go much below zero (without asset holders opting simply to hold cash), deflation may result in real interest rates (nominal rates *plus* the rate of deflation) that are

---

[18] The academic debate and the criticism of DSGEs by detractors go well beyond the points made here. Private financial institutions (for which accurate forecasting is highly lucrative) have, thus far, largely eschewed DSGEs.

too high to produce any countercyclical impact. These circumstances have given rise to quantitative easing (QE) – direct central bank purchases of financial assets, often with relatively long maturities. The aim is to ease monetary conditions beyond the constraints of the zero interest rate bound and directly influence longer-term yields (see section 4) and thus the shape of the yield curve. Along with QE, some central banks have also used *forward guidance* where, by making public their own forecasts, they have sought to influence market expectations more directly.

In circumstances of deflation and perceived secular weakness of demand, IT central banks have tried to keep interest rates as low as possible, through both conventional instruments and QE. But the full effects of such policies have yet to become clear. For example, savers, disadvantaged by low returns, may have to increase saving to realize their financial goals. Pension funds and corporate pension systems that have based their actuarial calculations on positive nominal interest rates within historical ranges may struggle to cover future obligations. In short, institutions that have commitments or portfolios based on interest rates in some historical range may face difficulties in a prolonged period of near-zero interest rates.

Before the 2008 financial crisis, the question of whether central banks should have objectives beyond inflation and output was much debated. Since the crisis, with heightened attention to other variables – especially excessive leverage, large capital flows, and asset price bubbles – this debate has sharpened. Some economists believe that monetary policy should not be burdened with these additional objectives; unless they have a direct bearing on the targeted inflation index, they should be dealt with through prudential instruments (see Chapter 6).[19] But others think that prudential instruments will sometimes be insufficient and that monetary policy should be both cognizant of and responsive to financial developments that threaten the resilience of the financial system.

3 Reading the Monetary Accounts

Regardless of the monetary policy framework, monetary accounts are similar across most countries. Here we work through how to read them – a prerequisite for understanding the conduct and assessing risks of monetary policy as covered in sections 4 and 5.

---

[19] Chapter 6 deals with prudential instruments, both those related to individual institutions and macro-prudential instruments focused on the financial system as a whole.

The financial system consists of the central bank, the commercial banks (which take deposits and make loans), and other institutions – credit unions (called building societies in some countries) that are mainly involved in mortgage or automobile financing, investment banks that focus on corporate finance, asset management companies that manage individual or institutional portfolios, and hedge funds that manage more risky portfolios. The actual landscape is more complex because some institutions (sometimes called "universal banks") are both conventional commercial banks and investment banks: they may, albeit through different arms, take conventional deposits and make loans, engage in corporate finance through managing or underwriting issues of equities or bonds, facilitate hedging by buying and selling derivatives, and trade in various assets and derivatives on their own accounts.

a The Basics

We will consider two balance sheets: one for the central bank and one for the commercial banking system.[20] These are simplified and stylized balance sheets, but they contain the essentials for analysis.

Let's start with a representative central bank balance sheet (Table 4.1). One key objective in constructing this is to track the monetary base – the sum of the liabilities of the central bank to the private sector – and the central bank assets that must, in aggregate, match it. Those liabilities comprise currency in circulation and bank deposits (also called reserves) at the central bank.[21] Bank deposits or reserves are further divided into those that are required (to fulfill any central bank regulation that commercial banks hold a certain percentage of their deposits as deposits at the central bank) and those in excess of the required amount.[22]

---

[20] In Chapter 6 a distinction will be made between the "trading book" and the "banking book" of universal banks. The latter, which covers conventional banking business, is the focus in this chapter.

[21] The range of financial institutions with deposits at the central bank differs between countries. Also, terminology differs: our generic "bank reserve deposits" here is termed DIs (balances of depository institutions) in the Fed accounts of section 4.

[22] Some central banks impose a reserve requirement and use the reserve requirement ratio (required reserves to deposits) as a policy instrument – higher reserve requirements reduce banks' funds for lending and thus make monetary policy more restrictive. Many central banks do not impose such requirements. Whether or not banks are required by regulation to hold reserves with the central bank, all banks do maintain central bank deposits for prudential reasons and to facilitate clearing.

TABLE 4.1 *Central bank balance sheet*

Assets	Liabilities
Net foreign assets (NFA₁)	Monetary base (or reserve money (MB))
Net domestic assets (NDA)	• currency in circulation (CiC)
• claims on banks (CB)	• currency in banks (CiB)
• net claims on government (NCG₁)	• currency outside banks (CoB)
• claims on other sectors (CO₁)	• bank reserve deposits with the CB (RD)
Other items net (OIN₁)	• required reserves (RR)
	• excess reserves (ER)

On the asset side of the balance sheet are net foreign assets or all foreign assets (which in most countries are identical to gross foreign exchange reserves) minus short-term foreign liabilities (those of less than one year maturity). This netting convention shifts to the asset-side liabilities of the central bank to foreign entities so that the liability side shows purely central bank liabilities to the domestic private sector. For simplicity we assume zero longer-term foreign liabilities (though if there were any we would net them out in the "Other items net" term). Central bank lending to banks, the government, and "other sectors" is shown under "Net domestic assets." As with central bank liabilities to foreign entities, we subtract government deposits in the central bank from the claims on government – hence *net* claims on the government – because they do not affect liquidity conditions in the private sector. "Other items net" is the aggregation of all other (usually small or relatively stable) items. It includes other assets minus other liabilities and the capital of the central bank (i.e., the part of its assets covered by equity or, alternatively stated, the difference between the central bank's total assets and total liabilities). Some presentations include OIN as a component of NDA.

The aggregate balance sheet of the banking system excluding the central bank follows a broadly similar structure (Table 4.2). Here the aggregates of primary interest are the monetary (or reasonably liquid) liabilities of the banking system to the private sector and its asset counterparts, particularly the credit extended to the economy.

TABLE 4.2 *Balance sheet of deposit institutions*

Assets	Liabilities
Net foreign assets (NFA2)	Total deposits (DEP)
Claims on central bank	• demand deposits (DD)
• currency in banks (CiB)	• time and savings deposits (TD)
• reserve deposits (RR + ER)	• foreign currency deposits (FXD)
Net claims on government (NCG2)	Loans from the central bank (CB)
Claims on other sectors (CO2)	
Other items net (OIN2)	

On the asset side we again combine foreign assets and short-term liabilities to get net foreign assets. Similarly, we combine claims on the government and government deposits to get net claims on government. "Other items net" for the banks includes all other assets and nets out the banks' capital (which may have various components), bank bonds issued, and all other liabilities not included in broad money.[23]

Analysts often look at a consolidated balance sheet for the central bank and the commercial banking system – called the *monetary survey* (Table 4.3). If one writes out the two balance sheet identities including all the subitems and then adds them together it is clear how the consolidation works. (Box 4.5 writes the balance sheet identities algebraically and shows this consolidation.) Item names (shown without "1" or "2") are the sum of the corresponding central bank and commercial bank items. Broad money (often called M2) is the measure of central and commercial bank money liabilities.

TABLE 4.3 *The monetary survey*

Assets	Liabilities
Net foreign assets (NFA)	Broad money (M2)
Net claims on government (NCG)	• Currency (CoB)
Claims on private sector (CO)	• Demand deposits (DD)
Other items net (OIN)	• Time and savings deposits (TD)
	• Foreign currency deposits (FXD)

[23] The capital of a bank is important for prudential reasons: it provides a buffer that protects deposits from losses on loans or any other assets. The importance of bank capital is taken up in detail in Chapter 6.

Box 4.5 **Algebraic Representation of Banking System Balance Sheets**

The balance sheets shown in Tables 4.1–3 are sometimes presented algebraically. Such a presentation adds no additional information, but is helpful in some contexts as a more compact view. The identities corresponding to each balance sheet in the text are as follows:

The balance sheet identity for the central bank corresponding to Table 4.1

$$NFA_1 + NDA + OIN_1 = MB \qquad (4.6)$$

$$MB = CiB + CoB + RR + ER$$

$$NDA = CB + NCG_1 + CO_1$$

The balance sheet for the commercial banking system corresponding to Table 4.2

$$NFA_2 + CiB + RR + ER + NCG_2 + CO_2 + OIN_2$$
$$= DEP + CB \qquad (4.7)$$
$$DEP = DD + TD + FXD$$

To get to the consolidated banking system (central bank and commercial banks) balance sheet, start by writing out each of the component balance sheets in detail.

$$NFA_1 + CB + NCG_1 + CO_1 + OIN_1$$
$$= CiB + CoB + RR + ER \quad \text{(central bank)} \qquad (4.8)$$
$$NFA_2 + CiB + RR + ER + NCG_2 + CO_2 + OIN_2$$
$$= DD + TD + FXD + CB \quad \text{(commercial banks)} \qquad (4.9)$$

We can add these two identities together and (a) net out common factors on both sides, (b) aggregate like factors in both balance sheets such that, e.g., NFA1 (net foreign assets of the central bank) plus NFA2 (net foreign assets of the commercial banks) becomes simply NFA (net foreign assets of the banking system). This yields a banking system (also called the monetary survey) identity:

$$NFA + NCG + CO + OIN$$
$$= CoB + DD + TD + FXD = M_2 \quad \text{(banking system)} \qquad (4.10)$$

Economists monitor several monetary aggregates because money is the liquidity in the economy that facilitates expenditure. They also keep a careful eye on the asset counterparts to increases in the money supply – credit expansion and changes in NFA.

Views differ on which monetary aggregate most influences demand and thus output and inflation.[24] The monetary base (MB) – sometimes called central bank money or reserve money – is the narrowest. It is directly created by the central bank and the base from which all broader aggregates originate. The so-called base multiplier (the ratio of a broader money aggregate, usually M2, to MB) summarizes this relationship. Narrow money (or M1) is usually defined as currency in circulation (i.e., held outside banks) plus demand deposits (CUR + DD) – this is a very liquid (readily available for spending) store of value. M2 adds "quasi-money" (TD, time and savings deposits) to M1. In practice the aggregates may be defined differently in different countries. M2 and even M1 may include foreign currency holdings and deposits.[25] Some countries go on to define and follow broader monetary and financial measures of liquidity, called M3, M4, and so on. These may include money market assets, treasury bills, commercial paper, and other financial assets.

b A Few Caveats about Inferences from Balance Sheet Aggregates

Changes in banks' asset preferences, in the asset preferences of the non-bank private sector, or in regulations (such as those governing required reserves) complicate inferences from the monetary accounts about the stance of monetary policy.

In circumstances where banks do not hold much in excess reserves and their lending is constrained by tight monetary conditions, an increase in required reserves constrains credit further and affects the ratio of the monetary base to a broader monetary aggregate (what are called the base multipliers). In such a case, banks are essentially being required by regulation to deposit a larger portion of their deposits with the central bank, thereby taking more of their deposits out of circulation. It would be erroneous in such circumstances to see an increase in the monetary base as expansionary.

[24] While this is something of a hangover from the money-supply-targeting policy regimes described above, the growth of money and credit aggregates contains useful information even if there is not a stable money-demand function.

[25] We usually define net foreign assets by residency rather than currency (though they are usually denominated in foreign currency). Foreign currency deposits are usually defined as residents' deposits denominated in foreign currency.

Similarly, the base multipliers fall (and monetary conditions are less expansionary than may be inferred from the central bank's balance sheet) if additional injections of liquidity are simply redeposited with the central bank as excess reserves. We will see such a development in the Fed's balance sheet after 2008 in the next section. Banks may be reluctant to use their liquidity to lend for various reasons: it may be that the demand for credit is subdued, it may be that would-be borrowers are all too risky, or it may be that bank lending is constrained by prudential regulations.[26]

Changes in private nonbank asset preferences in the aggregate can affect the velocity of any monetary aggregate (the ratio of nominal GDP to that definition of money) or, equivalently, the stability of demand for that monetary aggregate. An individual who decides to buy bonds from another resident does not change the money supply – the buyer's monetary holdings decline while those of the bond seller rise. But if residents in the aggregate decide to hold more bonds and less money, then the velocity of money rises (the demand for money falls) and a given money stock will be consistent with easier monetary conditions and greater aggregate demand. Financial innovations – such as the growth of near money substitutes – have had exactly this effect.

4 Countercyclical Policy and the Central Bank Balance Sheet in Practice

In this section we examine the balance sheet of an IT central bank carrying out countercyclical policy. Our example is the Fed during 2000–2014. The first eight years of this period saw a moderate cycle, from peak activity in around 2000 to a low point in 2003, followed by a strong rebound. The subsequent 2008 downturn was remarkably sharp and followed by a long, slow recovery. Countercyclical monetary policy during this latter period was unusual in that it was one of the first large-scale experiments with QE. Thus, while the post-2007 reflection of countercyclical policy in the Fed's balance sheet was atypically large, it illustrates starkly the path of the countercyclical efforts.

The Fed's monetary operations reflect specific aspects of the structure of US financial markets and institutions. The objective here is not to go into any detail on these complexities but rather to provide a concrete example in simplified enough terms for a broad understanding of how to trace these

---

[26] Chapter 6 explores this latter case more thoroughly. Insofar as banks are required to have a minimum ratio of equity capital to loans, this ratio may constrain lending even when liquidity is abundant.

operations on a balance sheet. We omit many details of the accounts and operations so as to focus on the big picture.

The period 2000–2007 illustrates two important tasks of a central bank in the course of a fairly conventional cycle.

First, central banks must ensure that the monetary base is (and thus broad measures of the money supply are) adequate to meet the transactions needs of the economy. Even without a reliably stable relationship between activity and the money supply, the latter must rise as transactions rise; if it does not, monetary conditions will tighten, initially pushing up interest rates and over time, in the extreme, causing deflation. Central banks generally increase (reduce) the monetary base by purchasing (selling) securities – typically the central bank operates in the government securities market because that is the deepest and most liquid financial market in most countries. This process is called open market operations (OMOs). In the central bank's balance sheet a purchase shows up as an increase in central bank holdings of government securities on the asset side and an increase in the monetary base on the liability side.[27]

Table 4.4 illustrates how this liquidity provision role played out on the Fed's balance sheet. It shows the consolidated balance sheet of the US Federal Reserve Banks for two points in time (end-2000 and end-2007) that the National Bureau of Economic Research identifies as at or close to cyclical peaks in the US economy.[28]

In this peak-to-peak snapshot, the expansion of the Fed's balance sheet primarily resulted from increases in base money to supply adequate liquidity to accommodate the growth of the economy. That is, the comparison is between two points with similar cyclical characteristics so the point-to-point expansion in the base money should not reflect any countercyclical actions. The increase in both currency (Federal Reserve Notes) and currency plus deposits of depository institutions (chiefly banks, "DIs" in the United States, that have deposits (reserves) with the Fed) was about 40 percent, almost identical to the cumulative growth of nominal GDP during the same period. Repos are

---

[27] In some (mainly developing) countries where the government bond market is thin (i.e., the government relies mainly on direct bank credits), central banks may buy and sell their own bills to carry out monetary policy.

[28] More precisely, the NBER identifies the cyclical peaks as March 2001 and December 2007. The central bank balance sheet of the United States is the consolidated balance sheets of the 12 district Federal Reserve Banks. The Federal Reserve System has three parts: the 12 Federal Reserve Banks (located in 12 Federal Reserve Districts), which are the operating arms of the system; the Board of Governors, located in Washington DC, and the governing body of the Federal Reserve System; and the Federal Open Market Committee (OMC) which sets monetary policy.

TABLE 4.4 *Consolidated balance sheet of the Federal Reserve Banks in two cyclical peaks, 2000–2007* (billions of US dollars)

	2000			2007	
Assets		**Liabilities**		**Assets**		**Liabilities**

2000				**2007**			
Assets		**Liabilities**		**Assets**		**Liabilities**	
Net foreign assets	29.6	Federal Reserve Notes	563.5	Net foreign assets	37.2	Federal Reserve Notes	791.7
GSE securities[a]	0.1	Balances of Dls	19.0	GSE securities	–	Balances of Dls	20.8
US gov't securities	511.7	Balances of US Treasury	5.1	US gov't securities	740.6	Balances of US Treasury	16.1
Repos	43.4	Reverse repos	0.0	Repos	46.5	Reverse repos	44.0
Other	29.4	Other (incl. capital)	26.6	Other	93.9	Other (incl. capital)	45.7
Total	614.2	Total	614.2	Total	918.3	Total	918.3

[a] Securities of government-sponsored enterprises. Fed holdings were trivial until after the 2008 crisis. See footnote to Table 4.7 for a fuller description.
Source: Federal Reserve Board, Annual Reports

government securities that the Fed has purchased with a commitment to return the security to the dealer on a set date. Reverse repos are government securities that the Fed has sold to a dealer with an agreement that the dealer will return them on a set date. Typically repos (reverse repos) are used to ease (tighten) monetary conditions when the Fed has a very short time horizon for its intervention. Reverse repos also provide a way for banks to park money with the Fed for a short period at an interest rate that might differ from that on excess reserves.

Second, between these two cyclical peaks, the Fed carried out counter-cyclical policy as output first fell below and rose back to and above estimated potential. The Fed articulates changes in monetary policy by announcing changes in its target for the Fed Funds rate (the rate at which banks lend overnight to one other to secure their desired level of reserve deposits at the Fed).[29] Figure 4.1 shows targets for the Federal Funds rate during 2000–2007.

The Fed does not intervene in the Fed Funds market. Rather it uses OMOs (with the typical instrument for operations being government securities) to ensure that the actual Fed Funds rate is at its target. When targeting an increase in the Fed Funds rate, the Fed sells securities so as to absorb banks' excess balances and thereby tighten conditions in the Fed Funds market.[30] In other words, a change in the Fed Funds rate typically requires changes in the Fed's balance sheet. Tables 4.5 and 4.6 show the Fed's balance sheet at more or less the points of the peak and trough for the Fed Funds rates – the initial peak (end-2000), the intermediate trough (end-2003), and the subsequent peak (end-2007).

Three clear differences show up between the easing phase (2000–2003) and the tightening phase (2003–2007):

- The overall balance sheet of the Federal Reserve Banks grew more rapidly during the first period, especially when compared with nominal GDP growth. It grew by 26 percent in the easing phase

---

[29] Balances at the central bank consist of required reserves – i.e., some regulatory fraction of banks' liabilities or deposits – in countries where such requirements are imposed, plus reserves held willingly in excess of any requirements for precautionary purposes or to facilitate transactions and clearing (excess reserves).

[30] In conditions when DIs hold large excess reserve balances, the Fed may also raise its deposit rate to influence the Fed Funds rate. The detailed mechanics of the Fed Funds market are complicated: they are influenced by which financial institutions are allowed to have interest-earning excess reserves with the Fed, by the rate on reverse repos, and by levies on banks' assets by the Federal Deposit Insurance Corporation. These institutional details are not important for the discussion in this chapter.

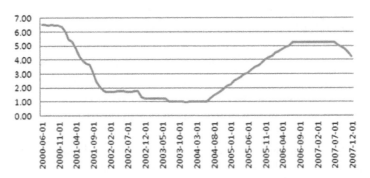

FIGURE 4.1 Target Fed Funds rate 2000–2007
Source: Federal Reserve of St. Louis, https://fred.stlouisfed.org/series/FEDFUNDS#0

(against nominal GDP growth of 12 percent) but by only 18.5 percent (against nominal GDP growth of 26 percent) in the tightening
phase.

- In absolute terms the faster expansion of the balance sheet during
  2000–2003 than during 2003–2007 arose from banknotes (currency).
  DI's reserves, however, rose during the first period and actually fell
  during the second. In other words, the easing of monetary policy
  resulted in a sizable accumulation of excess reserves that was partly
  reversed in the tightening period.
- OMOs to achieve the targeted changes in the Fed Funds target rate
  were significant. The sum of government securities holdings and
  repurchase agreements (repos) less reverse repos rose by 23 percent
  in the easing period compared with 8.5 percent in the tightening
  period.

Since the 2008 financial crisis, monetary policy and its reflection in the
balance sheets of central banks has changed drastically for many countries. In the United States, the need for exceptionally aggressive easing of
monetary conditions meant that the Fed Funds rate was cut over approxi-
mately one year from 4.25 to near zero (Figure 4.2). Facing the zero
interest bound, the Fed turned to mechanisms beyond reductions in the
Fed Funds rate. This led to several different specific policy-easing strategies, but by far the most substantively important was quantitative easing
(QE).

Generically, QE entails central bank purchases of securities with the
explicit aim of massively increasing liquidity in the financial system.

TABLE 4.5 *Consolidated balance sheet of the US Federal Reserve Banks during an easing cycle, 2000–2003* (billions of US dollars)

End-2000			
Assets		**Liabilities**	
Net foreign assets	29.6	Federal Reserve Notes	563.5
GSE securities	0.1	Balances of DIs	19.0
US gov't securities	511.7	Balances of US Treasury	5.1
Repos	43.4	Reverse repos	0.0
Other	29.4	Other (incl. capital)	26.6
Total	614.2	Total	614.2

End-2003			
Assets		**Liabilities**	
Net foreign assets	33.7	Federal Reserve Notes	689.8
GSE securities	–	Balances of DIs	23.1
US gov't securities	666.7	Balances of US Treasury	5.7
Repos	43.8	Reverse repos	25.7
Other	29.7	Other (incl. capital)	29.5
Total	773.8	Total	773.8

Source: Board of Governors of the Federal Reserve System, Annual Reports 2001 and 2004

TABLE 4.6 *Consolidated balance sheet of the US Federal Reserve Banks during a tightening cycle, 2003–2007* (in billions of US dollars)

End-2003					
Assets			**Liabilities**		
Net foreign assets	33.7		Federal Reserve Notes	689.8	
GSE securities	–		Balances of DIs	23.1	
US gov't securities	666.7		Balances of US Treasury	5.7	
Repos	43.8		Reverse repos	25.7	
Other	29.7		Other (incl. capital)	29.5	
Total	773.8		Total	773.8	

End-2007					
Assets			**Liabilities**		
Net foreign assets	37.2		Federal Reserve Notes	791.7	
GSE securities	–		Balances of DIs	20.8	
US gov't securities	740.6		Balances of US Treasury	16.1	
Repos	46.5		Reverse repos	44.0	
Other	93.9		Other (incl. capital)	45.7	
Total	918.3		Total	918.3	

Source: Board of Governors of the Federal Reserve System, Annual Reports 2004 and 2008

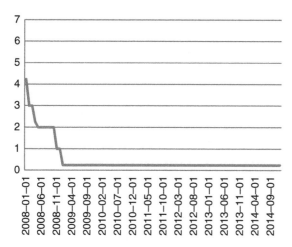

FIGURE 4.2 Target Fed Funds rate 2008–2014[a]

[a] Data after December 2008 are the ceiling on the Fed Funds rate reflecting the change in OMC procedures as the Fed Funds rate approached zero.

Source: Federal Reserve of St. Louis

It is similar to OMOs in the sense that it involves central banks acquiring assets and therefore increasing the monetary base. At least in the United States, however, it differed from conventional OMOs in three important ways: first it was undertaken not to achieve a target policy interest rate (the Fed Funds rate was already effectively zero), but rather to introduce stimulus through exceptionally liquid market conditions; second, it involved purchases of a far larger range of securities than OMOs or lending directly to financial institutions, with the aim of influencing directly the full range of interest rates instead of relying solely on a low Fed Funds rate to feed through to the structure of interest rates; and, third, it was aimed at segments of the financial market that were seen as having been unduly weakened by the financial crisis.[31]

The effect of QE on the Fed's balance sheet was dramatic. Table 4.7 shows the Fed's balance sheet at end-2007 and end-2014 (when peak QE positions occurred).

The monetary base rose 4½-fold over the seven-year period, against a cumulative rise of 20 percent in nominal GDP. Two component numbers

[31] For an explanation of these objectives of QE in the United States, see Bernanke, Ben, *The Federal Reserve's Balance Sheet: An Update*, October 8, 2009, www.federalreserve.gov /newsevents/speech/bernanke20091008a.htm

stand out. First, after varying over a range of $19–23 billion during 2000–2007, balances (for the most part excess reserves) of DIs rose sharply, accounting for about two-thirds of the 2007–2014 increase in the monetary base. Second, on the asset side, holdings of US Treasury securities (which traditionally accounted for upward of 90 percent of the Fed's assets) tripled; but by 2014 they accounted for less than 60 percent of total assets. Purchases of securities that allowed the Fed to directly affect conditions in specific asset markets (shown in Table 4.7 as GSE securities) were an equally important part of QE.

QE in both the United States and other countries took central banks into uncharted territory. It has spurred a debate among economists about whether new instruments are needed to counter exceptionally weak demand and the threat of deflation in the future. This has resurrected a discussion about direct, large-scale interest-free central bank financing of government spending – so-called *helicopter money* (see Box 4.6). Critical new topics have also emerged: do long periods of central bank action to hold down interest rates distort asset markets, encourage excessive leverage, and increase the financial sector's vulnerability to shocks? Can historically large central bank balance sheets be smoothly unwound as aggregate demand begins to grow more rapidly? We will come back to some of these questions in Chapter 6.

5 Monetary Policy and Vulnerabilities

Judgments about demand cycles and the nature and duration of shocks determine monetary policy. Even in an IT framework, where in principle meeting the inflation target is the sole goal of monetary policy, central banks constantly confront the need for judgments on both these issues. In doing so, policymakers (and those who analyze their actions) must first use the types of analyses developed in Chapters 2 and 3 to assess whether the economy is out of equilibrium in a way that monetary policy should address. Second, they must formulate and implement policy. Given ever-present uncertainties about the initial judgment on cycles and shocks and then about the appropriate policy response, it stands to reason that central bankers and analysts must have strong systems for assessing, in real time, signs of misjudgments on either front. Examining banking system balance sheets and considering vulnerabilities are central to this process.

In this section we examine how monetary policy decisions – even taken in an IT framework – can create or aggravate vulnerabilities to crisis and

TABLE 4.7 *Consolidated Balance Sheet of the US Federal Reserve Banks during the QE Period*[a] (in billions of US dollars)

	End-2007				End-2014		
Assets		**Liabilities**		**Assets**		**Liabilities**	
Net foreign assets[b]	37.2	Federal Reserve notes	791.7	Net foreign assets	35.3	Federal Reserve notes	1298.7
GSE securities[b]	–	Balances of DIs	20.8	GSE securities[b]	1775.5	Balances of DIs	2378.0
US gov't securities	740.6	Balances of US Treasury	16.1	US gov't securities	2461.4	Balances of US Treasury	223.5
Repos	46.5	Reverse repos	44.0	Repos	–	Reverse repos	509.8
Other	93.9	Other (incl. capital)	45.7	Other[a]	220.4	Other (incl. capital)	82.5
Total	918.3	Total	918.3	Total	4492.5	Total	4492.5

[a] Entries for GSE securities and US government securities do not include unamortized premia and discounts or accrued interest. Those items are included in "other" owing to the fact that Fed data do not differentiate those items according to GSE securities and government securities.
[b] Government-sponsored enterprise debt securities (including mortgage-backed securities) and Federal agency securities. GSEs are private enterprises sponsored by the government but their debt is not typically guaranteed by the government. These are instruments through which the Federal Reserve Banks acquired positions to influence credit markets directly. Other direct lending carried out early in the crisis had been largely unwound by 2014.
Source: Board of Governors of the Federal Reserve System, Annual Reports 2008 and 2015

Box 4.6 Money for Nothing, Goods for Free: Helicopter Money and the Accounts of the Central Bank[1]

In the wake of the great recession and especially in 2015–2016 some economists have revived the idea of helicopter money, first broached by Milton Friedman in 1969.[2] The basic notion is that the central bank would simply print money and distribute it to citizens.

Operationally the central bank would lend the government interest-free money forever. The government would use the money on higher subsidies, tax cuts, and/or public projects.[3] The seeming attractiveness is twofold. First, any government largesse is not constrained by the government's intertemporal budget constraint because the money never has to be repaid. Second, rising private disposable income would increase spending. Because the zero-interest loan is forever, this monetary expansion differs from quantitative easing (where the central bank buys government paper financed by issuing base money).

On the asset side of the central bank balance sheet, net claims on the government increase, and the new assets bear no interest and cannot ever be sold. On the liability side, the monetary base (cash and bank deposits) rises. When the economy moves out of recession and interest rates normalize, the fact that the central bank is stuck with interest-free government bonds forever means that its profits (and transfers to the government) will be reduced relative to the case where it can hold more normal interest-bearing paper.

If the monetary injection is modest and increases real output, the demand for cash may eventually rise and all will be well. This would be seigniorage financing without inflation. If the monetary injection elicits both a real and an inflationary response, part of the seigniorage derives from an inflation tax (on cash holders), not clearly preferable to any other sort of tax.

But, as shown in Table 4.7, a large increase in the monetary base is usually reflected in a jump in bank deposits with the central bank (often called bank reserves). The central bank may pay no interest on these reserves in abnormal recessionary circumstances. But what will it do when interest rates normalize? If the central bank pays interest, its profits drop (or its losses rise) insofar as it holds interest-free assets (government bonds) matched by interest-paying (excess reserve) liabilities. The net transfers of the central bank to the government (which may be positive or negative) fall; so that the interest-free government borrowing becomes, in effect, interest bearing.

Box 4.6 (*continued*)

If the central bank pays no interest on these reserves, it loses the ability to raise the short-term policy interest rate. The interest rate on reserves (or, at least, excess reserves) establishes a floor for the interbank money market (in that banks will not lend to other banks at a rate below what they can get from the central bank). If the central bank wants to reverse its substantial stimulus, the easiest, least disruptive mechanism is through raising this floor. But if cost concerns forestall any increase in the interest rate on reserves, banks will try to lend all excess reserves at any positive rate. So the central bank loses an essential instrument and it will be difficult to raise the official target rate.

If banks are loath to hold interest-free deposits with the central bank and are required to hold such reserves in excess of their desired level (to limit central bank losses), there is, in effect, a tax on the banks. So the helicopter money becomes tax revenue.

Friedman's helicopter money is more fable than prescription. The notion of free money is almost always illusory.

[1] See Borio, C., Disyatat, Piti, and Zabai, Anna, *Helicopter Money: The Illusion of a Free Lunch*, VOX CEPR's Policy Portal, May 24, 2016.

[2] Friedman, M., The Optimum Quantity of Money, in Milton Friedman, *The Optimum Quantity of Money and Other Essays*, Chapter 1. Aldine Publishing Company, Chicago, 1969.

[3] This would be a reversal of hard-won progress away from fiscal dominance and toward central bank independence.

how vulnerabilities might show up in balance sheets. To do this we examine two of the most common types of monetary policy judgments that can produce vulnerabilities: the first is monetary policy actions to address shocks – we shall focus on an external shock – to the economy, and the second is monetary policy actions when government financing needs threaten to crowd out private investment.

We consider actions of a central bank with an IT framework. However, reflecting the practices of most IT central banks, we assume that the framework is not followed in a pure form (i.e., a fully open EFA, a fully flexible exchange rate, and interest rate policy directed solely at the inflation target). Rather, this central bank blurs somewhat its adherence to the constraints of the impossible trinity by: intervening at times in the foreign exchange market to slow or stop unwanted changes in the exchange rate; using interest rate policy at times to influence the exchange rate or objectives apart from inflation; and/or putting in place restrictions on foreign financial flows.[32]

In general, in a reasonably pure IT framework, a shock sets in motion equilibrating mechanisms. These comprise changes in prices (the exchange rate, interest rates, and/or relative prices of goods and services) and/or EFA flows. They work to return the economy to an equilibrium path. A key question for policymakers, however, is *whether* to let these equilibrating mechanisms play out.[33] When a shock is likely to be reversed quickly, it is sensible for policy to prevent a market reaction that introduces unnecessary volatility with costs for domestic consumption and investment. But when a shock is more permanent, those equilibrating forces are needed to get the economy back to a sustainable path. Even then, it may be wise to spread the adjustment over time to ensure that market forces do not produce over-shooting. Yet shock-mitigating or smoothing policies carry risks of mistakes: when central banks act on a conviction that a shock is temporary, but it turns out to be permanent, eventual adjustments will usually be more disruptive and painful. One challenge for policy, therefore, is to judge the likely duration of any shock and watch for signs that policies are unsustainable.[34]

The essential insight in this analysis is that the major channels for monetary policy to create vulnerabilities involve actions to hold interest rates or the exchange rate at levels that prevent equilibrating adjustments to shocks or to the true cyclical position of the economy.

a Monetary Policy and External Shocks

Consider a country that starts from balance in both its external current account and its overall balance of payments and experiences a sudden, large increase in

---

[32] These can take a wide variety of forms from outright restrictions on some types of flows to more subtle policies to increase the costs of such flows or to put "sand in the wheels" of such flows. The latter might be prudential measures that discourage banks from accepting nonresidents' investments or making investments abroad.

[33] The scope for monetary policy to insulate domestic absorption from volatility depends on the source of the shock, the monetary framework, and openness to EFA flows. Consider an exogenous drop in export production. With a rigidly fixed exchange rate, a country can insulate domestic absorption at least in the short run by drawing down reserves or receiving financial inflows. In a pure floating IT framework, however, monetary policy cannot offset the negative effect on absorption (though it can influence whether it occurs through exchange rate or interest rate adjustment, with possibly different implications over time).

[34] For countercyclical policy this translates into the question: Is output truly deviating from potential (so that policy can facilitate an equilibrating closing of the output gap), or has potential changed so that what seems like a transitory cyclical problem is, in fact, a secular change?

import payments owing to a jump in the price of a major, price-inelastic import like oil.[35] This results in a current account deficit, some depreciation, and some increase in EFA inflows (as residents borrow to maintain absorption and FDI responds to cheaper domestic assets). Suppose financial inflows do not fully finance the higher import bill, possibly because the risk premium on the domestic currency increases, reflecting market concerns about the effect of the shock and how it will be handled. The authorities intervene (i.e., sell foreign currency) to contain the depreciation and prevent (what they see as) a short-lived reversible shock imposing excessively on domestic prices, real wages, and absorption, and threatening their inflation objective.

Table 4.8 illustrates this scenario in the central bank's balance sheet. (For simplicity we drop the OIN variable, which plays no part in this analysis, and the suffix "1.") NFA and the monetary base fall, thus tightening monetary conditions.[36] These changes are indicated by the arrows on the left side.

TABLE 4.8 *Balance sheet for a central bank with a managed float: the case of a surge in imports*

Assets	Liabilities
↓NFA	↓MB↑
NDA↑	

At this point, the intervention and resulting tightening of monetary conditions (increase in market interest rates) would attract more foreign inflows financing a larger share of the current account deficit. But they would likely also set off a series of second-round effects that would start equilibrating real changes: interest-sensitive domestic spending would slow; import volumes would also slow; and lower nontraded goods inflation would divert resources to traded goods production. All of these developments would tend toward reducing the current account deficit.

But the central bank, believing that the import price shock is a transitory aberration, does not want this tightening of monetary conditions to occur. So it sterilizes the monetary effects of the drop in NFA: it reverses the effects on the monetary base of its original sales of reserves by buying securities in the domestic market (arrows on the right side in Table 4.8). Box 4.7 provides a primer on intervention and sterilization.

---

[35] For ease of exposition, we will treat the import price increase as occurring in isolation; in reality, shocks may be numerous, simultaneous, and complex.

[36] Alternatively, the central bank could raise its policy rate to stop the depreciation. In this case, the counterpart to the drop in MB would be a drop in NDA rather than NFA.

If the authorities are correct in their assessment that the shock will soon be reversed, active policy may be the right response. The temporary current account deficit will have been financed by a combination of foreign inflows and use of central bank reserves. (The latter can be rebuilt through intervention at a later time.)

But what if the shock and its effects are sustained and the central bank continues to resist depreciation and monetary tightening? In the next period and again in the period thereafter NFA would drop and NDA would rise. The monetary base would stay on trend, but backed less and less by hard currency assets and more and more by NDA. Eventually NFA would reach a critical minimum, intervention would no longer be possible, and confidence in the currency would be eroded to the point where risk premia would rise. Financial outflows would then add to exchange market pressure.

In other words, a policy aimed at buffering a shock would have been based on a false judgment about the duration of the shock. The eventual disruption would be larger than would have occurred with earlier equilibrating adjustments. In the extreme, a currency crisis could ensue. Watching developments in the central bank balance sheet for early signs of diminishing reserves would be critical to a decision about when to stop the attempt to insulate the economy by holding exchange rates and interest

---

Box 4.7 Intervention and Sterilization

The interaction between monetary conditions, monetary policy, and the exchange rate regime depends on *intervention* and *sterilization*. *Intervention* occurs when the central bank intervenes in the market for foreign currency by buying or selling. It usually does this to influence the exchange rate. For example, an excess demand for foreign currency (usually because of an external payments imbalance – see Chapter 7) would drive up the price (which means a depreciation of the home currency). But the central bank could prevent or limit the depreciation by selling some of its foreign currency reserves – reducing its NFA. This intervention withdraws domestic currency cash from the economy (reducing the monetary base) to the extent of the domestic currency counterpart of the foreign currency sale.

In a fixed exchange rate regime the central bank pledges to buy or sell foreign currency to the extent necessary to prevent any change in the exchange rate, so the intervention is automatic and may be sizable

Box 4.7 (*continued*)

when there is a shift in the demand or supply of foreign exchange. In a pure floating exchange rate regime the central bank desists from any intervention in the foreign currency market, leaving exchange rates free to balance demand and supply. Perhaps the most common regime is one in which the central bank allows some flexibility in the exchange rate, but intervenes to "lean against the wind" – i.e., to smooth changes that are seen as too sharp or perhaps unwarranted.

Intervention entails changes in the NFA of the central bank and a corresponding change in the monetary base *unless the intervention is sterilized*. Sterilization means that the central bank offsets the change in the monetary base due to intervention by changing NDA. For example, if the central bank sells foreign currency to prevent a depreciation, the monetary base will fall by the amount of the domestic currency proceeds of the intervention. But if it then buys government bonds in the market (increasing NDA and injecting cash into the economy) in an amount equivalent to the intervention-induced drop in the monetary base, it will offset (*sterilize*) the monetary effect of the intervention.

Sterilized intervention in the face of persistent outflows will become unsustainable when (and usually well before) the central bank runs out of foreign exchange reserves. Sterilized intervention in the face of large and persistent inflows may be easier to maintain for some time. But, as some emerging market countries have discovered, such sterilization can be costly. It entails, in effect, buying low-yield foreign exchange assets (usually US Treasury bills) and selling relatively high-yield domestic assets. (The ex post yield differential becomes even larger if the central bank eventually succumbs to the appreciation pressures.) Thus the sterilization operation reduces the profits (or increases the losses) of the central bank, and reduces (increases) its transfers to (calls on) the government budget. Governments are usually loath to allow such policies to continue indefinitely.

Intervention and sterilization operations should be discernable in the central bank balance sheets. But unless they are dramatically large, it may require some persistence to disentangle them from myriad other transitory influences.

rates steady. Chapter 7 details the importance of central banks' official reserves in vulnerability analysis.

An important part of this analysis is that market concerns about the import price shock and the likely monetary policy response arose fairly quickly. Thus the risk premium on domestic currency increased early on. Had the risk premium adjusted more slowly, the country might have been able to cover the full current account deficit through foreign financing without central bank intervention and sterilization. But a buildup of external debt would eventually elicit a change in the risk premium and a corresponding (possibly sharp) discontinuity in interest rates and/or exchange rates. We would have been able to see the emerging vulnerability not in the central bank accounts, but only in a debt sustainability analysis – of the public sector (see Chapter 5) and/or the economy as a whole (see Chapter 7).

The building blocks of this section are the basis for assessing central bank responses to many developments – from other types of balance of payments shocks to changes in output gaps. Paradoxically, positive BOP shocks can create their own, but not totally dissimilar problems. After an inflow shock, the equilibrating mechanism is a nominal appreciation or an accumulation of NFA, which, in the absence of sterilization, eases financial conditions and pushes up prices of nontraded goods, services, and assets. In either case, the real appreciation may hurt exporters, and sterilized intervention frequently becomes an appealing option. But, as elaborated in Box 4.7, sustained sterilization to offset the monetary effects of this type of intervention is typically costly to a central bank, weakening its capital position, and reducing seigniorage transfers to the government. Moreover, analysis of such developments in Chapter 6 reveals the difficulties of maintaining financial stability in a rapidly growing EM economy with a sustained surge in financial inflows.

b Monetary Policy and Government Financing: Masking Excesses?

Now let's look at a shock that is domestic in origin: a shift to a more expansionary stance of fiscal policy. By examining the monetary accounts, it is possible to identify when an accommodating monetary response to higher government financing needs is producing a disruption to equilibrating monetary mechanisms. From a monetary perspective, this has similarities to an intervention-cum-sterilization response to the shock discussed in the previous section.

Assume an economy with output at potential and a government that embarks on an ambitious spending program not financed with higher taxes. Instead of the central bank balance sheet, we look here at the monetary survey covering all banks (Table 4.9). This broader focus is necessary because central banks are often legally prohibited from lending directly to the government in order to curb possible political interference in monetary policy. However, looking at the monetary survey we will see that this prohibition may make little difference to the final monetary effects of an increase in government borrowing. For clarity, we carry out this analysis in steps. However, ex post, the steps may seem to have occurred simultaneously within a single period.

TABLE 4.9 *Banking system balance sheet: increase in government bonds with tepid foreign interest*

Steps 1 and 2		Step 3	
Assets	Liabilities	Assets	Liabilities
NFA	M2↑	NFA↓	M2↑↓
↑NCG		↑NCG	
↓CO↑		↓CO↑	

Step 1: Because its direct borrowing from the central bank is restricted by law or regulation, the government offers bonds to the market – where either banks or foreign investors may purchase them. Assume first a scenario where foreign interest in the bonds is tepid.[37] To the extent that domestic banks pick up most of the bonds, monetary conditions tighten and banks cut exposure to the private sector (CO). The process in the domestic market is shown in the left arrows under Steps 1 and 2 of Table 4.9.

Step 2: The central bank must decide whether to validate this tightening by raising its policy rate or to adjust policy to prevent the tightening. Let's say that the central bank does not view the increase in the deficit as permanent or large enough to significantly alter the course of the economy. It therefore chooses not to change its policy rate and offsets any incipient

---

[37] This could be for one of several reasons: the market for the government's bonds is small and therefore illiquid; the government is relatively new to global financial markets and foreign investors shun exposure to a debtor without a track record; investors are concerned about the increase in the deficit and require a risk premium that (for reasons developed below) is resisted by the central bank.

interest rate increase by buying domestic assets from banks (perhaps the same assets the government sold to the banks). The monetary base increases, facilitating an increase in money (M2↑), and any actual or incipient crowding out of private credit is reversed (CO↑). The result is the same as if the central bank had monetized the deficit directly. The left-hand arrows under Steps 1 and 2 of Table 4.9 indicate what might have happened without the central bank action. The right-hand arrows indicate the additional effects of the central bank action; at the end of the process we see that M2 has increased with a rise in NCG as the asset counterpart.

As is clear from Chapter 2, however, monetary accommodation cannot create real resources. So the story cannot stop here.

Step 3: Insofar as the monetary accommodation of the government prevents a crowding out of private demand, it must be financed by foreign savings – i.e., an external current account deficit. Endogenous variables will change to make this happen – probably higher prices and a loss of competitiveness. These changes should put downward pressure on the value of the currency, but if the central bank remains of the view that the deficit is a temporary shock to be accommodated, it will intervene to defend the exchange rate. Thus NFA drops, and M2 falls back to its initial level, albeit backed by a different configuration of assets: higher NCG and lower NFA than in the original setting. In effect, the higher government deficit is being financed by a drawdown in central bank reserves to finance a resource transfer from abroad.

If the process is repeated again and again over many periods – i.e., aggregate demand continues to exceed potential output – the diminution in reserves will affect market judgments about the credibility of central bank policy and risk premia will rise.[38] The central bank will eventually be forced to change its policy with some combination of a higher interest rate and a depreciated currency. Insofar as risk premia are slow to adjust and an eventual (very large) adjustment comes at a point where reserves are dangerously low, a currency crisis may ensue.

In this scenario, the central bank made the decision to accommodate the government financing need because it believed it to be temporary with no threat to longer-term stability. This judgment turned out to be wrong, but as the balance sheet deteriorated a reasonable and independent central bank would stop the accommodation, and a responsible government would rein in its deficit. Problems arise when the signs of impending crisis are ignored,

---

[38] This may be because of some combination of residents seeking to move financial assets abroad (for fear of a sizable depreciation or a sovereign default) or nonresidents seeking to liquidate their holdings of domestic bonds for the same reasons.

most often because the government is unable or unwilling to reduce its deficit. In such cases, the central bank may have no alternative to abandoning its inflation target as a vicious circle of self-perpetuating depreciation, increasing inflation, and rising inflation expectations ensues. In effect, in situations like this (known as "fiscal dominance") there is no scope for independent monetary policy. Box 4.8 reviews the experience of Bulgaria in 1994–1997 when such a sequence of events occurred.

What if the central bank had been more cautious and had not accommodated the higher deficit financing from the beginning? This would have required that the central bank allow interest rates to increase following the initial tightening of monetary conditions. Now let's assume that the increase in interest rates whetted the appetite of foreign investors for domestic government bonds. The higher the response of foreign demand for domestic bonds, the less the monetary tightening, crowding out of credit to the private sector, and depreciation of domestic currency. This is not, however, a recipe for avoiding crises. Rather, it means that should the government persist in running inappropriately large deficits, the vulnerabilities will show up not in the bank balance sheets but in the government's exposure to foreign financing. In these circumstances, vulnerability analyses must focus on the sustainability of public debt, a topic to which we turn in Chapter 5.

Even if the central bank is cautious and strict in its pursuit of IT in such circumstances, considerations related to a weak fiscal position can gradually restrict its policy space. Two sources of such strain are common. First, with a prolonged and excessive fiscal financing requirement, risk premia will mount and ultimately slow inflows. Then, a gradual crowding out of private credit and higher interest on government borrowing can become a threat to growth and fiscal sustainability (as we will see in Chapter 5). Second, to the extent that foreign financing exposes borrowers (in this case the government) to exchange risk, persistent high dependence on foreign borrowing creates what is called "fear of floating." Central banks that allow market forces to drive foreign-exchange-denominated borrowing to high levels may be constrained in their exchange rate policy. Any significant depreciation could result in sizable capital losses (i.e., increases in the domestic currency value of debt liabilities) and unmanageable debt servicing costs for both the government and the parts of the private sector exposed to foreign exchange risk. This issue is explored further in Chapters 5, 6, and 7.

Box 4.8 Bulgaria: A Central Bank Balance Sheet Gone Awry, 1995–1996

The balance sheet of the National Bank of Bulgaria (BNB) during 1994–1996 traces a story of a banking crisis turned into hyperinflation and currency collapse via the actions of a central bank with no anchor and no independence from political decisions. It depicts the impossibility of employing monetary policy to stave off financial collapse resulting from the political failure to address bankruptcy in both enterprises and deposit money banks (DMBs). Table 4.10 shows the balance sheet and a timeline of the emerging crisis.

TABLE 4.10 *National bank balance sheet and policy indicators, 1994–1996* (billions of lev, except where noted)

	Reserve money	NFA	NDA	o/w Net credit to govt	o/w Credit to DMBs	OIN	CPI Inflation (eop from previous period)[a]	Lev/US$ (% change eop from previous period)[b]	Basic BNB interest rate[c]
Dec-94	83.0	−17.5	100.3	41.4	47.5	11.6	120.0	101.8	101.2
Dec-95	128.4	12.1	116.2	25.6	44.7	46.0	36.0	4.0	8.6
Mar-96	111.1	−25.6	136.7	59.8	61.9	15.0	8.1	11.5	12.4
Jun-96	129.9	−50.7	180.6	48.9	112.9	18.8	20.0	97.3	29.5
Sep-96	162.8	−124.2	287.0	98.3	144.0	44.7	69.0	47.9	38.2
Dec-96	247.0	−234.5	481.6	222.0	238.8	20.7	60.0	111.9	52.1

Source: IMF Bulgaria, Recent Economic Developments, 1999 www.imf.org/en/publications/cr/issues/2016/12/30/bulgaria-recent-economic-developments-and-statistical-appendix-2943
[a] For 1994–1995, end-of-period (eop) annual inflation rate. For 1996, end of quarter over end of previous quarter.
[b] For 1994–1995, end-of-period (eop) percentage change over previous year. For 1996, end of quarter over end of previous quarter.
[c] For 1994–1995, average of end-of-quarter rates at compounded annual rate. For 1996, end of quarter at compounded quarterly rate.

- **Background**: In 1994 the BNB provided large financing to the government and to banks (plagued by poor management and high nonperforming loans to state-owned enterprises), fending off a banking crisis. With the increase in liquidity, inflation rose to 120 percent. Despite heavy foreign exchange market intervention, the lev depreciated by 100 percent. In 1995, after the BNB's support operations relieved market concerns about a banking crisis, confidence in the lev rose. In fact, dollar purchases (raising NFA) were necessary to prevent a lev

Box 4.8 (*continued*)

appreciation, and the level of BNB credits to DMBs actually fell. A 55 percent rise in reserve money outstripped the 36 percent rate of inflation. This could be interpreted as the result of rising real money demand or as a surge in money supply that would erode the restored positive sentiment toward the lev and fuel a new round of inflation.

- **1996, first half**: Problems resurfaced in banks, crushing confidence in the banking system. Withdrawals of foreign currency deposits spiked, and the BNB sold dollar reserves aggressively to defend the lev. Falling NFA largely offset rising NDA, the latter reflecting substantial BNB lending to government and banks offset somewhat by a drop in OIN.[1] Reserve money rose modestly. The BNB raised its policy interest rate to help stabilize the exchange rate as NFA shrank. This increased government and bank financing needs but was insufficient to stabilize the lev. A vicious circle of depreciation, monetary accommodation, and inflation ensued.

- **1996, second half**: A government stabilization program in July brought short-lived calm. By September, the program had foundered. A sharp depreciation triggered another surge in intervention. BNB increases in the interest rate were substantial, but the interest rate exceeded the inflation rate only intermittently. Massive government and bank financing needs were accommodated in NDA expansion. In November, critically low foreign exchange reserves forced the BNB to halt intervention. In the last quarter a depreciation of more than 100 percent was a precursor to near-hyperinflation in early 1997.

[1] Large exchange rate changes complicate the central bank balance sheet. NFA here is marked to market while NDA is not. Reading the balance sheet requires care insofar as the valuation effects are rarely made explicit.

6 Exercises

1 Suppose you are employed by the foreign ministry to monitor economic developments in a particular country. The authorities characterize their framework as a flexible exchange rate regime with IT, but they acknowledge that the central bank intervenes to prevent excessive volatility in exchange rates and to offset short-term influences expected to reverse. Following

regional elections in March that went against the government, concern has grown about the political stability of the country and the default risk on its bonds in the event of domestic political disruptions. Rating agencies, which still see a low probability of political disruption, have not downgraded the rating of the country's debt, but they have raised questions about increased risks. The central bank has kept its policy interest rate unchanged, and no trend is evident in exchange rates vis-à-vis major trading partners.

(i) Consider the following highly aggregated, quarterly, central bank balance sheets:

   Can you come up with a narrative involving risk premia, exchange rates, interest rates, intervention, and sterilization that is consistent with these data? In what, if any, circumstances would this story raise alarms?

TABLE 4.11 *Central bank balance sheet (March 31)* (million pesos)

Assets		Liabilities	
NFA	1,000	MB	11,000
NDA	10,000		
OIN	–		

TABLE 4.12 *Central bank balance sheet (June 30)* (million pesos)

Assets		Liabilities	
NFA	500	MB	11,050
NDA	10,550		
OIN	–		

(ii) By the end of the year, the balance sheet is as follows (Table 4.13):

TABLE 4.13 *Central bank balance sheet (December 31)* (million pesos)

Assets		Liabilities	
NFA	200	MB	11,200
NDA	11,000		
OIN	–		

What would be your concerns about developments at this stage?

2 This exercise returns to the *transfer problem* of Chapter 2 and involves tracing the transfer through the monetary accounts under different scenarios. An international donor provides a grant to a poor developing country. The size of the transfer is large, several percent of GDP. In all scenarios except for the last one, (a) the exchange rate of the recipient country's currency is fixed to the US dollar; (b) the money is transferred in dollars from the bank account of the donor in New York to the account of the government in the central bank. The government then sells the dollars to the central bank for the domestic currency equivalent.

(i) Use the following stylized central bank balance sheet (Table 4.14, showing only three items as all others are assumed to be unchanged) to trace the transfer's initial effects, before the government spends the money. There is no need to use numbers, simply indicate with arrows and descriptively which items increase and which decline. Is the monetary base affected at this stage, and, if so, how?

TABLE 4.14 *Central bank balance sheet*

Assets	Liabilities
Net foreign assets (NFA1)	Monetary base (MB)
Net credit to government (NCG1)	

(ii) How does the central bank balance sheet change when the government spends the money that it received from the foreign donor?
(iii) What would happen, in the accounts and in the economy, if government spending all turned out to be on imports?
(iv) What would happen to the economy and the accounts if the country was at full employment and the government spending was all on nontraded goods?
(v) How would the answer to (iv) change if the economy was operating well below potential with substantial slack in all sectors.
(vi) Reconsider briefly (and verbally, i.e., without reference to the balance sheet) how your responses to questions (iii) and (iv) would change if the country had a pure flexible exchange rate.

3 This exercise is similar in its analytic requirement to question 2 above. It also returns to the issue of Dutch Disease, touched upon in Chapter 3 (see Box 3.4 and exercise 3 in that chapter); as was the case with that exercise, it will be possible to answer the questions more fully after reading Chapters 5–7, but a partial answer should be possible at this point.

Suppose, in a small open economy that has been close to full employment with a balanced external current account, there is a discovery of sizable reserves of natural gas that can be easily and profitably exploited. Prior to the discovery, the central bank's inflation targeting regime maintained inflation in its 2–5 percent target range. Its foreign exchange reserves were well below what it would have liked for prudential purposes. While it intervened in the foreign exchange market on occasion to counter sharp changes in exchange rates, it did not resist the gradual but sustained trend depreciation of its currency. Interest rates (real and nominal) on domestic currency loans and bonds were a couple of percentage points above those on comparable hard currency assets; this interest rate differential (which persists) reflects not only the currency risk premium (which, presumably, has diminished) but also the illiquidity of domestic currency assets due to the small size of the market.

Prior to the natural gas discovery, the country's principal exports were agricultural, and the production of these exports was profitable. To simplify the analysis, let's assume (a) that the exploitation and export of the natural gas follow very shortly after the discovery, (b) that exploitation of the gas, while broadly capital intensive, uses some domestic labor, and (c) that the gas is owned by a private domestic company that financed its initial exploration and exploitation operations by selling shares to residents; these shares have seen a large price increase, and profits, distributed as dividends, accrue to a wide swath of resident shareholders.

(i) The central bank decides to use the export bonanza from natural gas to build up its foreign exchange reserves and it does not initially sterilize the monetary effects of the intervention. Trace the monetary effects through the central bank balance sheets.

(ii) Summarize briefly what will likely be the effects of the exploitation and export of natural gas on relative prices and costs, and on the agricultural and domestic construction sectors.

(iii) Why might the central bank and the government be concerned about these sectoral developments and those in the balance of payments and the monetary accounts?

(iv) Suppose the central bank, while continuing to build up reserves, decides to sterilize the monetary impact of this buildup. What might constrain these sterilization operations?

(v) How could the government mitigate the effects of the advent of gas production on other sectors and help to sterilize the monetary effects? (This is a bonus question that should be reconsidered after Chapter 5.)

The Fiscal System

This chapter covers the macroeconomic influences of government spending and taxation. It aims at facilitating analysis in four areas:

1 *Reading the government accounts for a country (despite the complexities related to differences in national practices) and understanding both flows (like surpluses and deficits) and stocks (like government debt).*

2 *Assessing the credibility of budget projections.*

3 *Understanding countercyclical fiscal policy, the realism of the (sometimes heroic) estimates on which it is based, and the difference between automatic fiscal stabilizers and discretionary policy actions.*

4 *Judging fiscal sustainability based on debt dynamics under various scenarios.*

Fiscal policy is where political theory and ideology intersect with the everyday practice of governance, and, ultimately, the economics of budget constraints. Legislators have to make practical decisions on how much to spend, how to allocate this spending, which activities and citizens to tax and at what rates. The public debate usually appeals to broad principles – the appropriate role of government in the economy, the dangers of distorting market signals, and the balance between efficiency and equity – with positions reflecting ideological predilections. But actual decisions are often influenced more by electoral politics than lofty principles. Some political majorities may provide more services and greater protection from cyclical economic fluctuations than the tax base can support. Others may legislate tax cuts without corresponding reductions in spending. Thus policies may be myopic, with planning horizons that do not extend beyond the next election. Any necessary corrective action should be taken before crises emerge; but history is replete with failures in this regard.

Among professional economists, disagreement on the role of government is also substantial but there is broad agreement on the framework for analyzing the direct macroeconomic effects of the fiscal balance (i.e., the surplus or deficit on fiscal accounts). Specifically, it includes an assessment of the cyclical position of the economy, the characteristics of countercyclical policies, and the longer-term financial constraints that limit governmental largesse. Most, though not all, economists would support using fiscal policy to reduce the amplitude of cyclical swings. Most are concerned about the robustness or fragility of government finances over the longer term. Economists know that debt crises and balance of payments crises often originate in imprudent fiscal policies; they agree on the importance of forestalling these crises.[1]

This chapter presents the mainstream macroeconomic framework for analyzing the fiscal balance. It focuses on two important considerations in formulating fiscal policy: (i) smoothing economic activity through the cycle and (ii) ensuring that the longer-term fiscal outlook is financially sustainable. The former entails analysis of the scope for countercyclical fiscal policy. The latter involves ensuring that markets and the general public believe that budgets are credible and that the government will be able to honor and service its debt without disruptively harsh tax increases or spending cuts. Other aspects of fiscal policy – such as the structure of taxes, the reach of entitlement programs, and the government's provision of infrastructure – also have important macroeconomic effects. They are at the heart of a broader philosophical debate about the ideal role of government, and they work thorough microeconomic channels. Both the philosophical debate and the microeconomics of fiscal incentives and disincentives are beyond the scope we have set for this book.

The chapter starts with a brief review of the accounting framework for the government. It then provides a number of rules of thumb for assessing the credibility of budget projections – an essential task for holding governments accountable in the face of public pressures for lower taxes and greater expenditures. Frameworks for considering the effectiveness of fiscal policy in meeting two key macroeconomic objectives – short-term macroeconomic stabilization and longer-term fiscal sustainability – are taken up

---

[1] While a number of recent crises have originated in the private financial sector and unbridled leverage (see Chapter 6), here too problematic private behavior has often been exacerbated by implicit (or sometimes even explicit) government guarantees; or the crises have given rise to government bailouts that have left fiscal systems on the brink of unsustainability.

next. After that, the chapter discusses fiscal rules and their efficacy in insulating governments from short-term political pressures. The chapter concludes by revisiting some of the thought experiments from Chapter 2.

1 The Government Accounts

The boundaries of the fiscal (or public) sector are not clear-cut. Fiscal systems differ enormously between countries, reflecting differences in governmental structures, so analysis of any country requires an understanding of its institutional structure and the corresponding presentation of data.

The broad nonfinancial public sector accounts comprise the general government and nonfinancial public sector enterprises.[2] The importance of the latter depends on the degree of public ownership in the economy: in some countries coverage of public sector enterprises is a critical component of a fiscal analysis, in others it is insignificant.[3] We shall focus here chiefly on the general government. In some countries the general government is highly centralized, in others it is divided between a central (or federal) government, provincial (or state) governments, and municipal (or local) governments. In some cases all levels of government may be separately empowered to run deficits and to borrow (in bond markets, from banks, or through overdrafts with the central bank), in others lower levels of government may be required to balance their budgets.

Social insurance (sometimes called social security) funds are usually incorporated at the level of government in which they are run. A fully funded and autonomous social insurance system could be categorized as a separate entity in the nonfinancial public sector. But a pay-as-you-go system (one that collects fees or taxes and makes payments from those receipts in approximately the same period) is normally incorporated in general government.

---

[2] Public sector financial enterprises – e.g., the central bank and, perhaps, a development bank, a publicly owned commercial bank or trade financing institution – would be incorporated in a fully consolidated public sector. Here, we follow the convention of including any transfers between these financial institutions and the government (e.g., profit transfers from the central bank) in the budget, and treating the accounts of these institutions as part of the financial sector.

[3] In some countries much fungibility exists between these levels of the public sectors. For example, in such countries fiscal reform can be much like squeezing a balloon: greater austerity at the central government level is offset at other levels of government; when the aggregate general government is constrained, substantial deficits appear in publicly-owned enterprises. Effective analysis and policy formulation, therefore, requires understanding the interrelationships between the different components of the public sector.

a Reading the Accounts

The IMF's Government Finance Statistics Manual (GFSM) is a helpful source that seeks to systematize the reporting of fiscal data and to make them consistent with the National Accounts.[4] However, presentations of fiscal accounts are never identical across countries, even in IMF reports where the push for homogeneity is strong. They differ in the reach of the definition of the government and in exactly which expenditure and revenue items are placed above the line (as components that determine the deficit or surplus) or below the line (as financing items). That said, once the analytic framework of the GFSM is understood, most presentations of the data are easy to follow. In this section we present a generic framework based on the GFSM. Our presentation is notionally for the general government accounts but most elements are similar to those for the narrower central government accounts or broader overall public sector accounts. For many countries the fiscal year differs from the calendar year – e.g., it may run from April 1 through March 31. This complicates the integration of fiscal and income accounts.

Table 5.1 provides an example of the general government accounts using data for Poland. Budget tables may be presented in absolute nominal numbers (e.g., billions of zloty) or as ratios to nominal GDP as in Table 5.1; the latter are useful for scale – especially when comparing data across countries of different sizes – and for spotting discontinuities over time.[5]

We often call all the items above the line in Table 5.1 above-the-line items: i.e., categories of revenue and spending, *not* of financing. Total revenue minus total expenditure is called the overall balance (OB) or net lending. Below-the-line items are financing items. Therefore, if the government has a deficit above the line – so that *OB* is negative – below-the-line items show how this has been (or will be) financed.

Most sub-items of revenue and expenditure are self-explanatory. "Other revenue," however, includes three nontax items that bear explanation.

---

[4] The GFSM (www.imf.org/external/Pubs/FT/GFS/Manual/2014/gfsfinal.pdf) is updated periodically to improve conceptual clarity and to reflect changes in data compilation and common practices of fiscal accounting. Recent revisions have sought to integrate the flow presentation of government budgets with a statement of the government's net worth (a stock concept) and its components. This reflects the heightened attention in policy analysis to the government's longer-term financial position.

[5] An aside on terminology: when data are shown as percentages of GDP we cannot refer to a change of, say, 3.5 between two years as a change of 3.5 percent because the two numbers have different denominators. The change should be called a change relative to GDP of 3.5 percentage points.

TABLE 5.1 *Poland: general government operations (2015–2016)* (in percent of GDP)

	2015	2016
		Est.
Revenue (Rev)	39.0	38.8
Taxes	19.8	20.3
Personal income tax	4.7	4.8
Corporate income tax	1.8	1.8
VAT	7.0	7.1
Excises	3.5	3.6
Other taxes	2.8	3.0
Social contributions	13.6	14.0
Other revenue	5.6	4.3
Expenditure (Exp)	41.6	41.3
Expenses (C_g)	37.4	38.0
Compensation of employees	10.2	10.3
Use of goods and services	5.9	5.8
Interest	1.8	1.7
Subsidies	0.5	0.5
Social benefits	16.2	17.2
Other	2.8	2.5
Net acquisition of nonfinancial assets (I_g)	4.2	3.3
Net lending/overall balance (OB)	**−2.6**	**−2.4**
Net financial transactions	**−2.6**	**−2.4**
Net acquisition of financial assets	0.6	2.3
Net incurrence of liabilities	3.2	4.8
Memorandum items:		
Gross operating balance (GOB = S_g)	1.6	0.8
Primary balance (PRIM)	−0.8	−0.7
Structural fiscal balance	−2.6	−2.5
Primary structural balance	−0.8	−0.8
Public gross financing requirement (PGFR)	7.7	4.1
General government debt	51.1	54.4
Nominal GDP (zloty billions)	1,799	1,851

Source: IMF 2017 Article IV Consultation

These differ in importance from one country to another, and when large they usually are identified explicitly in budget tables and related discussions:

- Government operations in some of the least developed and poorest countries rely heavily on grants from richer countries or international aid agencies. For these countries, the steadiness or volatility of the "Grants" item in the budget is highly consequential.
- For most countries profit transfers from the central bank (see discussion of seigniorage revenue below and in Chapter 4) are a significant nontax revenue. Profit transfers from government-owned enterprises may also be sizable.
- Royalties, licensing fees, and various other kinds of fees may be important nontax revenues for some countries.

The placement of some items in the government accounts is not clear-cut but it can significantly affect public perceptions of the fiscal balance. Three stand out from recent experiences: privatization receipts, net acquisition of financial assets, and bank recapitalizations (which are relatively rare but can have large implications for government debt in a private sector financial crisis):

- *Privatization* receipts are those from government sales of nonfinancial assets, say buildings or land or shares in a state-owned company. These are usually put above the line as a (negative) part of the government's net acquisition of nonfinancial assets (thereby reducing government investment or I_g). If treated like this, privatization affects the OB: increasing the overall surplus (net lending) or reducing the overall deficit (a smaller negative number for net lending). In policy formulation, however, especially when we are thinking about how to finance government operations, we often think of privatization as a below-the-line financing option. In practice this difference in how it is recorded is not significant, though the optics are different.
- *Net acquisition of financial assets (often mainly policy lending)* by the government could be treated below the line as net lending – i.e., as an acquisition of a financial asset – on the grounds that placement of government financial resources in a loan is much the same as placement in an account with the banking system. Or it could be put above the line under other expenditure on the grounds that these are usually not commercial loans (but rather subsidized loans to

achieve some political or social objective), that they seldom decline, and that they may be difficult to liquidate. Where such lending exists, countries differ in their treatment of it.

- *Bank recapitalizations* by the government are rare but can have large implications for government debt in a banking crisis. There is no common practice in how they are treated. They usually entail the government providing interest-earning government bonds to a bank in exchange for an equity share in the bank. The acquisition of the equities could be put above the line with the correspondingly larger deficit then covered by the equivalent issuance of bonds. But usually the transaction is excluded entirely from the flow accounts and treated only in the government's stock (net worth) accounts (see below) as a swapping of bonds for equities. The transaction increases government debt, and subsequent interest payments on the bonds are included in expenditure. Correspondingly, any dividends from the equities would be nontax revenues.

Leaving aside privatization, policy lending, and recapitalizations for now, we can write down the basic budget identities using the acronyms from Table 5.1.

$$OB = Rev - C_g - I_g \qquad (5.1)$$

If expenditure exceeds income – so that OB is negative – the gap is financed by borrowing (at home and/or abroad): domestic borrowing comprises net credit from banks (including the central bank) plus net bond issuance (i.e., new bonds issued to domestic residents minus amortizations); foreign borrowing consists of bonds issued abroad minus amortization plus net borrowing from foreign banks. Seigniorage – i.e., revenue from the printing of money by the central bank – may also be treated as part of government financing. It is more usually included above the line in nontax revenues as profit transfers from the central bank.[6]

Often analyses refer to the overall deficit defined as OD = −OB.

The government's saving-investment balance, a key component of the overall economy's saving-investment balance discussed in Chapter 2 (recall

---

[6] To the extent that the central bank holds interest-bearing government notes bought from the private sector by printing money, it makes seigniorage profits that are transferred to the government. If, instead, seigniorage takes the form of interest-free loans from the central bank to the government, it is part of net credit from the banking system, and it reduces the effective average interest rate on government debt. Boxes 4.1 and 4.6 have more thorough analyses of seigniorage.

Box 2.7), is embedded in the general government accounts. Government saving is defined as its revenue less its current spending.[7]

$$S_g = Rev - C_g \qquad (5.2)$$

Since, by definition,

$$OB = Rev - C_g - I_g \qquad (5.3)$$

Then

$$OB = S_g - I_g \qquad (5.4)$$

In other words, the government's saving-investment balance is identical to its overall balance or net lending.

The fiscal accounts should be on an accrual basis (i.e., items should be recorded when they become due, not when they are actually paid), not on a cash basis. This convention makes the fiscal accounts compatible with the National Accounts, which are on an accrual basis. But some countries still present on a cash basis. It is essential to know the practice of a country when examining its fiscal accounts. If a government is under financial pressure, the cash deficit may be distorted by arrears on wages and salaries to public employees and on payments to suppliers of goods and services. In such circumstances the reported deficit will be smaller if measured on a cash basis than if on an accrual basis. But the cash deficit will present a false picture.

The government's net worth – a stock concept as opposed to the flow data in Table 5.1 – reflects the accumulated changes in stocks of assets and liabilities; these result from flow operations and changes in asset and liability valuations. While net lending (or the overall balance) is the flow that affects the stock of the government's financial assets and liabilities, the net worth of the government also includes its nonfinancial assets. If a negative overall balance reflects substantial investment (i.e., acquisition of nonfinancial assets), the government's financial assets would fall but its net worth would rise if this investment exceeded the absolute value of the negative overall balance. The gross operating balance, or government saving, is defined as revenue minus expenses ($GOB = Rev - C_g$) if capital consumption (depreciation) *is not* included in expenses.[8] While the overall balance changes the government's stock financial position, the operating balance changes the government's net worth.

The GFSM seeks to link flow data from the budget to the stock (net worth) data. Conceptually, these links are important for interpreting the

---

7   As is clear from Table 5.1, this is identical to the *gross operating balance* – or *net operating balance* if capital consumption (depreciation) is included in C_g. See below.
8   As indicated in Table 5.1, the term "expenses" is used synonymously with current expenditure. If capital consumption *is* included in expenses then the corresponding concept (revenue minus expenses) is a *net operating balance* (NOB).

health of the fiscal accounts. For example, a government's assets might include ownership shares in an enterprise. The dividends that the enterprise distributes each year are flow revenues for the budget. But if the value of that asset (the net worth of the enterprise) drops – because of mismanagement or bad luck – the government's net worth declines even though its flow accounts may continue to look healthy. A statement of the government's net worth would capture this weaker overall position when the budget flow accounts would not.

Many countries do not have the data and valuations required for a complete and consistent stock-flow presentation, and determining the present (stock) value of contingent liabilities and the flow of future social security obligations is even more difficult. As a result, fiscal analyses are often based on flow data, with stock considerations restricted to government debt, rather than net worth.

This section has picked up features of government accounts that are typically the most important quantitatively or operationally. Myriad other definitional and accounting issues related to the government accounts are covered in the GFSM. Not all countries' data and presentations will reflect current "best practice." At the risk of insulting the statisticians by giving short shrift to the subtleties and nuances of public sector accounting, we will move on now to some fiscal analytics.

b Judging the Credibility of Budget Projections

Suppose one is presented with a country's budget and asked to assess its credibility. A typical question is: "Has the government slanted its budget projection to look more favorable than a true central projection, so as to avoid admitting the need for tax increases or spending cuts?" Assessing the credibility of the budget is the first step in reaching a judgment on whether a budget is serving countercyclical objectives and on whether it is creating potential sustainability problems. What are the standard components of such an assessment?

(i) Revenue
On the revenue side, projected receipts are highly contingent on economic developments in the tax base – income taxes on projections of incomes, profits taxes on company profits, customs duties on imports, and so on. With enough time one could build an econometric model to project each revenue component. But, short of this, and given a plausible set of projections for the National Accounts aggregates, one can usually get a quick fix

on the broad components of revenue by looking at tax elasticities and buoyancies – two ways of measuring the responsiveness of revenues to changes in tax bases.

The elasticity of each tax is the percentage change in the revenue from the tax divided by the percentage change in the tax base – *given an unchanged statutory tax rate and base*. Thus, with no change in the tax system, the elasticity of the individual income tax would be calculated as the ratio of the percentage change in actual income tax collections to that in nominal personal incomes or perhaps nominal GDP (in a rougher calculation). This calculation is straightforward if tax rates or structures are unchanged; however, when changes occur the elasticity calculation has to correct for them. Tax buoyancy is a cruder measure insofar as it does the same calculation but without correcting for any changes in tax rates or definitions of the base. One may estimate the elasticity or the buoyancy with the previous year as the base (if that year had no unusual characteristics) or by calculating the relationship between the growth of revenue from a tax and the growth of its base over several years.

Buoyancy or elasticity calculations provide a relatively easy first check on the plausibility of the government's revenue projections and their consistency with the national accounts projections on which the budget is based. First, if the buoyancy of the income tax historically has been between 0.9 and 1.3 but in the current budget projections it is 1.8, there is an obvious question to ask: What is the government doing to bring in revenues from this tax that are so far above the historical norm? If the statutory tax rate has increased, one needs to discuss how easy it will be to collect taxes at this higher rate and whether the increased rate will elicit avoidance. The oldest story in excessively sanguine budgeting is that a high buoyancy will result from "better tax collection efforts." This narrative may prove correct (see Box 5.1), but it often proves to be fiction.[9]

Second, if the buoyancy ratios seem sensible but the official national accounts projections are implausibly sanguine, one can use the buoyancy ratios with independent (i.e., more realistic) national accounts projections to get a better fix on revenue projections. At a highly aggregated level,

---

[9] It is true that buoyancy is sometimes increased significantly by better tax design. For example, a simplification of VAT by reducing the number of different rates has, on occasion, increased compliance.

Box 5.1 Buoyancy: Disentangling Underlying Influences

For the most part, it is sensible to start with a buoyancy assumption of
1, or an assumption based on recent history. But insofar as the projected revenue buoyancy differs from this prior, the next step must
always be to delve into the specifics of the country involved.

Besides changes in statutory tax rates, it is sometimes true that better
design (usually simplification) of the tax system or improved enforcement of tax laws (reduced evasion) increases tax buoyancy. Buoyancy
can also be influenced by shifts in the composition of GDP. For
example, in Poland (Table 5.1) the high tax buoyancy (1.9 in 2016)
reflects a substantial increase in the share of wages in GDP (which
affected personal income taxes and social contributions) as well as
better enforcement of VAT. Buoyancy calculations can also be thrown
off by sharp changes in growth rates. For example, if the tax accrual
system has a built-in one-quarter lag and the economy falls into
recession in 2018, taxes for the year will remain high because they
reflect the booming economic activity in 2017.[1]

[1] The lags between activity and tax accruals are becoming shorter with the digitization
of tax systems.

$$revenue\ change\ (in\ percent) = buoyancy$$
$$\times\ nominal\ GDP\ change\ (in\ percent)$$
$$(5.5)$$

Tax revenues are usually the greater part of budget revenues. Some other
components (like social insurance contributions and fees) may be amenable to similar analysis – i.e., closely related to projections for growth of the
base. But other parts (like "other revenues") may be more idiosyncratic. For
the latter, an assessment of the budget projections may depend on discern-
ible trends, some other pattern evident in revenue data, or simply the
plausibility of the underlying narrative and assumptions. Estimates of grants
from foreign donors are usually based on a pipeline of undisbursed commitments by donors and some normal disbursement rate.

(ii) Expenditure
On the expenditure side, assessing the credibility of projections entails two
different sorts of exercises. One part of spending, called "nondiscretionary
expenditure," consists of items where spending is set by contract or by law.

Interest payments on the government debt are set by debt contracts, and social security payments (pensions, unemployment benefits, some medical benefits) must conform to existing laws. If one has a reasonable projection of the underlying base – e.g., the stock of debt, level of unemployment, number of pension recipients, and any cost-of-living adjustment – one can make a fair projection of the related component of nondiscretionary expenditure. A quick approximation may be calculated using the elasticity of the spending category to its base.

The other part of expenditure is "discretionary expenditure." Some of its parts are also amenable to fairly straightforward calculations. Spending on wages and salaries depends on wage rates (which in turn may be influenced by cost-of-living adjustments) and the number of employees in the civil and military services. Often a government bent on retrenchment will project a reduction in employment. Such projections need to be assessed for their plausibility in the political circumstances.

But assessing the credibility of other parts of discretionary spending – that on goods and services and on capital projects – is far more nuanced. The government can speed up or slow down many of these expenditures depending on circumstances. Some current spending may be reasonably predictable insofar as there is a minimal amount of spending on, say, infrastructure maintenance or school textbooks that is consistent with normal operations. Capital projects, however, are often truly discretionary and tend to change most severely as governments seek to contract or expand spending.[10]

(iii) Public Gross Financing Requirement (PGFR)
The annual PGFR is often the focus in assessing a country's fiscal robustness or fragility. It comprises the repayment obligations on the government's short-term debt plus the amortization of the government's medium- and long-term debt minus the overall balance from the budget. (A negative overall balance – i.e., a government deficit – adds to the PGFR.)

Assessing the feasibility of the projected scale and composition of financing is critical to reaching a judgment on whether the budget will strain market access. If analysis leads to doubts about whether markets will fund the PGFR at reasonable interest rates, the prudent course is for the government to go back to the drawing board of budget formulation. This is frequently a critical part of negotiations between a country facing financing difficulties and the IMF when IMF financial support is sought.

---

[10] Capital spending is especially vulnerable to retrenchment: it is relatively easy to cut by slowing down project disbursements. But it may be less responsive to expansion insofar as identifying new and worthwhile projects is usually a much slower process.

Short-term debt is usually rolled over by creditors but in circumstances of financial stress, a rollover rate of less than 100 percent may be a prudent assumption. Projections of interest rates at which the government will be able to issue new medium- and long-term debt are guided by assessments of global market conditions, expected inflation, and any changes in market perceptions of the probability of default by the government.[11]

2 Assessing the Macroeconomic Effects of Fiscal Policy

Fiscal policy plays a central role in macroeconomic stability. The two most important aspects of this role are the smoothing of economic activity over the cycle and, from a longer-term perspective, making sure that the spending and taxation policies of the government are consistent with a sustainable debt burden. The latter objective entails ensuring that there is little risk of the government being unable to meet its debt obligations (without a substantial and disruptive change in the main parameters of fiscal policy) at some future date. This section provides the analytical tools needed to assess whether fiscal policy is meeting these two prerequisites for macroeconomic stability.

a Fiscal Policy and Macroeconomic Stabilization over the Cycle

The government's budget should help stabilize the economy over the cycle. This may happen in two ways: first, through *automatic stabilizers* (the GDP-stabilizing changes in revenues and expenditure that occur automatically during periods when actual GDP departs from potential GDP) and, second, through *discretionary policy actions* (deliberate fiscal policy actions to reduce the amplitude of GDP cycles). Distinguishing between these two channels for countercyclical fiscal effects is important for two main reasons. First, though automatic stabilizers occur in the absence of any policy action during cycles, in some circumstances they will not provide all the countercyclical heft that may be desirable. Therefore, quantifying how much stimulus/ contraction is likely to come from automatic stabilizers is the first step toward

[11]   Most advanced countries issue debt in their own currencies, while, historically, most EMs have had to issue debt in a major currency and bear the currency risk (so-called *original sin*). But in the past two decades, many EMs have been able to issue own-currency debt, thus transferring currency risk to creditors. In this case, the price of debt (the inverse of the interest rate) incorporates two risk premia: one for default risk and the other for currency risk. As stated in Chapter 3, if a country's fiscal position is sound, it may have little or no default risk premium; but interest rates on own-currency EM debt will still be higher than on the equivalent US dollar debt insofar as creditors require an interest rate premium against perceived depreciation risk.

deciding whether discretionary policy action is also necessary. Second, automatic stabilizers and discretionary fiscal action may have quite different implications for the government's debt position over time – i.e., long after a particular phase of a cycle ends.

The starting point for distinguishing between automatic stabilizers and discretionary policy is the concept of the *structural fiscal balance*.[12] This is the overall balance that would occur for any given revenue and expenditure policies *if the economy were operating at full employment* (i.e., actual Y_r equals *potential* Y_r (Y^*)).[13] The structural balance is calculated by adjusting the actual balance to remove the cyclical influences on revenue and spending that occur when economic activity is not at potential. As discussed in Chapters 2 and 3, estimating potential GDP – where capital and labor are fully utilized – is difficult. But the aim is to identify some point in the average cycle where the unemployment rate is as low as it can go without putting upward pressure on inflation. In economies with significant structural or price distortions that keep unemployment rates high throughout the cycle, there is often a vigorous debate about how much of unemployment is cyclical – and, therefore, potentially responsive to countercyclical policies – and how much is structural.

(i) Automatic Stabilizers

When GDP is below potential, employment, household incomes, and business profits are below the "full employment" level. This weaker tax base reduces government revenues. At the same time, some government spending obligations, such as those for unemployment insurance and other programs to alleviate the effects of the downturn, increase. Thus the government's overall balance falls (the deficit rises). But in the absence of discretionary fiscal policy changes, the *structural balance* (surplus or deficit) remains unchanged. The automatic changes in the fiscal balance caused by a cyclical divergence of activity from its potential level are called the *automatic stabilizers*. For the same gap between actual and potential GDP, the

---

[12] The literature sometimes distinguishes between the cyclically-adjusted fiscal balance and the structural fiscal balance. The latter adjusts the former for any one-off irregular influences in the government accounts. We use the term structural fiscal balance to mean the cyclically-adjusted balance because we do not posit any such irregular changes.

[13] *Full employment* does not mean that unemployment is zero (as discussed in Chapters 2 and 3). Moreover, the unemployment rate that is considered "full employment" differs between economies and even over time in one economy because of institutional ("structural") characteristics that may either prolong *frictional* unemployment or reduce the proportion of the working-age population that is willing or able to work. In the remainder of this section we use the terms *full-employment* GDP and *potential* GDP interchangeably (denoted as Y^*).

size of the automatic stabilizers differs between countries, depending on the elasticities of revenues and spending with respect to the cycle.

The analysis of the structural fiscal balance typically focuses on the *primary balance* – defined as total revenue minus noninterest ("primary") expenditure. This is because interest spending has a limited, if any, cyclical component insofar as a large share of government debt at any point is subject to fixed interest rates and multiyear maturities. We start the cyclical analysis in an illustrative fashion by assuming that revenue and primary spending both have constant elasticities to nominal GDP. At any point in the cycle, the primary balance is equal to the primary structural balance (that which would obtain if GDP were equal to potential) plus the fiscal effects of the deviations of GDP from potential.

$$PRIM = \textit{primary structural balance} + \textit{cyclical effects}$$
$$= Rev^* - PExp^* + (Rev - Rev^*) - (PExp - PExp^*) \qquad (5.6)$$

PRIM = primary balance
PExp = noninterest spending
* denotes the structural (or cyclically-adjusted) value of a variable

Now let's derive the structural revenue and expenditure estimates by adjusting actual revenue and expenditure for the deviations of nominal GDP from potential nominal GDP. Since we are using elasticities of revenue and expenditure to nominal GDP we have to use logarithms:

$$Ln(Rev^*) = Ln(Rev) - \gamma_r Ln(Y_n/Y_n^*) \qquad (5.7)$$
$$Ln(PExp^*) = LnPExp - \gamma_e Ln(Y_n/Y_n^*) \qquad (5.8)$$

γ_r = elasticity of revenue with respect to GDP
γ_e = elasticity of expenditure with respect to GDP

The elasticity of revenue to GDP is usually a positive number close to unity, while that of expenditure is usually a small negative number or zero. The expenditure elasticity is a larger negative number where unemployment insurance and welfare systems are more generous.

From equations (5.6–5.8), the primary fiscal balance can be separated into structural and cyclical components.

These equations are oversimplified: we could compute elasticities of different categories of revenue and spending to different bases – income tax to household incomes, customs revenues to imports, and so on. But while the additional arithmetic may be important in the actual analysis, it adds nothing conceptual and is thus omitted here.

We scale budget balances by GDP: the actual balance as a ratio to nominal GDP, the structural balance as a ratio to potential nominal GDP. The *stance* of fiscal policy is indicated simply by the structural balance: expansionary if the structural balance is in deficit (so that even when GDP is at potential the government is adding to demand) and contractionary if the structural balance is in surplus. If the government took no discretionary fiscal action in response to deviations of actual from potential GDP, changes in the primary balance ratio would all be attributable to automatic stabilizers. In these circumstances, while the fiscal accounts would exert countercyclical effects, the *stance* of fiscal policy would be unchanged.

(ii) Discretionary Policy Action

Often the government wants to go further than merely allowing the automatic stabilizers to play out. It may want to take discretionary action to pull the economy out of recession faster than the automatic stabilizers alone would do.[14] If it does so, the conventionally-measured deficit increases by more than is attributable to the *automatic stabilizers* alone. Thus the *stance* of fiscal policy changes – i.e., the primary structural deficit increases relative to potential GDP. (An increase in the structural primary deficit is sometimes referred to as a positive *fiscal impulse* or a *discretionary injection of fiscal stimulus*.) It follows that unless fiscal impulses are symmetric over the cycle – i.e., discretionary stimulus is followed by discretionary contraction when the economy moves from recession to boom – the structural deficit will rise over time.

Discretionary fiscal stimulus is a potentially powerful countercyclical tool.[15] But it can also be a difficult genie when let out of the bottle. It is much easier to increase spending and cut taxes in a recession than to reverse these actions subsequently, and politicians, even in democracies with well-informed voters, will be tempted to postpone fiscal retrenchments any time close to an election. If government investment exceeds government saving as an economy returns to full employment, the government will be in competition with private investors for private saving. Then by

[14] For simplicity of exposition, in the discussion of discretionary fiscal action we will focus on situations of stimulus rather than contraction (often called withdrawal of stimulus).

[15] This is true even though expansionary fiscal policy is usually offset in part by increased private saving. The doctrine of *Ricardian Equivalence* posits that the offset will be complete because rational private agents will save to cover future tax obligations (or reduced future government transfers or services). Thus, full Ricardian Equivalence would emasculate fiscal policy as a countercyclical tool. Ricardian Equivalence is mathematically elegant in a complete intertemporal, general equilibrium model; but empirically the private offset to government expansion is usually estimated to be about 0.5. That is, about half of the direct effect of a countercyclical fiscal expansion on GDP is usually offset by higher private saving. Fiscal policy is, therefore, typically an effective countercyclical tool.

driving up real interest rates and discouraging private investment, the government deficit will crowd out private sector activity. Debt dynamics will also be affected, as discussed later in this section.

(iii) Automatic Stabilizers vs. Discretionary Action: A Snapshot of the Debate

Most economists engaged in policy formulation would support having higher fiscal deficits when an economy is in recession. The hawks among them would typically favor relying on automatic stabilizers alone; the doves on adding discretionary stimulus. The policy debate is often framed around two issues: the extent of spare capacity in the economy (and thus the amount of stimulus needed to increase demand enough to push output back to its potential level) and the size of the fiscal multiplier, that is, the percentage change in real GDP that will result from a given amount of discretionary fiscal stimulus (the latter measured as the change in the structural balance in percentage points of potential GDP).[16]

The first component in this debate – the difficulty of estimating the extent of spare capacity in the economy – was taken up in Chapter 2 in the discussion of estimating potential output. Box 5.2 provides a graphic illustration of the fiscal implications of getting this estimate wrong in the United Kingdom during the early 2000s.

Box 5.2 Output Gaps and Structural Fiscal Balances

It is difficult to predict recessions and more so if the economic downturns are extreme. In the pre-recessionary period, governments and even independent analysts tend to think that the high level of economic activity is normal – or, at least, not massively abnormal – and that activity at close to this level will be sustainable. Once the recession hits, questions emerge about whether the activity in a particular sector – housing, perhaps, or finance – was in fact reflective of a bubble.

(continued)

---

[16] In recessions, when interest rates are typically low, it is often argued that the time is ideal for government infrastructure investment – because of both the need for stimulus and the low cost of financing. But time lags are problematic. The government may not have "shovel-ready" investments with a rate of return that warrants incurring debt, and long planning and implementation lags may mean that the additional stimulus hits the economy after the cyclical weakness has bottomed out. Some would argue that almost any discretionary spending in a deep recession is better than none but this position is contentious. We will not explore this part of the debate further because it quickly gets into the quality of governance and institutions.

Box 5.2 (*continued*)

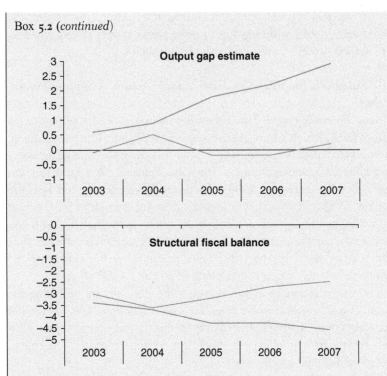

FIGURE 5.1 United Kingdom: output gaps and structural fiscal balances (percent of potential GDP)
Source: IMF WEO October 2007 and October 2017

The top panel in Figure 5.1, recalling Chapter 2, shows estimates of the output gap – actual output minus potential output – from two different vintages of the IMF's WEO. The bottom panel in Figure 5.1 shows the corresponding estimates of the structural fiscal balances. The blue lines represent estimates from the October 2007 WEO; the red lines from October 2017 WEO.

It is clear that in 2007, on the eve of the great recession, output was not viewed as substantially above potential. The cyclical adjustment, therefore, was small and the structural fiscal balance (a deficit of about 2.5 percent of potential output) was estimated to be not very different from the actual fiscal balance.

(*continued*)

> **Box 5.2** (*continued*)
>
> After the great recession, however, there was a fundamental reassess-
> ment of the economic conditions that had prevailed in 2007. As is
> evident from the red lines, the retrospective estimate of the output gap
> in 2007 was much larger (at almost 3 percent of potential GDP), the
> magnitude of the cyclical adjustment to derive the structural fiscal
> balance was, therefore, much more significant, and the resulting struc-
> tural fiscal balance was a deficit of about 4.5 percent of potential GDP.

The second component – assessing the size of the fiscal multiplier –
raises a different set of complexities. It is a hot issue in any discussion of
fiscal policy options.

The most simplistic calculation of the government spending multiplier
starts with a closed economy with exogenous private investment and government spending. The fiscal stimulus has a direct effect on aggregate
demand and income and then a subsequent effect through higher income
on private consumption.[17] In this simple view

$$\Delta Y_r = \Delta Exp(1/(1 - mpc)) \tag{5.9}$$

mpc = marginal propensity to consume

Thus, for instance, if the mpc is 0.7, the multiplier would be 3.3. In other
words, for every dollar increase in government spending, GDP rises by over
$3. This is simplistic insofar as it omits various offsetting influences and
results in an unrealistically large multiplier.

The conventional textbook closed-economy Keynesian model (sometimes called the Hicks–Hansen or, as in Box 4.4, the IS–LM model)
expands this simple analysis to admit possible effects of increased government spending on interest rates and in turn on private investment.[18] In this
model, the multiplier is larger the smaller the effect of the fiscal stimulus on
the interest rate. In the real world, fiscal stimulus in circumstances of weak

---

[17] The time dimension of the multiplier is usually not well defined. It could refer to the effect
of fiscal stimulus in a given year on GDP in that year, the effect of fiscal stimulus in
a given year on GDP over a longer period, or the effect of a multiyear fiscal stimulus on
GDP over the same or a more extended period.

[18] The model, described in Box 4.4, includes an equilibrium locus for the goods market (the
IS curve, where interest-sensitive investment equals income-sensitive saving) and an
equilibrium locus for the money market (the LM curve, where the supply of money is
exogenous and its demand – what Keynes called *liquidity preference* – depends on both
income and the interest rate).

demand (with the economy below potential) may well elicit very little interest rate reaction, both because monetary policy is likely to be accommodative and because there is likely to be a saving glut. Thus the multiplier will be larger the more slack in the economy. Fiscal stimulus is more likely to crowd out private demand as the economy gets closer to full employment, with investment constrained by saving and less accommodative monetary policy.

In a model that admits price changes and varying risk premia, other influences affect the efficacy of fiscal policy. Crowding out may be effected through real resource constraints and price changes: e.g., additional government investment may exacerbate supply constraints in some critical sectors – such as electricity or building materials – and crowd out private investment by increasing prices of these essential inputs. The efficacy of fiscal policy may also be sensitive to the level of government debt: if debt is raised to a precarious level, risk premia may rise and push interest rates higher.

Estimates of the multiplier are further complicated in an open economy. Once trade is introduced, some of the increase in demand from a fiscal stimulus will "leak out" through higher imports, mitigating the effect on domestic output. Exchange rate arrangements are also determining. The open-economy Mundell–Fleming model (discussed in Box 4.4) concludes that in a fixed exchange rate setting (where additional financing can be found in global financial markets without any increase in interest rates), the multiplier will be higher than in a floating exchange rate setting (where, in the absence of an easing of monetary policy, the effect of a fiscal expansion on aggregate demand will be muted by both higher interest rates and the likely resulting currency appreciation). Box 5.3 draws on recent data from the fiscal crisis in Greece to illustrate some of these considerations.

Box 5.3 The Difficulty of Pinning Down the Size of the Fiscal Multiplier: The Case of Greece

Changes in the fiscal stance influence real growth through various and complex channels. Besides the initial effect on demand and the secondary effects on income and private expenditure, fiscal adjustments typically have other influences through interest rates, prices, exchange rates, perceptions of fiscal sustainability, and expectations about future obligations and policy changes. In addition, other changes in the economic environment may occur at the same time as the fiscal action. Estimated econometric models with solid

Box 5.3 (*continued*)

microeconomic optimizing behavior that might be capable of estimating or projecting multipliers do not exist. Not surprisingly, therefore, the debate about the size of multipliers is vigorous and unsettled.

Consider the case of Greece. In April 2010, when negotiations on economic projections and policies for a standby arrangement (SBA) between the IMF and Greece were at an advanced stage, the IMF's April 2010 WEO projected a reduction in Greece's structural government deficit relative to potential GDP of 5.25 percentage points during 2009–2011.[1] Real GDP was projected to drop by just under 3 percent during 2009–2012. These projections assumed a multiplier of 0.5 (other influences were close to a wash). The GDP projection proved overly sanguine by a large margin: during 2009–2012 real GDP dropped by about 20 percent.[2] Does this mean that the program projections were based on too low a fiscal multiplier (some economists have argued ex post that the assumed multiplier should have been substantially above 1)? Or was the assumed multiplier justifiable but then augmented by other factors not adequately foreseen?

Three types of other factors were significant:

 (i) The SBA projections were based on a modest rise in yields on government debt; in fact yields rose sharply – that on debt with a 10-year residual maturity from 5 percent in late 2009 to above 25 percent by mid-2012. This jump, as well as a quantitative credit crunch, severely affected private interest-sensitive spending.

 (ii) Various setbacks raised doubts about the feasibility of financing the programmed fiscal deficit. The targeted fiscal adjustment was therefore increased to about double the amount initially planned.

(iii) Other parts of the policy program (especially structural reform) were not fully implemented, and external competitiveness did not improve as projected.

All of this means that it is difficult to assess alternative narratives.

In one story, the original projection of the fiscal multiplier was too low, and the larger-than-projected drop in GDP elicited a vicious circle of detrimental influences. In this view, less fiscal adjustment (financed by more official lending to the government) would have been more effective in achieving program objectives.

An alternative narrative downplays any error in the assumed multiplier, arguing that creditors from the outset doubted the realism of the program – the improvement in competitiveness, the government's

(*continued*)

Box 5.3 (*continued*)

ability to stick to fiscal and structural commitments, and thus the projections for GDP. These doubts, along with banking system fragilities, led to higher risk premia and a virtual credit freeze for private businesses. The problem, therefore, was not a faulty assumption about the fiscal multiplier. Rather it was unrealistic projections for competitiveness, market confidence in the program, risk premia, and interest rates that produced a drop in GDP far larger than that attributable to fiscal retrenchment.

It is doubtful that we will be able to determine definitively which of these stories is correct.

[1] Of the several types of lending arrangements between the IMF and member countries, the SBA is the most common. It entails funding from the IMF that is disbursed in tranches over a one- to three-year period; each disbursement is contingent on the borrowing country having in place pre-agreed macroeconomic and structural policies designed to set the economy on a path to recovery. Repayments of each tranche are scheduled over 3.25–5 years after each disbursement. The SBA with Greece began in May 2010.

[2] Both fiscal retrenchment and falling GDP continued after 2012.

If one believes that governments are capable of assessing the cyclical position of the economy and injecting and withdrawing stimulus accordingly, there is a case for discretionary fiscal policy. As noted, however, the political economy of fiscal policy tends to favor expansionary over restrictive interventions. In extreme circumstances this can lead to debt rising over several cycles and, eventually, an unsustainable fiscal position.

b Fiscal Policy, Debt Dynamics, and Sustainability

Fiscal balances determine the amount of borrowing a government must undertake. The vast majority of countries have a stock of debt (usually calibrated, for analytic purposes, as a ratio to nominal GDP) due to past borrowing to finance steady moderate deficits or countercyclical policies in downturns that are not fully offset in economic upturns. Usually government debt is of a relatively high quality and is readily tradable; it is a liquid asset for banks and businesses to hold, a vehicle for central bank open market operations, and its yields serve as a benchmark for interest rates at all maturities. Moreover, insofar as government investment produces future dividends (in the form of higher growth) it makes sense to spread the cost of this investment over current and future generations through debt financing. So a modest stock of government debt is considered manageable and even desirable.

Instances abound, however, when governments borrow excessively for long periods and the level of debt becomes problematic. Sometimes these situations are resolved through fiscal austerity measures (cutting deficits or running surpluses), which are typically painful for citizens and politically unpopular. Sometimes, when the politics of austerity are untenable, high and unsustainable government debt leads to a crisis that can be resolved only by restructuring the debt (changing the terms on outstanding debt with creditor approval) or, in extreme circumstances, outright default.

Fiscal crises typically occur when investors fear that the government may be incapable of meeting its financing requirements at some future time. The onset may be sudden. A typical example is a country that has run a sizable fiscal deficit for some time. Risk premia may have drifted upward and growth may have slowed gradually. Then some precipitating event, such as a political change or crisis in a neighboring country, focuses investors' concerns on the precarious debt dynamics – the likely path of debt determined by future growth, interest rates, and fiscal positions as described below – and the risk that the government may not be able to service and repay its debt at some future date.

When such concerns become acute, investors either stop buying or rush to sell government paper (what is sometimes referred to as a "sudden stop" in financing flows), and risk premia rise sharply relative to those in safer comparator countries. The government may then not be able to meet its financing needs (its PGFR) at any reasonable interest rate, and a potential future problem is brought into the present with sharply disruptive effects.

Analysis of the longer-term sustainability of the government's finances is, therefore, as important as the countercyclical considerations of the last section. Today's fiscal policy determines tomorrow's debt burden. Because investors are always looking to the future – in effect, conducting their own sustainability analyses – financial markets translate concerns about future debt back to today's market signals. Continuous analysis of the fiscal situation and early correction of incipient financing problems is thus critical to sound policy. A debt sustainability analysis (DSA) is therefore a central feature of the IMF's annual review of each member country's macroeconomy and can be found in the resulting reports (Article IV Consultation Reports). Box 5.4 describes the IMF's approach to fiscal sustainability.

Box 5.4 What is the IMF's Standard for Sustainability of the Fiscal Position and Public Debt?

In general terms, public debt can be regarded as sustainable when the primary balance needed to at least stabilize debt under both the baseline and realistic shock scenarios is economically and politically feasible, such that the level of debt is consistent with an acceptably low rollover risk and with preserving potential growth at a satisfactory level. Conversely, if no realistic adjustment in the primary balance – i.e., one that is both economically and politically feasible – can bring debt to below such a level, public debt would be considered unsustainable.[1]

The IMF also points out the judgments that enter its debt sustainability analysis (DSA) for market access countries (MACs), as distinct from low-income countries, which mostly finance from official sources.

In practice, assessing debt sustainability for MACs involves probabilistic judgments about the trajectory of debt and the availability of financing on favorable terms. In making such an assessment there are several important considerations: (i) are debt burden indicators projected, at a minimum, to stabilize at levels consistent with an acceptably low rollover risk and with preserving growth at a satisfactory level, taking into account cyclical considerations, ... in the baseline scenario ... [and] under plausible stressed scenarios? (ii) are the level and trajectory of the debt burden indicators underpinned by realistic projections for primary balance adjustment? (iii) are the assumptions for other key macroeconomic variables (e.g., growth and interest rates) realistic? and (iv) is the debt profile well balanced in terms of maturity, currency composition, and investor base so as to facilitate continued market access?[2]

---

[1] IMF, Staff Guidance Note for Public Debt Sustainability Analysis in Market-Access Countries (May 2003), www.imf.org/en/publications/policy-papers/issues/2016/12/31/staff-guidance-note-for-public-debt-sustainability-analysis-in-market-access-countries-PP4771

[2] Ibid.

(i) Fiscal Sustainability Narrowly Defined

The simplest standard for a fiscal sustainability is having a fiscal balance that, if maintained, will result in a stable ratio of debt to nominal GDP at least by some point in the foreseeable future.[19] Often, "the foreseeable future" is called the medium term, which can be taken to be about five years. The intuition here is that as long as the debt ratio is (and is expected to remain) stable, current investors should have no reason to reduce their positions and will roll over debt as it matures. Therefore the risk of a large increase in the risk premium or a sudden stop in financing is low.[20]

Algebraically, the public debt ratio is constant if the percentage change in debt is equal to the percentage change in nominal GDP.

$$\Delta D_t / D_{t-1} = \Delta Y_n / Y_{n,(t-1)} = gr_{n,\,t} \tag{5.10}$$

D = stock of government debt

gr_n = percentage change in nominal GDP

We know that the change in outstanding debt in period t (i.e., the change in the stock of debt between the end of period $t - 1$ and the end of period t) is equal to interest payments in period t (determined by the stock of debt at the end of period $t - 1$ times the interest rate in period t) minus the primary balance in period t.

$$\Delta D_t = i_t D_{t-1} - PRIM_t \tag{5.11}$$

Substituting equation 5.11 into 5.10, we get the debt-stabilizing condition.

$$\Delta D_t / D_{(t-1)} = i_t - prim_t [Y_{n,t} / D_{t-1}] = gr_{n,\,t} \tag{5.12}$$

$$prim = PRIM_t / Y_{n;t}$$

The policy variable in this expression is the primary fiscal balance. Thus, the minimum condition for debt sustainability is that the primary balance be no more negative than is consistent with a percentage increase in debt

[19] The terms "fiscal sustainability" and "public debt sustainability" are often used interchangeably, including in this book. Moreover, "debt sustainability" is frequently used as shorthand for "public debt sustainability" even though an important but separate topic is "external debt sustainability." Chapter 7 provides more detail on the latter and addresses the complementarity between the two types of sustainability.

[20] This is a rather limited definition. If the debt ratio is high there is a danger of a loss of confidence and higher interest costs in the event of any shock to the economy, and this may set off a vicious circle of rising deficits and debt leading to an unsustainable financial situation even without discretionary fiscal action.

no greater than that in GDP over the medium term. This primary balance is given by rearranging equation (5.12), yielding

$$prim_t = [D_{t-1}/Y_{n,\,t-1}][Y_{n,\,t-1}/Y_{n,t}]\ (i_t - gr_{nt})$$
$$= (D_{t-1}/Y_{n,\,t-1})[(i_t - gr_{n,t})/(1 + gr_{n,t})] \qquad (5.13)$$

Thus the primary balance that stabilizes the debt ratio depends on the starting debt ratio but also on the difference between the interest rate and the growth rate. If growth is high relative to the interest rate, it may be possible to stabilize the debt ratio with a larger primary deficit (or smaller primary balance). Note that the relevant interest rate here differs from the current market interest rate because most debt will have been contracted at interest rates prevailing well before the current year. The effective interest rate is calculated as the actual (or estimated future) interest bill divided by the debt stock.

In thinking about sustainability we are thinking about the future, and about trends rather than cycles. So it makes sense to think about the *primary structural balance* that will stabilize the debt ratio over time.

So far we have been working with nominal variables – nominal GDP and its growth, and nominal interest rates. But it is reasonable to ask whether inflation affects the analysis. The short answer is that changes in inflation can have significant effects on both government deficits and fiscal sustainability.

First, changes in inflation can complicate the projections of deficits, primary deficits, and the influence of government saving and investment on the economy. The effects of changes in inflation can work through myriad influences such as changing relative prices and differences between automatic adjustments for inflation on various items in the fiscal accounts. These depend on the precise characteristics of the change in inflation and the institutions of individual countries (especially different practices vis-à-vis indexing and tax bracket creep). It is difficult to generalize these. One general influence, however, works through debt servicing where the change in interest obligations relative to GDP depends on the extent to which inflation is anticipated in the effective interest rate on government debt. When higher inflation is not anticipated in the interest rate on government debt, increases in inflation reduce the deficit ratio. Box 5.5 elaborates on this latter channel.

Box 5.5 Inflation and the Government Deficit

We know that the deficit (*Def*) is affected by the primary balance (*PRIM*) and that inflation affects both primary expenditures and revenues. But the automatic, interest-payment effects due to inflation depend on the level of debt (D), the nominal effective interest rate (i), inflation (π), expected inflation (π^e), and the real interest rate (r). Assume initially that the entire stock of debt is rolled over every year. The deficit in year t equals interest payments minus the primary balance.

$$Def_t = D_{(t-1)}\{(1 + \pi_t^e)(1 + r_t) - 1\} - PRIM_t \qquad (5.14)$$

Now, recalling that Y_{nt}/Y_{nt-1} is equal to $(1 + \pi_t)(1 + gr_{r\,t})$, we can write the deficit ratio as

$$Def_t/Y_{n,t} = (D_{(t-1)}/Y_{n,(t-1)})[(1 + \pi_t^e)(1 + r_t) - 1]/[(1 + \pi_t)(1 + gr_{r,t})]$$
$$-(PRIM_t/Y_{n,t}) \qquad (5.15)$$

Let's drop the terms $r_t\pi_t^e$ and $gr_{rt}\pi_t$ (which are products of two fractions and usually too small to make a significant difference). We can then simplify the equation to

$$Def_t/Y_{n,t} \approx (D_{(t-1)}/Y_{n,(t-1)})[(r_t + \pi_t^e)/(1 + gr_{r,t} + \pi_t)] - (PRIM_t/Y_{n,t})$$
$$\approx (D_{(t-1)}/Y_{n,(t-1)})[i_t/(1 + gr_{r,t} + \pi_t)] - (PRIM_t/Y_{n,t})$$
$$(5.16)$$

We want to isolate the automatic effect of inflation on the deficit ratio in period t. Therefore, for simplicity, assume (i) the debt ratio has been constant at 100 percent (i.e., $D_{t-1}/Y_{n,(t-1)} = D_{(t-2)}/Y_{n,(t-2)} = 1$), and (ii) that in both periods $t-1$ and t there is primary balance. Maintaining the extreme assumption that debt is rolled over every year and assuming further that inflation is fully and correctly anticipated in interest rates (i.e., $\pi = \pi^e$), we can eliminate real influences by setting both the real growth rate and the real interest rate at a steady 2 percent. In this polar case, inflation raises the deficit ratio substantially. If inflation jumps from zero in period $t-1$ to 10 percent in period t without any change in real variables, then

$$Def_{(t-1)}/Y_{n,(t-1)} \approx 0.02/1.02 \approx 2\% \qquad (5.17)$$

$$Def_t/Y_{n,\,t} \approx 0.12/1.12 \approx 10.7\,\% \qquad (5.18)$$

(*continued*)

Box 5.5 (*continued*)

At the other extreme, assume that all government debt is long term at fixed nominal interest rates. (A realistic middle-ground case would assume this for some significant portion of the debt.) Then a jump in inflation from zero to 10 percent (a shock insofar as it is not anticipated in the effective nominal interest rate) reduces the deficit ratio from 2 percent to about 1.79 percent.

The effects of inflation complicate macroeconomic diagnostics. Consider the first case, with inflation raising the deficit ratio, and recall the adding-up constraint from Chapter 2: the private sector investment–saving gap plus the government investment–saving gap is equal to the external current account deficit

$$(I_p - S_p) + (I_g - S_g) = CAD \tag{5.19}$$

where all variables can be defined as ratios to nominal GDP. If the government deficit ratio changes owing to inflation, should we expect an equivalent change in the current account deficit, or, alternatively, an offsetting change in the private investment–saving gap? The answer, after working through the inflation accounting in the private sector, is that a change in the government deficit ratio due solely to inflation (without any real change or change in competitiveness) will likely be offset by the private investment–saving ratio and not elicit any appreciable change in the current account deficit ratio.

Second, the influence of inflation on debt dynamics is important. The basic intuition is that inflation would not change the debt dynamics if the effective interest rate on government debt always correctly anticipated inflation. However, because some debt is almost always of long maturity and at fixed nominal interest rates, inflation that is not fully anticipated in the interest rate on government debt ("inflation surprises") lowers the real interest rate relative to the real growth rate (or raises the nominal growth rate relative to the nominal interest rate) and thus reduces the government debt ratio. This means that a government with a debt problem will have an incentive to produce inflation surprises. (This is the problem, described in Chapter 4, for central banks charged with safeguarding the value of the currency.)

Yet another complication arises when part of government debt is denominated in foreign currency so that debt dynamics are also sensitive to the exchange rate. In such circumstances, a depreciation of the domestic currency increases the domestic currency value of the stock of foreign-currency-denominated debt, the ratio of debt to GDP, and the cost of debt servicing. Box 5.6 spells out the algebra of a generalized debt sustainability analysis, laying out all of the possible effects on debt dynamics through changes in growth, inflation, the exchange rate, and the primary balance. The interaction between inflationary effects and exchange rate effects is particularly important in cases where some debt is in foreign currency.

Box 5.6 Debt Dynamics with Inflation, Exchange Rate Changes, and Other Effects

Start with equation (5.11) but divide debt into foreign currency (dollar-denominated) debt and home currency debt. Debt and interest rates are shown with superscripts "f" and "h" for foreign currency and home currency, respectively. For simplicity assume the exchange rate is unity in period $t - 1$. Debt in period t will be equal to that in period $t - 1$, plus interest paid on the initial debt level, plus the effect of the percentage change in the exchange rate (ε) on both the stock of foreign debt and the interest on it, minus the primary balance, plus any other off-budget relevant changes (OTH).

$$D_t = D^f_{(t-1)} + \varepsilon_t D^f_{(t-1)} + i^f_t D^f_{(t-1)} + \varepsilon_t i^f_t D^f_{(t-1)} + D^h_{(t-1)}$$
$$+ i^h_t D^h_{(t-1)} - PRIM_t + OTH_t \tag{5.20}$$

Dividing through by nominal GDP, recalling that $Y_{n,(t-1)}/Y_{n,t} = 1/(1 + gr_{n,t})$ where $gr_{n,t}$ is the rate of growth of nominal GDP, converting upper case letters to lower case letters to denote ratios to GDP, and rearranging terms, yields

$$d_t = \Phi_t[(1 + \varepsilon_t)(1 + i^f_t)d^f_{(t-1)} + (1 + i^h_t)d^h_{(t-1)}] - prim_t + oth_t$$
$$\Phi_t = 1/(1 + gr_{n,t}) \tag{5.21}$$

But we want the debt dynamics – i.e., the change in the debt ratio, Δd_t – so, subtracting $d_{(t-1)}$ from both sides and rearranging yields

$$\Delta d_t = \Phi_t \left[d_{(t-1)} \left\{ i^f_t (d^f_{(t-1)}/d_{(t-1)}) + i^h_t (d^h_{(t-1)}/d_{(t-1)}) \right\} \right.$$
$$\left. - gr_{(n,t)} d_{(t-1)} + \varepsilon_t (1 + i^f_t) d^f_{(t-1)} \right] - prim_t + oth_t \tag{5.22}$$

(continued)

Box 5.6 (*continued*)

Note that the interest rate variable attached to d_{t-1} in the first term is simply a weighted average of the home and foreign rates and is thus the effective overall nominal rate of interest.

If we want to show inflation explicitly in the debt dynamics, we can recall that $gr_{n,t} = [(1 + \pi_t)(1 + gr_{r,t}) - 1]$. Therefore we can rewrite equation (5.22) for Δd_t as

$$\Delta d_t = \Phi_t \Big[d_{(t-1)} \big\{ i_t^f (d_{(t-1)}^f)/d_{(t-1)}) + i_t^h (d_{(t-1)}^h)/d_{(t-1)}) \big\} \\ - gr_{r,t} d_{(t-1)} - \pi_t (1 + gr_{r,t}) d_{(t-1)} + \varepsilon_t (1 + i_t^f) d_{(t-1)}^f \Big] \\ - prim_t + oth_t \qquad (5.23)$$

We can separate the change in the debt ratio into five components:

- An interest rate effect: $\Phi_t[d_{(t-1)}\{i_t^f(d_{(t-1)}^f/d_{(t-1)}) + i_t^h(d_{(t-1)}^h/d_{(t-1)})\}]$. Higher rates increase the debt ratio.
- A nominal growth effect: $\Phi gr_{n,t} d_{(t-1)}$ (or, alternatively, a real growth effect $\Phi_t gr_{r,t} d_{(t-1)}$ plus an inflation effect $\Phi_t \pi_t (1 + gr_{r,t}) d_{(t-1)}$), both of which reduce the ratio.

Sometimes these two effects are shown as an "interest rate-growth differential" as both growth and the effective interest rate have the same coefficients. In doing projections, we can also write the equation showing the real interest rate–real growth differential and using the projected inflation as the expected rate of inflation component of the domestic nominal interest rate. Projections are also needed for all of the other variables: the exchange rate, the foreign interest rate, the primary balance, and other influences.

- An exchange rate effect: $\Phi_t[\varepsilon_t(1 + i_t^f)d_{(t-1)}^f]$. A depreciation ($\varepsilon_t > 0$) increases the debt ratio when some debt is in foreign currency.
- A primary balance effect: $prim_t$. A larger primary balance reduces the debt ratio.
- Other off-budget effects. Examples: recapitalizing banks by issuing them government debt increases the debt ratio; privatization and/or a debt restructuring agreement with creditors might lower it.

(*continued*)

Box 5.6 (*continued*)

Equations (5.20–5.23) depict the most inclusive circumstances. But we can consider more restricted cases.

Consider an important practical case: the effect of inflation where all (or even most) debt is in domestic currency. Debt dynamics and thus sustainability are unaffected by inflation *only if* the effective real interest rate on government debt is impervious to inflation. In the real world, however, insofar as part of government debt is long term and at fixed nominal interest rates, higher inflation can reduce the effective real interest rate on government debt and thus the government debt ratio. This "inflating away" of the government debt means that governments have an incentive to produce inflation surprises – a problem for monetary policy alluded to in Chapter 4. Equally problematic: disinflation with legacy high fixed nominal interest rates can raise the effective real interest rate to the detriment of debt sustainability. The analytics below use a restricted version of the more general equations above.

Consider first the extreme case where debt is rolled over each period and there are no inflation surprises (i.e., $i_t = [(1 + r_t)(1 + \pi_t^e) - 1]$ and $\pi_t = \pi_t^e$). We know that debt dynamics can be influenced by *prim*, other factors, and by the difference between the real interest rate and the real growth rate. So to isolate the effect of inflation we set *prim* = *oth* = o and $r_t = gr_{r,t}$. It is easy to show, in these circumstances that equation (5.21) collapses into $d_t = d_{t-1}$ so that inflation has no effect on the debt dynamics.

However, if, more realistically, we assume that some government debt is longer term and at fixed interest rates that do not perfectly anticipate inflation (i.e., inflation is a surprise insofar as it is not reflected in the effective nominal interest rate) then a jump in inflation reduces the debt ratio. In the extreme case where all debt is domestic, i_t is impervious to inflation, and we maintain *prim* = *oth* = o, equation (5.21) becomes $d_t = d_{(t-1)}[(1 + \bar{i}_t)/(1 + \pi_t)(1 + gr_{r,t})]$. Thus, for example, if inflation rises from zero in year $t - 1$ to 10 percent in year t, real growth is steady at 2 percent, the effective nominal interest rate on government debt is fixed at 2 percent (implying a real rate of 2 percent in year $t - 1$ and a real rate of about −7.25 percent in year t), then the debt ratio will drop by about 9 percent owing solely to inflation (or, equivalently, to the fall in the effective real interest rate on government debt). If the debt ratio is 40 percent in year $t - 1$, it will drop to 36.4 percent because of the

(*continued*)

> **Box 5.6** (*continued*)
>
> 10 percent inflation surprise. If it is 100 percent in year $t - 1$, it will drop to
> 90.9 percent because of the inflation surprise.
>
> As is clear from equation (5.23), the ability of the government to
> inflate away debt is curtailed to the extent that debt is in foreign
> currency. In the extreme case where all debt is in foreign currency
> and the inflation surprise is coupled with a depreciation to preserve
> competitiveness, the negative inflation effect on the change in the
> debt ratio $(\Phi_t \pi_t ((1 + gr_{r,t}) d_{(t-1)}))$ is offset by a positive exchange rate
> effect $(\Phi_t \varepsilon_t (1 + i_t^f) d_{(t-1)})$.

The interplay between changing risk premia on domestic government
debt, interest rates, and exchange rates also presents an enormous challenge
for policymakers (and therefore analysts). Consider the fairly common
situation in which, because of actual or prospective developments in the
balance of payments, the risk premium on the home currency rises.
The monetary authorities can respond in one of two ways: they can either
facilitate a rise in the policy interest rates to cover the higher risk premium
while holding the exchange rate constant, or they can resist the interest rate
increase and let the currency depreciate to the point where an appreciation
(equivalent to the change in the risk premium) is expected.

To the extent that debt carries fixed long-term interest rates the former
path tends to minimize, at least in the near term, the effect of the rising risk
premium on the debt ratio. To the extent that debt is denominated in
foreign currency, the latter path will increase the debt ratio at least temporarily and could call fiscal sustainability into question or even trigger
a crisis of confidence. Specifically, if a significant part of government debt is
in foreign currency (and, especially, if debt is longer maturity and thus less
sensitive to changes in interest rates) the central bank may well choose the
first option even though this path may prevent a needed improvement in
competitiveness. This is one variant of the so-called *fear of floating* phenomenon (to which we shall return in later chapters).

(ii) A Fuller Perspective on Fiscal Sustainability

Most of the foregoing has been mechanistic – fiscal policy has been defined
as sustainable if in a forward-looking analysis it is expected to produce a stable
ratio of public debt to GDP at some point over a medium-term time horizon.
Judgments arise only in connection with projections for variables affecting
the debt trajectory – the effective interest rate, real GDP growth, inflation,
the exchange rate, and the primary balance. In the vast majority of countries,

DSAs find that in at least this rather mechanistic analysis, public debt is sustainable. However, in some countries, even those with ample market access, a DSA finds considerable scope for concern about sustainability. Box 5.7 provides an illustration of such concerns, drawing on the IMF's 2017 Annual Article IV consultation with Brazil.

Box 5.7 What Do Difficult Debt Dynamics Look Like? The DSA for Brazil, 2017

Assessing the sustainability of government finances is not an exact science. The mathematics presented in the text (and more fully in Box 5.6) are the foundation, but interpreting actual data requires peripheral vision. The IMF is charged with this task and assesses every member's fiscal sustainability, usually annually. Here we give the IMF's standard for sustainability and an application in the 2017 annual surveillance report on Brazil.

In its annual consultation with Brazil, the IMF concluded that despite efforts to consolidate and reform the fiscal sector, "fiscal sustainability has not yet been secured."[1] The fiscal problem was attributed to a recession, triggered by large macroeconomic imbalances and a loss of confidence, and added setbacks from declining terms of trade, tight financing conditions, and a political crisis. The IMF projected a recovery from the cyclical weakness but not one strong enough to fully reverse the adverse debt dynamics. Reproduced in Table 5.2 (in edited form) is the IMF's Public DSA.

Five main observations from these data inform the IMF's conclusions.

First, by far the largest problem is the excess of the effective real interest rate over the real growth rate (what the IMF calls "automatic debt dynamics"). During 2017–2022, the projected gap contributes over 15 percentage points to the 14 percentage point increase in the debt ratio. After the 2015–2016 recession, real growth is projected to recover slowly and be well below the 2008–2013 average. But real interest rates remain high owing to (a) disinflation (as inflation falls in the projections, high nominal interest rates on legacy debt keep the effective interest rate high) and (b) a steady 100 bps risk premium over Libor.

Second, other items in the DSA are therefore more or less a wash over time. A stubborn primary deficit requires debt financing through

(continued)

TABLE 5.2 *Brazil: debt sustainability analysis for nonfinancial public sector – baseline scenario*

	Actual data					Projections			
	2014	2015	2016	2017	2018	2019	2020	2021	2022
Key input variables (in percent)									
Nominal gross public debt/GDP	62.3	72.5	78.3	81.5	85.8	88.6	90.5	91.7	92.4
Public gross financing req-mt/GDP	15.9	19	20.6	14.3	17.2	18.0	20.7	25.3	25.1
Primary balance/GDP	0	-2.1	-0.3	-0.9	-0.8	0	0.6	1.1	1.6
Real GDP growth	0.5	-3.8	-3.6	0.3	1.3	2.0	2.0	2.0	2.0
Increase in GDP deflator	7.9	8	8.3	7.4	4.7	4.7	5.0	5.0	5.0
Nominal GDP growth	8.4	3.8	4.4	7.8	6.1	6.8	7.1	7.1	7.1
Effective nominal interest rate	11	13.7	12.6	10.8	10.5	10.1	10.0	9.8	9.7
Debt stabilizing primary balance/GDP									2.2
Contributions to changes in public debt/GDP (in percentage points)									
Primary deficit/GDP	0	2.1	0.3	0.9	0.8	0	-0.6	-1.1	-1.6
Automatic debt dynamics	1.8	7.5	4.9	2.2	3.4	2.7	2.4	2.3	2.2
Interest rate/growth differential	1.4	5.9	5.7	2.2	3.4	2.7	2.4	2.3	2.2
of which real interest rate	1.7	3.6	3.2	2.4	4.5	4.2	4.1	4	4
of which real GDP growth	-0.3	2.3	2.5	-0.3	-1.0	-1.6	-1.6	-1.7	-1.7
Exchange rate depreciation	0.4	1.6	-0.7	...	...	...	...	...	...
Other (projection period includes change in ex. rate)	0.4	0.6	0.3	0.1	0.1	0.1	0.1	0.1	0.1
Total change in public debt/GDP	2.2	10.2	5.5	3.2	4.3	2.8	1.9	1.3	0.7

Box 5.7 (*continued*)

2018 under current policy plans. Thereafter, the primary position moves to surplus, though well below the debt-stabilizing surplus of 2.2 percent of GDP calculated for 2022 and beyond. The projected exchange rate depreciation adds only slightly to the debt ratio.

Third, another negative in the risk assessment is the public gross financing requirement PGFR/GDP – what Brazil must borrow to finance the primary deficit, interest, and rollover of maturing debt. The PGFR rises from an annual average of about 17.5 percent of GDP during 2014–2017 to well over 20 percent during 2020–2022. For market access countries (MACs), which comprise EMs plus advanced countries, the IMF has established a "high-risk threshold" for the gross financing requirement of 15 percent of GDP. Brazil's risk is somewhat mitigated by the fact that (1) almost a third of publicly held debt is held by the central bank, which has a continuous rollover policy, and (2) interest payments are an accrued measure, when Brazil has a significant share of zero-coupon bonds on which cash payments are zero until maturity so that actual borrowing needs in the near term are less than indicated in the PGFR.

Fourth, stress tests examining a variety of shocks to GDP, the planned improvement in the primary balance, and the real interest rate reveal that for shocks within plausible bounds both the debt/GDP and the PGFR/GDP could rise to as much as 117 percent and over 30 percent, respectively.

Fifth, some strengths in the structure of Brazil's existing debt (the debt profile) – the small shares of short-term debt, foreign currency debt, and nonresident holdings in total debt, and the large central bank holdings – are a mitigating factor in the risk assessment.

[1] IMF, Brazil – 2017 Article IV Consultation (July 2017), www.imf.org/~/media/files/publications/cr/2017/cr17215.ashx

But even if the debt ratio can be shown to stabilize at some point in the medium term based on central estimates for the input variables, other considerations may lead us to question the sustainability of the government finances:

- The level at which the debt ratio stabilizes is important. A stable ratio at 40 percent is less vulnerable to shocks than a ratio that stabilizes at

120 percent. There are no hard-and-fast ceilings but the IMF subjects countries with debt ratios above a threshold – 85 percent for advanced countries and 70 percent for emerging market countries – to the highest level of scrutiny for potential debt problems.

- The annual PGFR is relevant. This is a flow concept, measuring the total amount of fiscal financing a government is expected to need each year over the medium term. As described in section 1 b (iii), it includes financing for the overall balance, rollover of short-term debt, and amortization of medium- and long-term debt. Again there are no hard-and-fast ceilings but the IMF uses thresholds of 20 percent of GDP for advanced countries and 15 percent of GDP for emerging market economies to determine whether intense scrutiny for potential financing problems is warranted.

- Sensitivity to shocks is important. A baseline projection of the debt ratio may level off at an acceptable level; however, if that trajectory is very sensitive to unexpected but plausible shocks, a larger margin for safety should be built into the targeted debt ratio. The only way to establish sensitivity to shocks is to consider alternative sets of input variables to the calculation of the debt ratio trajectory and to determine whether some that are not remote tail scenarios produce excessive debt ratios or ratios that do not converge to a stable path.

The IMF has pioneered the analysis of fiscal sustainability and its sensitivity to shocks through its periodic DSAs of all member countries. It is useful to review its approach. A DSA uses the framework described above and central (or baseline) medium-term projections for the key macroeconomic input variables – real GDP growth, increases in the GDP deflator, the path of the nominal exchange rate, the average interest rate on government debt (which takes into account its maturity structure, currency composition, and whether it is fixed rate, floating rate, or indexed), a credible path for the primary balance, any nondebt financing (such as privatization proceeds), and the recognition of any of the government's contingent liabilities. The aim is to project a baseline path for the debt ratio in order to determine whether, and at what level, the debt ratio will stabilize. If this level is not excessive (see the first bullet above), the DSA shows the projected primary balance that will maintain this ratio indefinitely.[21]

---

[21] If the debt ratio is excessive, the DSA makes the imperative of fiscal retrenchment explicit by showing the change in the primary overall balance necessary to stabilize the debt ratio at a lower level. Note that the DSA is a secular rather than a cyclical analysis: the primary

The variables put into the projections may differ from historical patterns. For example, the authorities may have embarked on a changed policy path such as a new multiyear privatization program, a tax reform, or an infrastructure investment plan. If so, a DSA using projections based on historical patterns can be compared with the baseline to see what the effect of the policy changes on the debt path will be.

The most interesting aspect of the analysis, however, is the *sensitivity-to -shocks* part. This entails rerunning the spreadsheet with shocks to critical input variables to assess the effect of the shocks on fiscal sustainability over time. Four variants of the simulation are common: (a) real interest rates at two standard deviations above baseline (calculated on an historical measure of variability); (b) real growth two standard deviations below baseline; (c) the exchange rate depreciated by two standard deviations; and (d) a combination of all three of these shocks with each set at one standard deviation from the baseline. Additional or "tailored" shocks may be chosen: e.g., lower-than-projected privatization receipts or proceeds from some change in the tax structure. Once again, this analysis, while apparently mechanistic, entails judgment: in the choice of shocks, in the size of shocks, in the duration of shocks, in whether short-lived problems trigger contingent liabilities (such as debt guarantees to quasi-public entities) that exacerbate problems and lengthen their effective duration.

Sensitivity analysis of this kind has weaknesses. In particular, it does not include possible endogenous feedback from the private sector – e.g., changes in risk premia as debt ratios increase or investment disincentives from certain types of tax increases. Also, standard deviations derived from an historical period with low volatility may be too small to capture potential shocks. Nevertheless, if undertaken thoughtfully, sensitivity analysis can provide some sense of the robustness or vulnerability of the public finances to various contingencies.

3 Fiscal Rules: A Bulwark against Short-Term Political Pressures

Fiscal policy is formulated by elected officials subject to political pressures. Before an election it may be difficult for them to support a tax increase or a reduction in spending on a program dear to the hearts of voters. But such policy changes may be warranted by economic conditions or even urgently needed to put debt dynamics on a stable path. Fiscal rules seek to counteract the pressure of politics in fiscal decisions by enshrining in guidelines (in the extreme even with the force of law) limits on spending levels, deficits or

balance will change with cyclical influences but the focus is on the average position over the cycle.

public debt. If entrenched and accepted, fiscal rules both constrain elected officials and provide them with cover: unpopular policies can be attributed to the rules, not the insensitivity of officials to the wishes of their constituents.

Broadly, a fiscal rule involves some kind of instruction on spending and taxation when deficits or debt reach levels deemed inconsistent with macroeconomic stability (including leaving space for future countercyclical policy). Most countries do not have a fiscal rule or have one but frequently violate it. Violations usually occur in a cyclical downturn, when past policies have not left adequate space for stimulus. Those arguing that the rule is too rigid usually prevail in the policy debate. Still, fiscal rules have served some countries, such as Chile and Switzerland, reasonably well over more than a full economic cycle.[22]

Fiscal rules take many forms. One sensible rule requires "structural balance" – i.e., that the budget has to be balanced on average over the cycle. This means that automatic stabilizers and even discretionary stimulus can operate in downturns but must be offset in boom periods when output is above sustainable levels. Because stimulus is easier than retrenchment, such a rule inevitably leads to a great technical debate about where exactly the economy is in the cycle at any particular budget date. Politicians tend to overestimate potential GDP during high-growth years when everyone is hopeful that the boom is sustainable, and to overestimate economic slack in recessions. Practical difficulties with the structural balance rule are illustrated in Box 5.8.

Box 5.8 Practical Difficulties with the UK Fiscal Rules in 1996–2007

While estimating the structural balance may be conceptually straightforward, in practice the estimate is only as good as that of potential output, and, as recognized in Chapter 2, estimating potential GDP is hazardous. A stark example of the importance of quantifying potential output and the cyclical position of the economy is in the fiscal policy rule that the United Kingdom operated during 1996–2007. A key aspect of that rule was that the fiscal position was required to be in balance on average over the business cycle. In other words, the rule allowed the budget to be in deficit in years when actual output was below potential but there had to be offsetting surpluses in years when output was above potential.

---

[22] A country-by-country summary of fiscal rules can be found in www.imf.org/external/datamapper/fiscalrules/Fiscal%20Rules%20at%20a%20Glance%20-%20Background%20Paper.pdf

Box 5.8 (*continued*)

Putting this rule into practice required that there be a view not only on the cyclical position of the economy in the current budget year but also on the trajectory of potential output, which was the basis for calculating future revenues and therefore future deficits or surpluses. If potential was overstated, estimates of future revenues would be too high and current policy too expansionary to meet the rule over time. If potential was understated, the opposite would occur. Even relatively small errors in calculated potential relative to actual output over the business cycle would mean that the actual policy was either tighter or easier than was appropriate or intended. A reasonably high degree of confidence in estimates of potential output was critical to getting fiscal policy right.

The UK government's estimates of potential in the few years before the great recession were overly sanguine by a substantial margin (as is clear from subsequent revisions). This undermined their fiscal rule and, of course, their estimates of future deficits and debt ratios.

The UK authorities were not alone in making this mistake. Indeed, governments of almost all major economies made similar errors, as did other experts. As illustrated in Box 5.2, the errors in the IMF's WEO estimates of the prerecession potential GDP and structural fiscal balances were large, albeit not as large as those of the government.

Another sensible rule – the *golden rule* – is that the government should not borrow for current spending, or, equivalently, that government borrowing should not exceed government investment. This makes sense insofar as the benefits of investment will accrue over a long time and should be paid for over that time span. But squabbles inevitably arise about how exactly to define investment and, when tested, the rule can elicit creative accounting practices.

In some countries or currency unions the authorities have also set a government debt ceiling as a ratio to GDP. In the euro zone, for instance, along with a rule that deficits should be below 3 percent of GDP except in special circumstances, there is a rule that government debt should not exceed 60 percent of GDP; this rule (hardly enforced since its inception at the time the euro was created) has proved genuinely ill-suited to lengthy downturns.

As part of a fiscal rule, some governments appoint an apolitical, independent, and authoritative body to make or review budget projections and/or act as the guardian of the rule. Fiscal policy is too close to the heart of governance for politicians in a democracy to cede control to unelected appointees as is the case with monetary policy; however, even without executive power such a body can sway opinion. In the United States, where there is, at best, a weak fiscal rule, the Congressional Budget Office plays the role of an honest interpreter of fiscal conditions. Its success depends on the credibility of its reporting and on avoiding politicization.

4 Thought Experiments

Here we extend the thought experiments from earlier chapters to flesh out the diagnostics by adding the framework for fiscal analysis.

Suppose we see a disturbingly large (or growing) current account deficit in the economy we are assessing. We know (from Chapter 2) that this must reflect either high absorption or low output, which in turn reflects some combination of saving-investment imbalance in the private sector and the government:

$$CAD = ABS - GNDI = \left(I_p - S_p\right) + \left(I_g - S_g\right) \tag{5.24}$$

with the last parenthetical term equivalent to the government deficit.

If we find that the problem is not a drop in output (relative to potential) but a sharp increase in demand, and if it turns out that the government saving-investment imbalance is the culprit, it warrants further fiscal analysis. A jump in the government deficit is unlikely to be cyclical in circumstances of excessive aggregate demand (when the automatic stabilizers should be reducing the deficit), and an increase in the structural primary deficit does not make macroeconomic policy sense when demand is above potential output. So it would seem there is a case for fiscal retrenchment. Nevertheless it is worth digging deeper to examine the origins of the widening structural deficit, and whether it threatens the sustainability of the government debt dynamics. (When a widening external imbalance is due solely to fiscal policy, a coincidence between fiscal and balance-of-payments financing problems – the so-called twin deficit problem – is likely.)

If, alternatively, the widening of the current account deficit reflects a drop in output rather than a surge in demand, it is quite likely that automatic fiscal stabilizers, by cushioning demand, will be exacerbating the effect. Whether the increased current account deficit should be countered (by contractionary policies), or sustained, or even increased (through discretionary fiscal expansion to further mitigate the drop in income) will depend upon a number of judgments: Is the output drop temporary and, if so, what is its likely duration? Does the country have enough reserves (or borrowing capacity through its credibility in global financial markets) to cover the likely transitory external financing need? How would a currency depreciation influence debt dynamics? How quickly could the country's reputation for fiscal and financial prudence be eroded? How easy (in political economy terms) will it be to restore fiscal policy to its pre-shock parameters when output picks up? None of these judgments is easy but clarity on the specifics (even as to the identifiable unknowns) helps in reaching a policy consensus.

Another thought experiment, carried over from earlier in the book and reflected in much economic commentary in recent years, is as follows. Assume that government debt is high enough that sensitivity analyses show that a prolonged negative shock could threaten fiscal sustainability or highly prized expenditure programs. The economy is recovering slowly from a pure Keynesian (deficient demand) recession so that the economy is still operating well below potential. Given weak private final demand, private investment is anemic, and export demand also is too frail to pull the economy out of recession. Should the government allow the deficit to widen through the automatic stabilizers, putting on hold any fiscal correction needed over the longer run? Should it go further and put in place expansionary discretionary fiscal policies (i.e., increase the structural deficit) to speed up the recovery?[23]

These are difficult questions. Most of the simple analytics so far are based on identities and an understanding of the economic data. Without behavioral equations we have no real sense of the ability of the private sector to adjust to the vicissitudes of the economic environment. So thoughtful policy formulation calls for some estimates of behavioral equations, a good sense of the political scope for current fiscal stimulus and future retrenchment, and a clear notion of the limits to government financing (after which negative debt dynamics become threatening). Sometimes, however, the situation is clarified by the harshness of

---

[23] The generalization that automatic stabilizers should be allowed to operate in all cases but discretionary expansion should be eschewed is problematic. Insofar as the power of automatic stabilizers differs substantially between countries, the effect of automatic stabilizers on the deficit in one country may be larger than a combination of both stabilizers and fiscal action in another.

the environment – i.e., the simple debt sustainability analysis and the external financing environment may severely limit the scope for fiscal support.

5 Exercises

The country Balnibarbi has been under some pressure from its creditors to adopt a less expansionary fiscal stance. You are part of a team hired to visit the country to provide advice on the fiscal situation. Summary fiscal data are provided in Table 5.3 below.

1 The data for 2020 are government projections and one task is to assess their credibility:
   (a) Based on the tax buoyancy implicit in the projection for 2020, what question would you ask to assess the plausibility of the projections?
   (b) What numbers on the expenditure side of the budget for 2020 raise questions?
2 Another task is to assess the influence of the economic cycle on the fiscal position and whether fiscal policy is appropriately countercyclical:
   (a) Can you infer from the data where GDP is relative to potential GDP in 2018, 2019, and 2020? If so, explain your inferences.
   (b) Taking the data at face value, what is the fiscal stance and the fiscal impulse in 2019?
   (c) To what extent is the change in the overall balance projected for 2020 due to cyclical effects rather than discretionary fiscal policy actions?
3 Consider the sustainability of debt:
   (a) What primary balance ratio would stabilize the debt-to-GDP ratio in 2020 at the 2019 level? Explain how this is derived.
   (b) What would happen to (i) the overall balance, (ii) the primary balance, and (iii) the debt ratio if a jump in the risk premium in 2020 raised the effective interest rate on government debt from 7.1 percent to 8.5 percent (assuming, somewhat unrealistically, that this had no effect on nominal or real GDP)?

TABLE 5.3 *Balnibarbi: general government operations (2018–2020)*
(percent of GDP except where specified)

	2018	2019	2020
Revenue (Rev)	38.5	38.8	41.6
Taxes	32.5	31.9	34.8
Social contributions	4.1	4.3	4.2
Other revenue	1.9	2.6	2.6
Expenditure (Exp)	44.6	47.5	46.1
Expenses (C_g)	40.3	42.7	41.7
Compensation of employees	11.4	12.6	12.3
Use of goods and services	5.8	5.9	5.7
Interest	3.0	3.8	3.8
Subsidies	0.7	0.9	0.8
Social benefits	16.4	16.3	15.9
Other	3.0	3.2	3.2
Net acquisition of nonfinancial assets (I_g)	4.3	4.8	4.4
Net lending/overall balance (OB)	−6.1	−8.7	−4.5
Net financial transactions	−6.1	−8.7	−4.5
Memorandum items:			
Nominal GDP growth (in percent)	4.8	5.6	4.3
Real GDP growth (in percent)	2.4	2.7	2.7
Primary balance (PRIM)	−3.1	−4.9	−0.7
Structural fiscal balance	−6.0	−8.9	−4.5
Primary structural balance	−3.0	−5.1	−0.7
Government debt (dirham billions, end of period)	910.0	1077.3	1167.6
Nominal GDP (dirham billions)	1,821	1,923	2,006
Effective interest rate on government debt	6.0	8.0	7.1

CHAPTER 6

Financial Stability

This chapter covers the scope for and prevention of macroeconomic instability stemming from the financial sector. It focuses mainly on banks, which in most countries are the core of the financial sector. Five topics are addressed:

1 *The scope for procyclical leverage to amplify cycles, produce asset price bubbles, and lead to severe crises.*
2 *Bank balance sheet vulnerabilities – capital inadequacies, unstable sources of funding, and illiquidity.*
3 *Efforts to improve both micro- and macroprudential policies.*
4 *Common characteristics of financial crises in EMs and mitigating policy options.*
5 *Crises in advanced countries and financial sector oversight in a sophisticated financial center.*

A strong financial sector is a force for good. It intermediates funds from savers to borrowers, facilitating both investment and intertemporal consumption smoothing. Without this intermediation, economic activity would be severely constrained. Leverage, that portion of an undertaking financed by borrowing rather than owners' equity, makes it possible for a resource-constrained entrepreneur to undertake a profitable venture. Insofar as the returns on the investment exceed the cost of borrowing, leverage amplifies the rate of return on equity.

However, leverage also amplifies the losses that must be borne by equity holders in unsuccessful ventures. Where promising investments attract considerable credit financing but turn out to be ill-considered, enterprises incur large losses. Insofar as these lead to an inability to service and repay bank loans, the bank incurs a loss on its loan.

If a bank's losses (due, in this case, to nonperforming loans) can be absorbed by a reduction in the value of shareholder equity, the bank is not insolvent and other liabilities (like deposits) are cushioned from losses. However, because banks are generally also highly leveraged (i.e., their equity capital is small relative to their aggregate assets or liabilities), non-performing loans can lead to losses too large to be absorbed simply by a diminution in the valuation of equity capital. In this case a bank would, in the absence of government intervention, be unable to fully repay depositors and bond holders. In principle, it should be declared insolvent: its equity capital written down to zero, the proceeds from its good assets distributed to its creditors, and the residual losses borne by creditors depending (inversely) on the seniority of their claims.

In practice, even the idea that a big bank might be declared insolvent can cause the financial system to seize up: at the first hint of trouble, holders of maturing debt of the bank may refuse to roll it over; the interbank lending market may cease to operate smoothly with detrimental implications for all banks; and depositors may rush to withdraw deposits (a run on the bank). Also, clients and other financial institutions that have outstanding contracts with the bank to hedge risks on their own balance sheets (e.g., through credit default swaps to insure risky assets) may be vulnerable to contagion (the spread of a problem in one institution to others) if the risk of default on those contracts rises.

Such a panic can spread. Depositors might lose trust in the banking system more generally, credit would be sharply cut back even for worthy borrowers, banks could cease to be effective intermediaries between savers and investors, and the whole economy could suffer. Just as a breakdown of the power grid – a cessation of electrical power – has an effect on all sectors that can add up to be far larger than the losses in the electricity sector itself, a financial sector disruption can exert spillover effects across the economy that are disproportionate to the value-added in finance. It is not the size of the sector but the fact that banks' balance sheets link all other sectors that explains its importance.

Moreover, it is not unusual for distress in the financial sector to spread to government finances. First, in many countries the government guarantees bank deposits, usually up to some specified maximum amount (beyond which it is assumed that large depositors will have done their own due diligence on the soundness of the bank). Second, some financial institutions are "too important to fail" (TITF) because of their size or their interconnectedness with other institutions. In other words, conventional insolvency procedures would impose so severe a cost on the whole economy that the government is forced to bail out the institution. Although banks are generally privately owned, their operations contribute to the public benefit of financial stability. It is likely, therefore, that governments will step in to provide some sort of financial backstop for most sizable financial institutions (and certainly for TITF institutions) well before a hint of insolvency appears.

Most crises since the mid-1990s have been either the result of or have been amplified by vulnerabilities on banks' balance sheets. The crises may appear first in another part of the economy: for example, excessive government debt or a real-estate price bubble. But these crises have counterpart vulnerability in bank balance sheets. Indeed, the crises may well be fostered by imprudent lending: e.g., through new lending instruments with risks that are not adequately assessed or restrained by the regulatory system. Regardless of where the initial vulnerability resides, the repercussions of the unfolding crisis on banks' balance sheets generally exacerbate the crisis.

Given these considerations, the regulation and supervision of the financial sector, with the objective of promoting sound intermediation and forestalling crises, is an essential part of effective macroeconomic policy. It is also extremely difficult to do because of the complexity of the financial system and the pace of financial innovation. If profitable opportunities arise that seem sensible even though they do not quite fit into the current regulatory regime, bankers often create new instruments or institutions to accommodate them. This innovation may be benign and even beneficial; however when it entails excessive risk the authorities may not amend regulations in time to forestall problems. The objective is to establish a regulatory regime that is broad enough to capture changes in the financial sector, sufficiently permissive to facilitate benign innovation, while still rigorous enough to prevent excessive risk.

The regulation, monitoring, and supervision of the financial sector is an area fraught with difficulty, subject to intense debate, and, especially since 2008, evolving rapidly. We will focus on the broad issues that the experiences – in particular the actual financial crises– of the past 30 years indicate are critical to macroeconomic stability. We will not, however, seek to capture all of the intricacies of current debates.

1 Bank Regulation: An Intuitive Sketch of Prudential Considerations

Chapter 4 looked at banks' balance sheets in the aggregate but did not go into detail about banks' capital, noting simply that it was a liability component of the aggregate "Other items net," which was not particularly important for the purposes of that chapter. Now we look at capital more explicitly. Consider the simple and highly stylized balance sheet shown in Table 6.1.

TABLE 6.1 *Balance sheet of a bank*[a]

Assets	Liabilities
Net foreign assets	Deposits in broad money (DEP)
Claims on the central bank	Local currency demand deposits (DD)
Currency	Local currency time and savings
	deposits (TD)
Reserve deposits	Foreign currency deposits
Net claims on government	Loans from the central bank
Claims on private sector (including	Loans from other banks
banks)	
Domestic currency claims	Other loans and bonds
Foreign currency claims	Equity capital
Other assets	

[a] In this balance sheet, "Net foreign assets" are net claims on nonresidents. "Foreign currency claims" and "foreign currency deposits" are those on and by residents.

The balance sheet balances. Therefore the value of equity capital is equal to the value of all the assets minus the other liabilities – it is the net worth of the equity owners of the bank. If the founders of the bank put up $1 million in equity capital (their own money) and get deposits of $9 million, then the bank has $10 million to invest in assets. This means it initially has a capital–asset ratio of 10 percent. It might then place $500,000 on deposit with the central bank and invest the other $9.5million in interest-bearing assets. At the end of each year, if the bank makes a profit (from interest earned on its assets), it may distribute some of this profit to its shareholders and leave some in the bank for reinvestment; to the extent that profits are not distributed, the value of equity capital rises. If, however, at the end of the year the bank makes a loss – perhaps assets have to be written down because borrowers do not pay interest and/or default on loan principals – the value of equity capital declines. So far, so simple.

Now, in light of this stylized balance sheet, consider three main things that could go wrong:

- Capital may be insufficient to cover losses. In that case, the bank would be insolvent, and some of the losses would result in a writing down of other liabilities – loans, bonds, and even deposits. We call this an "insolvency" (or "capital inadequacy") problem.

- Loans and bonds from investors and other banks (liabilities that the bank is using to finance its lending) may fall. If investors develop fears about the bank's solvency, they may refuse to roll over loans to the bank when they come due. Moreover, any diminution of confidence in the bank would probably mean that all "wholesale" sources of funding would dry up at the same time. We call this a "stable funding" problem.

- In the face of a drop in market confidence about the quality of a bank's assets, a sudden surge in withdrawals (a "run" on the bank) can occur. This risk is important because banks engage in maturity transformation – i.e., their liabilities are of shorter-term average maturity than their assets. To the extent that longer-maturity assets are illiquid, a bank may not have the cash to meet a surge in withdrawals.[1] We call this a "liquidity" problem.

Bank regulation should seek to reduce the probability of these three sorts of shocks occurring and to dampen their effect if they do occur. Therefore, there are three classes of regulations.

- Regulations that try to ensure that banks have sufficient capital relative to their assets to cover potential losses and reduce the likelihood of insolvency. But how much capital is sufficient? Obviously if a bank's assets consist only of cash and the treasury bills of a sound government, the safe ratio of capital to assets would be lower than if its assets comprise mainly high-risk loans. So the question of how much capital is appropriate implicitly requires some assessment of the riskiness of the bank's total assets, an exercise that is far from straightforward.

- Regulations that guard against a sudden drying up of funding sources. Insofar as conventional deposits from bank customers are more stable than short-term wholesale borrowing, a regulation might consider the extent to which the bank relies on these stable funding sources as opposed to wholesale borrowing.

- Regulations that seek to ensure that a bank has sufficient liquid assets in its overall portfolio of assets to cover outflows for a specified period (in the event of some shock to confidence). A bank's relationship

---

[1] Maturity transformation is the business of banks. For some long-maturity assets there are highly liquid markets so they can be swapped for cash quickly and easily. For others there are no liquid markets. The liquidity mismatch vulnerability is due to this latter category of assets.

with the central bank helps to cushion any sudden shock to liquidity. Central banks perform a lender-of-last-resort function: if a bank faces a run on deposits, the central bank lends it enough money to cover withdrawals until it can liquidate sufficient assets. This function is meant to guard against illiquidity by bridging a period until assets can be liquidated. But bank supervisors and central bankers would prefer to see such appeals to the lender-of-last-resort function of central banks as rare occurrences and to put in place regulations that ensure this. (It is often difficult, in the heat of a crisis, to determine whether a bank is facing a liquidity crisis or a solvency crisis; central bank liquidity provision is not a solution to a problem of insolvency.)[2]

2 Bank Regulation: Terms, Definitions, and Difficulties

a Regulating Bank Capital, Funding, and Liquidity

The intuitions of the last section are a guide to understanding the fundamentals of prudential bank regulation. But any discussion of regulation, even in the press, is littered with esoteric terminology and detail. Until 2013 "capital" was not simply owners' equity; it came in many forms, and what should be included in capital differed depending on regulatory purposes and across countries. Banks' assets are often weighted by risk for regulatory purposes, and the weighting schemes were subject to debate. While we focus on the "banking book" of financial institutions, there is also a "trading book" for a different set of financial transactions, and this is regulated somewhat differently (the distinction between banking and trading books is defined at the end of this section). This section tries to cut through the thicket of terminology and explain some of the concepts.

A bank's capital is the first part of its liabilities to be at risk in circumstances of a drop in the value of its assets; as such, it is the protective buffer for other liabilities like deposits. Capital provides

---

[2]   Some countries require banks to hold liquid deposits ("required reserves") with the central bank in some proportion to their deposit base. Whether required by regulation or not, all banks hold some such reserves. But required reserve regulations are motivated more by monetary policy considerations than prudential ones. Historically, some countries have also required banks to hold a minimum ratio of specified liquid assets (usually government bills) to deposits. Such liquid asset ratios were sometimes justified on prudential grounds although they may have been motivated by monetary policy or government financing considerations.

protection against unexpected losses. Expected losses should be covered by provisioning – i.e., a preemptive setting aside of capital to cover an expected loss.

The Basel Committee on Banking Supervision (BCBS) has led the international process of establishing a framework for bank regulation. This has gone through three phases – Basel I, Basel II, and Basel III – since the late 1980s.[3] The 2008 global banking crisis greatly influenced Basel III. The plan was to phase in the changes gradually through 2018. (Box 6.1 provides a primer on the Bank for International Settlements (BIS) and the BCBS.)

Box 6.1 Why does Basel, Switzerland Feature so Prominently in Discussions Related to Financial Stability?

First, Basel is the location of the headquarters of the Bank for International Settlements (BIS). The BIS, established in 1930, is an international financial organization owned by 60 member central banks, representing countries from around the world that together make up about 95 percent of world GDP. The mission of the BIS is to serve central banks in their pursuit of monetary and financial stability, to foster international cooperation in these areas, and to act as a bank for central banks. The BIS disseminates statistics on international banking and financial activities that are critical to policymaking, research, and public discussion; and it is an important center of research, analysis, and commentary on issues of relevance for monetary and financial stability. The BIS acts as a prime counterparty for central banks in their financial transactions, and it serves as an agent or trustee in connection with official international financial operations.

Second, while the Basel Committee on Banking Supervision (BCBS) is an independent entity from the BIS, its secretariat is

(*continued*)

---

[3] Basel III is the agreed regulatory standard for large internationally active banks but the basic coverage of banks and other depository institutions differs between countries. For example, in the European Union, all banks and investment firms are covered. In the United States, institutions other than small bank holding companies (defined as those having less than $1 billion in consolidated assets and not doing significant nonbanking business) are covered (as well as intermediate holding companies of foreign banking organizations with more than $50 billion in nonbranch assets).

Box 6.1 *(continued)*

also located in Basel at BIS headquarters. The BCBS was established by a group of central bank governors of major advanced countries in 1974. Its membership is now much wider. It is the primary global standard setter for the prudential regulation of banks, and it provides a forum for cooperation on banking supervisory matters. Its mandate is to strengthen the regulation, supervision, and practices of banks worldwide with the purpose of enhancing financial stability. The BCBS does not possess any formal supranational authority. Its decisions do not have legal force; rather, it relies on its members' commitments to achieve its mandate. BCBS members include organizations with direct banking supervisory authority and central banks.

Sources: www.bis.org and www.bis.org/bcbs/charter.htm

Since 2013, under Basel III, the definition of "capital" has been tightened substantially, and most of the jurisdictional differences (i.e., difference across countries) have been eliminated. Capital comprises Tier 1 capital and Tier 2 capital. Tier 1 capital consists of *Common Equity Tier 1* (CET1) capital – chiefly common shares and retained earnings – and Additional Tier 1 (AT1) capital.[4] The larger is CET1, the stronger the buffer against losses. But AT1 capital also cushions depositors and creditors (other than those included in AT1) against losses. Tier 2 capital (all components of which have maturities of five years or longer and for which dividend or coupon payments are not sensitive to a deterioration in credit ratings) provides an additional cushion.

Regulators impose a *capital requirement* on banks and some other financial institutions. This is a minimum amount of capital that an institution must hold. It is calculated as a percentage of risk-weighted assets – i.e., each type of asset is assigned a weight reflective of its riskiness (as measured by the bank's own model or standard supervisory models), and the denominator of the ratio is that weighted aggregate.[5]

---

[4] The essence of this additional Tier 1 capital is that it is subordinate to depositors, general creditors, and regular subordinate debt; that it is perpetual (i.e., has no maturity date); and that dividend or coupon payments are entirely at the discretion of the bank.

[5] The generic term *capital adequacy ratios* covers both those based on risk-weighted assets and those for which assets are not weighted by risk (see below).

Some safe assets, like cash or the highest rated treasury bills, may be given a zero weight and thus excluded from the aggregate.[6]

Capital requirements under Basel III are as follows:

- A minimum *CET1 ratio* to risk-weighted assets of 4.5 percent.
- An additional *capital conservation buffer* phased in through January 1, 2019 to total 2.5 percent of risk-weighted assets.
- A *surcharge on global systemically important banks (GSIBs)* phased in through January 1, 2019 to total between 1 percent and 2.5 percent of risk-weighted assets (depending largely on the size of the bank).
- A *countercyclical buffer* of CET1 between zero and 2.5 percent of risk-weighted assets; the maximum phased in through January 1, 2019. Imposition of this buffer – a macroprudential instrument (see below) – will be at the discretion of national regulators.
- A minimum *Tier 1 capital ratio* of 6 percent of risk-weighted assets.
- A minimum *total capital (Tier 1 and Tier 2) ratio* of 8 percent.

Note, first, that target ratios are higher than the minimum ratios, and, second, that national regulators may impose more exacting requirements or phase in requirements ahead of schedule.

Under Basel III there is also a *leverage ratio* requirement (Tier 1 capital equal to or greater than 3 percent of total exposure). This ratio does not weight the exposures of the financial institution and thus seeks to counter problems of undercapitalization that may be due to the weighting rules. Also, it covers not only assets on the banking book but also derivatives and other off-balance-sheet items. A leverage ratio surcharge for GSIBs (along the lines of the risk-weighted requirement described above) remains under discussion.

Two other standards have been agreed upon to improve liquidity risk management. The *net stable funding ratio* aims to ensure that banks rely more on capital and relatively stable retail deposits than on short-term wholesale funding, which can be easily available when market liquidity is buoyant but can disappear in periods of illiquidity.[7] The *liquidity coverage*

---

[6] The Basel framework calls for minimum regulatory requirements commensurate with the underlying risks, as indicated by the issuer's *probability of default* and *loss given assumed default*. In principle, therefore, loans to governments and their central banks are assigned positive risk weights for all but the highest-quality issuers. National authorities, however, have the option – but not the obligation – to allow lower risk weights for sovereign exposures denominated and funded in domestic currency; these often receive a zero risk weight.

[7] The net stable funding ratio is the ratio of "available stable funding" to "required stable funding" and the minimum is targeted at 100 percent. Available stable funding measures a bank's sources of funding, weighted by their stability characteristics. Required stable

ratio seeks to ensure that banks have sufficient cash and other liquid assets (i.e., assets that can be quickly liquidated without loss) to cover a month of potential outflows in a stressed situation.[8]

Tables 6.2 and 6.3 summarize these various prudential measures.

Banks typically divide their activities into two groups – banking and trading – and they notionally book them differently because they are subject to different regulatory and accounting rules. The *banking book* covers traditional bank activities and thus financial instruments not actively traded and usually intended to be held to maturity – e.g., loans to corporate customers. The *trading book* covers financial instruments held for trading purposes, to help customers trade, and/or to profit from bid-ask spreads in prices – e.g., mortgage-backed securities that are bought from and sold to clients. Assets in the trading book are not intended to remain on the books until maturity or are off balance sheet to start with (e.g., in the case of derivatives). Trading book assets are marked to market – i.e., valued at current market price in any accounting period. Banking book assets are generally held at acquisition value, written down to account for expected losses.

While both books are subject to capital and liquidity regulation (e.g., leverage regulation is concerned with overall exposure), for the trading book model-based metrics such as value at risk (VAR) are particularly important inputs into banks' risk assessments and corresponding capital requirements.[9]

---

funding is a measure of a bank's assets and off-balance-sheet exposures weighted by liquidity characteristics and residual maturities.

[8] On September 3, 2014, the US Federal Reserve voted to impose a *liquidity requirement* (to be phased in by the end of 2016) on large US banks. It required 15 banks with more than $250 billion in assets to hold enough cash, government paper, and other high-quality liquid assets to meet liquidity needs for 30 days of outflows in stressed circumstances. The number of days is reduced to 21 for banks with between $50 billion and $250 billion in assets, and the requirement is not applicable to smaller banks. In practice, the change probably represented an easing of the liquidity requirement for all but the largest 15 banks and, moreover, the definition of liquid assets was broadened somewhat. The change did not entail a significant portfolio adjustment for the banks, but the regulation may prevent a move to a less liquid portfolio if credit demand strengthens with economic activity.

[9] VAR models assess the probability that the value of a portfolio will fall by more than a specified threshold amount in a given time frame. They thus have three important components: threshold loss value, probability, and time frame. A two-week 1 percent VAR of $10 million means that there is one chance in a hundred that the value of the portfolio will fall by $10 million or more in any two-week period. Obviously the probability distributions are culled from some historical experience. For the VAR to be useful the volatility (or variance) in this historical experience must be representative of current and near-future conditions.

TABLE 6.2 *Basel phase-in arrangements*
(all dates as of January 1 in the year shown)

Leverage ratio	2016	2017	2018	As of 2019
	Parallel run until 1 Jan 2017 Disclosure started 1 Jan 2015		Migration to Pillar 1	
Minimum CET1 ratio	4.5%	4.5%	4.5%	4.5%
Capital conservation buffer	0.625%	1.25%	1.875%	2.50%
G-SIB surcharge		Phase-in		1.0%–2.5%
Minimum common equity plus capital conservation buffer	5.125%	5.75%	6.375%	7.0%
Phase-in of deductions from CET1 (including amounts exceeding the limit for DTAs, MSRs and financials)	60%	80%	100%	100%
Minimum Tier 1 capital	6.0%	6.0%	6.0%	6.0%
Minimum total capital	8.0%	8.0%	8.0%	8.0%
Minimum total capital plus capital conservation buffer	8.625%	9.25%	9.875%	10.5%
Capital instruments that no longer qualify as Tier 1 capital or Tier 2 capital	Phased out over 10-year horizon beginning 2013			
Liquidity coverage ratio	70%	80%	90%	100%
Net stable funding ratio			Introduce minimum standard	

Source: Basel III Monitoring Report (September 2017), Basel Committee on Banking Supervision, Bank for International Settlements (on BIS website www.bis.org/bcbs/qis)

TABLE 6.3 *Minimum and target risk-based capital and leverage ratio requirements* (fully phased-in Basel III in percent)

	Fully implemented risk-based requirement			Fully-implemented leverage ratio requirement
	Minimum	Target non-G-SIBs	Target G-SIBs	Minimum and target
CET1 capital	4.5	7.0	8.0–9.5	
Tier 1 capital	6.0	8.5	9.5–11.0	3.0
Total capital	8.0	10.5	11.5–13.0	

Source: Basel III Monitoring Report (September 2017), Basel Committee on Banking Supervision, Bank for International Settlements (on BIS website www.bis.org/bcbs/qis)

Two problems involving banks' trading books contributed to the 2008 financial crisis. First, VAR models proved excessively sanguine about risks to banks' trading books. Based on a recent period of history in which volatility had been low, the models understated the value at risk and provided a false sense of confidence. Second, banks engaged in regulatory arbitrage by switching assets from banking to trading book (or off balance sheet entirely) and thus increasing leverage to dangerous levels. These problems have been significantly redressed: arbitrage between banking and trading book is now more constrained by regulation; trading book capital requirements are more stringent; evolving rules will limit (or ring-fence) proprietary trading – that is, trading by banks for their own account as against that for clients – to reduce the exposure of depositors to this risk; and estimates of volatility in VAR models are generally now more conservative.[10]

The appropriate levels of the various *capital adequacy ratios* have been hotly contested. Those favoring higher ratios than the targets under Basel III see them as necessary to safeguarding deposits, the viability of deposit insurance schemes, and the public finances. But others argue that higher ratios would reduce banks' effectiveness in intermediating savings, especially to small and medium-size enterprises, and would thus be detrimental to actual and potential growth. In circumstances where banks are constrained by capital rather than funding, the effectiveness of a countercyclical easing of monetary policy in getting banks to lend more

---

[10]   The so-called Volker rule in the United States, a proposal by the European Union, and the Vickers Report in the United Kingdom all focus on limiting exposure to proprietary trading.

is diminished. But the arguments behind the general claims of those opposed to more stringent capital requirements are less plausible.

b Macroprudential Regulation

So far our discussion of prudential regulation has been largely at the level of the individual financial institution. But for some time economists (especially those at the BIS) have advocated a regulatory regime that goes beyond the individual institution to focus on the financial system as a whole – i.e., *macroprudential regulation*.[11]

There are two aspects to macroprudential regulation: (i) how to constrain the evolution of systemwide risk over time (the "time dimension"), and (ii) how to assess and constrain the level and distribution of systemwide risk at a point in time (the "cross-sectional dimension"). Both seek to deal with developments that might seem exogenous from the point of view of an individual institution but are endogenous to the system as a whole.

The time dimension is largely concerned with cyclical risks. During economic upswings it is common to see higher asset prices (that seemingly improve collateral values), increased risk tolerance by institutions, greater market liquidity, and thus rapid credit expansion.[12] During economic contractions these tendencies reverse. Leverage, therefore, tends to be procyclical, and financial markets can increase the amplitude of cycles and systemwide vulnerability with potentially devastating results. In each phase the actions of individual financial institutions seem sensible from the point of view of these institutions; however, the procyclicality of credit is destabilizing from a systemwide perspective. Insofar as macroprudential regulation focuses on the time dimension – the evolution of the financial system – it will seek to dampen this tendency toward procyclical leverage by adjusting prudential ratios. The *countercyclical buffer* (discussed above) is an example: supervisory authorities may increase capital requirements when system incentives show a tendency to excessive credit creation.[13]

---

[11] See Borio, Claudio, The Macroprudential Approach to Regulation and Supervision, VOX CEPR's Policy Portal http://voxeu.org/article/we-are-all-macroprudentialists-now (April 2009) for a succinct history and exposition.

[12] For example, think of housing prices and the collateral for mortgage lending. But housing finance is only one example of the incentives for procyclical credit expansion.

[13] In September 2016, the US Federal Reserve Board of Governors released a framework for a countercyclical capital buffer. It envisages a 250 basis point increase in the Tier 1 common equity requirement (for banks with at least $250 billion in assets) if a financial bubble is determined to be forming.

The cross-section dimension is concerned primarily with the interconnectedness, correlation across institutions, and concentration of risks. At any point in time there may be critical systemwide vulnerabilities that are difficult for individual institutions to appreciate. Common (or correlated) exposures across institutions are one example. In 2008, for example, many US financial institutions had significant holdings of mortgage-backed securities, which seemed a reasonably safe bet from the perspective of an individual institution. But when the risk premia on these assets jumped, all the holders sought to sell at the same time – analogous to a fire in a theater that sends a horde of people rushing for the single narrow exit.[14] The distribution of risk across institutions is another example: very large and interconnected financial institutions – those that are in the so-called TITF class – contribute disproportionately to system risk and should, therefore, be subject to especially rigorous regulation.

TITF banks present particular challenges. Some systemically important banks are too big or too interconnected to fail without threatening major economic disruption; they are therefore virtually assured of government support in a crisis. As such, they benefit from the perception of being less risky and from consequently lower funding costs. But, given this advantage and the potential costs of failure to the taxpayer and the economy, it is argued that significantly higher capital buffers are appropriate for these institutions. Most of these institutions are global and (as noted earlier and in Tables 6.2 and 6.3) the Basel III package comes with a macroprudential overlay that includes – among other things – an internationally agreed framework for global systemically important banks that entails capital surcharges.

c Other Issues

A few additional issues related to prudential management are worth mentioning.

First, international agreement on minimum standards is essential to ensuring a more-or-less level playing field between jurisdictions and limiting regulatory arbitrage – i.e., banks moving operations to the jurisdiction

---

[14] The situation was exacerbated by additional factors: the dubious intrinsic value of some of the underlying loans in these structured instruments, the fact that many were held off balance sheets with little capital backing, the effective liquidity mismatch insofar as assets with a seven-year average tenor were financed with short-term commercial paper, and the fact that many were held in the trading book where they had to be marked to market in circumstances where the market had collapsed.

with the least regulation – which could undermine the objectives of regulators in the more conservative countries.

Second, we have focused on banks but in many countries the nonbank financial sector is large and important. Progress has been made in advanced countries in extending the supervisory net to these institutions. In the United Kingdom, for example, while supervisory scrutiny and stress testing of insurers, central counterparties, and asset managers is not as comprehensive as that of banks, they nevertheless provide some assurances of resilience. But especially in some EMs, unregulated segments of financial markets are still significant and potentially problematic.

Third, related to prudential supervision of large financial institutions is the question of how, in the event of severe distress and insolvency, these institutions will be resolved without undue social or fiscal costs. Such resolution is required when conventional insolvency proceedings for a failing bank would destabilize the financial sector and harm the economy more generally. A resolution of this kind inevitably entails using the capital cushions required by prudential regulation and "bailing in" (i.e., writing down the value of) liabilities other than deposits before seeking public assistance. Resolution may seek to sustain some critical functions and the viable parts of the bank. In the United States, the Dodd–Frank law (of 2010) requires large banks and designated nonbank financial companies to periodically submit resolution plans ("living wills") that describe how orderly resolution would be achieved in extreme circumstances. In the European Union, a *bank recovery and resolution directive*, adopted in 2014, spells out the rules for bank resolutions. Other countries have also made progress in this area but this progress is far from uniform.

Fourth, "stress testing" has been alluded to – e.g., the liquidity coverage ratio envisages liquid assets being able to cover 30 days of outflows in a stressed situation – but not discussed. It will be discussed briefly in section 4.

Finally, implicit in the discussion thus far has been the question (also raised in Chapter 4) about the evolving relationship between monetary policy and macroprudential regulation. Prior to the 2008 crisis, most central bankers were wedded to the idea of monetary policy targeting an index of inflation, and paying attention to broader financial conditions – rapid credit expansion, asset price inflation, and potential bubbles – only to the extent that they were likely to affect inflation. Even after the crisis, many prefer to assign macroprudential policies to the task of containing credit surges and related developments, chiefly by tightening regulatory requirements on capital and lending to contain leverage and forestall the development of asset price bubbles.[15] Increasingly, however, some economists and central bankers are questioning whether macroprudential policies suffice in these circumstances, and whether monetary policy should, at a minimum, stand ready to support macroprudential policies when necessary.

We now turn to a discussion of how financial (or balance sheet) crises have unfolded in recent years and how efforts to anticipate them have been adapted.[16] We will address EM crises first and then advanced country crises.

3 The Anatomy of an EM Balance Sheet Crisis

EM crises have unfolded in many different ways but most have a few broad characteristics in common:

- Rapid growth that reduces the per capita GDP gap with advanced countries (e.g., because of structural reforms of the sorts discussed in Chapter 2 that raise productivity).
- Financial innovation (as in advanced economies but generally at a lower level of sophistication) that often involves opening the domestic financial system to foreign institutions and investors.
- Weak governance, often in the form of fledgling prudential regulation and supervision, implicit government guarantees for private or publicly owned businesses, and/or large government deficits.
- Limited exchange rate flexibility.

Here we trace an illustrative crisis involving an element of each of these factors, remembering that the specifics of actual vulnerability buildups and crises vary widely. Some overlap with the analyses of vulnerabilities in Chapters 4 and 5 is unavoidable: the underlying influences in those types of crises often bring the financial system into a central role in how the crisis unfolds. We then consider why assessing balance sheet vulnerabilities is so

---

[15] Besides adjustments in capital adequacy ratios, such tightening may include other measures. In the case of a surge in mortgage lending, for example, stricter loan-to-value and/or loan-to-income ratios may be useful additional macroprudential instruments.

[16] There is a tendency for commentators to use the terms "balance sheet crisis" and "financial crisis" synonymously, but they may not be identical. A financial crisis is also a balance sheet crisis when the stock of debt in the balance sheet at a point in time and in particular circumstances is unsustainable – it cannot be serviced and repaid. But another type of financial crisis may occur even without a debt-stock problem if, for example, a country simply cannot borrow enough to finance its budget or balance-of-payments deficit, and this flow problem elicits a sharp and painful change in circumstances.

difficult and conclude the section with a comment on the changing land-scape of financial sector policies.[17]

a An Example of an EM Crisis

Consider an EM country that has recently implemented wide-ranging structural reforms to raise the pace of income catchup to advanced-country levels. Wishing to tap foreign savings to help finance its catchup potential, the country, which has historically been mostly closed to foreign capital, gradually allows financial inflows (a form of financial innovation). The country has a long-standing policy (a hangover from the time when most small countries pegged their exchange rates and imposed strict con-trols on EFA flows) of limiting movements in the exchange rate.

Various favorable developments occur in the few years after these reforms: exports grow strongly, motivating higher investment; productivity and profits rise (especially in the manufacturing sector); wages increase; and prospects for continued income growth are perceived as excellent. These developments give rise to the Balassa–Samuelson process described in Chapter 3. Prices of nontraded goods and assets (mainly real estate) rise, while, with the stable exchange rate, traded goods price inflation remains low. Initially this is not seen as problematic: as income rises, higher prices of nontraded goods (and real assets like housing) call forth higher supply and are equilibrating in a rapidly growing economy. But as residents see a housing price boom they climb aboard the bandwagon: they borrow to finance purchases of bigger homes, second homes, or rental properties.

Their borrowing to finance these purchases puts upward pressure on interest rates on domestic currency loans. To meet the surge in private credit demand, domestic banks turn to foreign banks for funding. They find that they can cover their foreign exchange exposure by on-lending these funds in foreign currency. Domestic borrowers, encouraged by the history of limited exchange rate movements (seen as an implicit exchange rate guaranty), are happy to accept lower-interest foreign currency loans.

What is happening is a real-estate bubble: price increases initiated at home by the rapid income catchup, and then reinforced by buoyant expectations and easy access to global financial markets. The analysis in Chapters 2–4 point to the developments that may accompany this process: a real currency

---

[17] As is evident from recent history, a financial crisis in a country – like the United States or United Kingdom – that is a financial center for the global economy has global ramifica-tions. A crisis in an EM country may be more contained. But because of various linkages even these crises have had serious contagion effects on other countries.

appreciation (brought about by rising inflation insofar as the nominal exchange rate is broadly fixed), and a widening current account deficit (despite lingering export growth) financed by the financial inflows and reflecting the import content of surging investment and private consumption. Fiscal excesses, due, perhaps, to the cyclical rise in tax revenue fueling excessive optimism about future tax receipts, and/or to the lure of low-interest-rate foreign borrowing opportunities, may add to the general euphoria.

The central bank may be untroubled by any exchange rate pressures as long as external financing is readily available. An understanding of rising vulnerabilities would have to be diagnosed from developments covered in other chapters – an analysis of the real exchange rate, rising inflation, credit expansion, the cyclically-adjusted fiscal position, the current account deficit, and the buildup of external debt. But at least as important as all of these considerations are the leverage ratios, liquidity, and funding circumstances of banks, and the foreign exchange exposure of the private sector – the so-called balance sheet vulnerabilities.

What might trigger a crisis? In these circumstances, any one or combination of several events: a drop in real-estate prices, a rise in country-specific or global risk premia, higher global interest rates, and/or a large adverse change in the terms of trade. Such events can result in a complete halt (or reversal) in foreign inflows (often called a "sudden stop") necessitating abrupt corrective action to cut domestic demand and to shore up banks with severe losses.

The specifics of an actual crises (illustrated in the next section) may differ. But most have a few similar characteristics: a sudden stop in foreign financing or, at a minimum, a sharp increase in interest rates in external markets and/or a large depreciation of the domestic currency. These ructions may make government debt unsustainable. Or they may bankrupt highly indebted private enterprises that are sensitive to interest rates and/or exchange rates leading to a spike in banks' nonperforming loans (NPLs) such that some banks become insolvent (with contagion effects) or require government support to stay in business (with detrimental effects for government finances). At this point, most countries turn to the IMF for financing in support of a comprehensive program to address the crisis conditions and mitigate the underlying vulnerabilities that produced the crisis. IMF support helps cushion the drop in external financing, thereby alleviating the need for draconian measures to curb public and private spending, and provides assurance to external markets that policies to adjust are in place. Nevertheless, the adjustment policies are painful.

b Why is Assessing Balance Sheet Vulnerabilities So Difficult?

The evolving vulnerabilities described above seem clear. Why then is there so much debate about how to judge the seriousness of balance sheet vulnerabilities of a country experiencing very large inflows? First, the kinds of developments described are rather common in rapidly catching-up EMs, and most do not experience crises: two sets of circumstances with essentially the same structure of vulnerabilities will not necessarily end in the same outcome. Tipping points (or crisis trigger events) are unpredictable, and the challenge for policy is to make the financial system robust to these unpredictable events. Second, investors and governments are loath to dampen the euphoria or to bridle the much-vaunted process of catching up to income levels in advanced countries. Third, in an economy where growth is rapid for good reasons (in our example recent structural reforms and rising productivity) the balance sheet changes that we have described may be financing sustainable growth. Let's look at how the balance sheet developments described above may be difficult to diagnose.

Suppose you are asked to assess the risks in the country described above. Suppose that that you do not have good information on the housing market or the housing story is one part of a more complex rapid catchup situation. Let's say you are simply given data on the foreign-exchange-denominated assets and liabilities of the government (including the central bank), the banking system, and the nonbank private sector.[18] The data may look like those in Table 6.4 (copied from an article in *Finance and Development* for a mythical country called Xanadu).[19]

The top block of data shows the central bank, the second block banks, and the third block the private nonfinancial part of the economy. The bottom block shows aggregates.

The central bank's reserves amount to $40 billion. This covers 80 percent of total short-term FX liabilities of all sectors – not the 100 percent or more we would like in an ideal world but not obviously dire.

Banks have a balanced FX book with two possible vulnerabilities. First, maturity transformation: short-term liabilities funding longer-term assets. But maturity transformation is the normal business of banks, and we don't know anything definitive about the liquidity of these assets. Second, most of the longer-term FX-denominated assets on the books are, in fact, loans to

---

[18] Such data are not always readily available or easy to construct but reasonable proxies can usually be found.

[19] Lipschitz, Leslie, Wising Up about Finance, *Finance and Development* (March 2007), 24–27.

TABLE 6.4 *Xanadu's balance sheet*
(foreign-exchange-denominated assets and liabilities, in billions of US dollars)

	Assets	Liabilities	Net assets
Central bank (vis-à-vis nonresidents)	40	10	30
short-term	40	2	38
medium- and long-term	0	8	−8
Commercial banks	37	37	0
short-term (vis-à-vis nonresidents)	3	28	−25
medium- and long-term (vis-à-vis nonresidents)	4	9	−5
medium- and long-term (vis-à-vis residents)	30	0	30
Nonbanks	1	75	−74
short-term (vis-à-vis nonresidents)	1	20	−19
medium- and long-term (vis-à-vis nonresidents)	0	25	−25
medium- and long-term (vis-à-vis domestic banks)	0	30	−30
Total	**78**	**122**	**−44**
short-term (vis-à-vis nonresidents)	44	50	−6
medium- and long-term (vis-à-vis nonresidents)	4	42	−38
medium- and long-term (vis-à-vis residents)	30	30	0

Note: In this example the government has no foreign-exchange-denominated assets or liabilities

domestic borrowers. We need to know more about their liquidity and riskiness.

The nonfinancial part of the economy has a substantial ($74 billion) FX exposure. How serious is the risk in this exposure?

The financial data alone could be consistent with a benign situation. If nonbank FX exposure were mostly on the part of exporters with large FX earnings relative to exposure, the exposure is naturally hedged. A shock – say an increase in the risk premium on FX borrowing – is unlikely to have dire effects; given their FX revenues, exporters would probably be able to roll over exposures at slightly higher interest rates. More extreme circumstances could induce the central bank to allow the currency to depreciate. Such a depreciation would result in a capital losses for the FX borrowers but it would be unlikely to bankrupt the naturally hedged exporters. If banks experienced difficulties in rolling over short-term FX liabilities, the central bank would be able to provide liquidity to cover the outflow by drawing down reserves. If necessary, this could be supplemented with government borrowing or IMF purchases. In short, banks might have a liquidity but not solvency, problem.

On the other hand, the situation might be malign. What if nonbank FX exposures were concentrated in naïve mortgage borrowers or a construction industry that failed to understand the risk of low-rate, long-term, FX-denominated mortgages or simply took a gamble on the fixed exchange rate. Any shock to which the authorities responded by breaking with the fixed exchange rate would produce a capital loss or, if FX exposures were large, a solvency problem for such borrowers. Banks would then face circumstances much more dire than temporary illiquidity: their FX-denominated loans to domestic borrowers – $30 billion of total FX assets of $37 billion – would be at risk of default, and their overall solvency questionable.

This is usually such a frightening scenario for the authorities that it induces *fear of floating*. As is clear from the configuration of foreign exposures, the authorities see that letting the exchange rate depreciate could produce a crisis or worsen a crisis that is in its early stages. Gambling for redemption, by avoiding a depreciation, accepting a significant loss of reserves while defending the exchange rate, and hoping for some fortuitous turn of events is obviously an attractive option. Yet in many cases, at the point where the balance sheet exposures have become severe, a crisis is inevitable whether or not the government tries to delay the depreciation as long as possible.[20] And delay has significant costs in terms of lost reserves effectively financing a continuation of the buildup of foreign exposures.

To assess the risk of foreign exchange exposures for depositors, the financial system, and the government finances, we need data on how large this FX exposure is relative to the overall size of the banking system and the capital buffers. If the FX exposures are small in relation to the aggregate balance sheet and banks are well-capitalized, any writing down of the value of FX-denominated assets could be absorbed by equity holders without putting the depositors, financial system, and government finances at risk.

We also need data on whether any given FX exposure is concentrated in one or a few very large banks. A large exposure in a small bank cannot be ignored but it is less systemically destabilizing than a problem in a large bank or group of banks. A government cannot allow a large bank to fail in

---

[20] Staving off depreciation requires higher interest rates consistent with the higher risk premium; these will exert a contractionary influence on the real-estate sector, which is usually sensitive to interest rates.

the way it could a small bank or corporation that becomes insolvent. If nonperforming FX assets are large enough to threaten an important bank with insolvency, the government will likely act preemptively by extending capital support to the bank in question (probably by issuing government bonds to the bank in exchange for an equity stake), and, perhaps, by organizing the transfer of nonperforming assets from the balance sheet of the bank to an institution (sometimes called a "bad bank") charged with maximizing their value. In the latter transaction, the transfer price might include a less-than-transparent measure of fiscal support, thereby weakening government finances.[21]

Malign scenarios involving excessive private sector leverage usually require a degree of moral hazard – i.e., an expectation, based on past policies, that borrowers will somehow be protected from the adverse consequences of their decisions. Thus, in balance sheet assessments, two institutional characteristics are viewed as mitigating risks.

- At least some degree of exchange rate flexibility. Borrowers that are cognizant of exchange risk will shun sizable foreign exchange exposure.
- Strict bankruptcy laws and efficient liquidation procedures. These reduce economywide disruptions from private insolvencies and help to dispel borrowers' beliefs in implicit government guarantees.

In countries with these characteristics, and especially those with a history of significant exchange rate volatility, it may not be necessary to dig too deeply beneath the data on foreign exchange exposures.

A history of rigorous application of the regulatory ratios defined above would also have militated against FX components of the balance sheets threatening stability. Capital adequacy ratios would have buffered bank deposits and senior debt. A minimum stable funding ratio would have limited reliance on short-term foreign wholesale funding. Liquidity coverage regulations would have constrained maturity transformation unless the loans involved were liquid.

Prudential measures, however, have their limitations. If domestic borrowers in a booming real-estate market are bent on low-rate FX loans for leverage, a tough regulatory regime may simply encourage disintermediation from the banking system – i.e., either direct borrowing abroad or borrowing through new, unregulated channels involving nonbank parts of the financial

---

[21] It is arguable that, in the absence of government financial support, the fiscal costs of an implosion of the financial sector might be even larger.

sector. Assessing balance sheet vulnerabilities in the conditions discussed in this section, therefore, must also take into account the degree to which macroeconomic policies and diagnostic instruments – debt sustainability analysis (of both the government and the economy as a whole [see Chapters 5 and 7]), countercyclical fiscal policy analysis, interest rate policy, and capital flow management – are being employed to contain risks.

In some cases, surging foreign financial inflows help to fund credit expansion in domestic currency, a process that relies on central bank intervention to limit appreciation. Box 6.2 provides a graphical description of the types of policies that frequently need to play a role in managing the effects of such surging financial inflows.

c A Framework for Assessment in EM Countries

Since the spate of EM balance sheet crises in the 1990s, international surveillance of financial sector policies in EM countries has become more systematic. In 1999 the IMF and World Bank introduced the Financial Sector Assessment Program (FSAP) through which formal assessments of financial policy frameworks in individual countries are carried out.[22] FSAP assessments evaluate the quality of a country's regulatory framework and its supervision rather than the robustness of the country's financial sector; but the two are not unrelated and FSAPs provide useful information on the resilience of a country's financial sector. For most EMs these assessments are voluntary: governments of close to 100 EMs have participated in the program. Motivated by the severity of balance sheet crises during the 1990s, the growing sophistication of their financial markets and linkages with global markets, many governments have made significant improvements in financial sector policies.

In the many EM crises that were broadly similar to the generic case above, banks' capital, leverage, liquidity, and stable funding ratios would probably not have been compatible with the now more rigorous standards.[23] And even without these standards, an assessment of these ratios would have served as a useful diagnostic device. It is notable that in many EMs the authorities are now using prudential regulations and indicators to discourage short-term, volatile capital inflows that lead to excessive credit expansion. Moreover, the

---

[22] FSAPs contain a financial stability assessment (produced by the IMF) and, for emerging and developing countries, a financial development assessment (produced by the World Bank) that assesses the extent to which the financial sector is capable of supporting development. For a brief description of the FSAP see www.imf.org/external/np/fsap/fssa.aspx

[23] Consider the slew of crises from Mexico in the mid-1990s, through the Asian and Russian crises toward the end of that decade, the Eastern European crises in the following decade, and even, to some extent, the recent crises in Spain, Ireland, and Portugal, among others.

Box 6.2 Coping with Surging Capital Inflows

In the example in the text we saw an emerging market economy facing a credit-fueled real-estate bubble where private sector leverage was financed by substantial capital inflows. Figure 6.1 is a decision chart on how the authorities might deal with such an inflow. The implicit assumption here, however, is that the foreign borrowing is converted into domestic currency to fuel credit expansion.

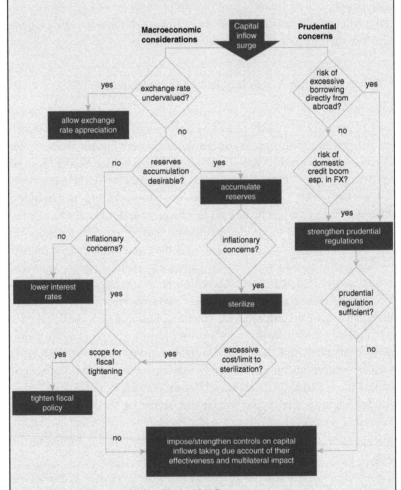

FIGURE 6.1 Policies to deal with capital inflows

Source: Jonathan Ostry, Atish R. Ghosh, Karl Habermeier, Marcos Chamon, Mahvash S. Qureshi, and Dennis B. S. Reinhardt, *Capital Inflows: The Role of Controls*, IMF Staff Position Note (February 2010)

Box 6.2 (*continued*)

It is possible that prudential measures might suffice. If not, they may be supported by macroeconomic instruments – a combination of currency appreciation, interest rate policy, reserve accumulation (with the latter sterilized if there are inflationary concerns), and fiscal policy. But to the extent that there are limits to all of these instruments – discussed in some detail in the foregoing chapters – it may be necessary, as a last resort, to impose capital controls.

---

range of prudential measures being used extends beyond those discussed above; they include additional capital requirements on FX-denominated lending and/or punitive additional reserve requirements on FX-denominated liabilities.

But these considerations do not mean that further improvement is unnecessary. Really successful surveillance of financial sectors requires imagination. The next EM financial crisis will probably involve, at least in the first instance, financial innovation motivated by large profit opportunities, institutions or instruments that may not yet exist or are not understood by supervisors, and nonbank financial intermediaries that fall below the radar of prudential scrutiny.

4 Balance Sheet Crises and Financial Assessment in Advanced Countries

As in EMs, financial crises in advanced countries come in a variety of forms. A common thread, in crises that are not fiscal in origin, is that some domestic agents – businesses or private individuals – borrow excessively, driven by expectations of rising asset prices. Banks accommodate this borrowing, moved by similar expectations and higher collateral values, and enabled by either lax regulation or financial innovation with which regulation has not caught up. Leverage turns a boom into a speculative bubble and, when prices overshoot a sustainable level, the bubble bursts. It is worth reiterating that the increase in credit, however motivated, is often facilitated by financial innovations that change the financial environment in a way fully appreciated only in retrospect. In this section we describe briefly some factors that contributed to the recent advanced country crises, and then we consider how the IMF assesses financial sector policies in advanced countries

a Crises in Advanced Countries

The 2008 financial crisis in the United States had as essential elements both a period of rapidly rising house prices and financial innovation. The latter included:

(i)   burgeoning issuance of structured financial products (loans packaged together and securitized in various risk tranches) that weakened the scrutiny of borrowers by the initial lenders (as loans were sold off rather than held on the books of the loan-originating institutions);

(ii) banks' ability to arbitrage between banking and trading books and even to hold many assets entirely off balance sheet, thus effectively reducing their capital-to-loan ratios;

(iii) liquidity imbalances between longer-maturity assets that proved illiquid under duress and highly liquid short-maturity liabilities;

(iv) value-at-risk calculations based on ill-considered estimates of volatility; and

(v)   a complex and gigantic web of interconnected derivatives that could hedge risky positions effectively only if all parts of the web remained intact.

Housing prices may have risen even without the influence of financial innovation; but without the ebullient support of the financial sector the price bubble would probably not have grown so large and its bursting been so consequential.

Some crises – like those that crept up on Japan at the end of the 1980s and on Ireland in 2008–2010 – were particularly insidious, although they bore some resemblance to the EM crisis described in section 3.[24] Both of these crises followed a long history of very strong economic performance, seemingly robust external finances, and substantial increases in living standards. It was natural (and equilibrating) in these circumstances that prices of nontraded goods (especially real estate, the essential nontraded asset) should rise more rapidly than other prices. But crises ensued when these relative price increases elicited a surge of highly leveraged speculative investment, overshot any reasonable assessment of equilibrium, and created a bubble that eventually burst with dire consequences.

---

[24] The disequilibria were initially domestic rather than external, although the sustained credit surge in Ireland was eventually financed to a large extent by wholesale funding of Irish banks from abroad.

b Assessing Financial Sector Policies in Advanced Countries

Designing policies to assess the health of an individual bank in an advanced country is difficult but getting a good fix on the health of the overall financial sector is even more so. The profitability of an individual institution together with the capital and leverage and liquidity ratios discussed above give some sense of the robustness of a bank, and in most normal circumstances the actual ratios should be well above the minimum required levels. Additional issues arise in the assessment of a country's financial system as a whole:

- The positions of individual banks and other financial institutions will differ, and it is important to have some notion of (i) the potential spillover effects from the failure of a large institution, or of (ii) systemic implications from shocks to many smaller institutions where vulnerabilities and risks are correlated.
- International spillovers between related institutions can be large, and the rigor of supervision may differ between jurisdictions.
- An assessment of the health of financial institutions in "normal" circumstances does not necessarily show how they will respond in stressed circumstances. Many thought the circumstances in the US financial sector between 2005 and 2007 were "normal"; the bubbles that burst were only retrospectively apparent. While it is difficult to foresee events that may trigger financial distress, insightful stress tests, based on exigent but plausible scenarios, are essential.
- In some countries the broad financial infrastructure – including clearing houses, insurance companies, hedge funds, other asset managers, and nonbank credit institutions – is hugely complex. The myriad interrelationships, both between institutions within the country and with institutions abroad, make for very difficult analysis and supervision. But the rigor of analysis of these relationships is critical to an assessment of the financial sector as a whole.

Advanced countries also participate in the Financial Sector Assessment Program. In 2010, the IMF made FSAPs mandatory for 29 jurisdictions with "systemically important financial sectors," and FSAPs for those 29 countries are carried out by the IMF alone. FSAP documents do not make for easy reading or immediately transparent conclusions but, in principle, the main conclusions of an FSAP for these 29 countries are reflected in summary form in the IMF's staff report for its annual Article IV consultations with each country.

IMF surveillance of the financial sector in the United Kingdom is a useful example, and a technical note from the 2016 FSAP with the United Kingdom illustrates the complexity of a major financial center and the challenges of assessing robustness.[25] However, given the potential for both domestic and international spillovers from such systemically important centers, the importance of assessing and mitigating their vulnerabilities cannot be overstated.

The IMF's 2016 Article IV Consultation Report for the United Kingdom (hereafter the *Report*) gives a good sense of London's significance as a financial center and the difficulty of monitoring it.[26] The financial assets of UK-domiciled financial institutions amount to about 10 times UK GDP; the United Kingdom's insurance sector, fund management industry, and equity trading platforms are huge by global standards and are globally interlinked; four banks and two insurance companies in the United Kingdom are classified as globally systemically important; and London hosts two of the largest central counterparties in the world.[27]

The *Report* starts by assessing financial soundness indicators over time (Table 6.5).

It also compares the CET1 and leverage ratios with other major European banks, and funding, liquidity, asset quality, and profitability with banks in the United States and Europe (see Figure 6.2). As of 2015 capital adequacy ratios were above regulatory minima and generally in line with those in other European centers, credit growth relative to GDP was unremarkable, asset quality had improved substantially (fewer NPLs) relative to 2011–2013, and funding was more reliant on deposits (less on short-term wholesale borrowing) than in the years immediately after the financial crisis. Liquidity had also improved, though not to quite the same extent as in other European banks. Noninterest expenses were high and this had reduced the rate of return on assets.

Two stress tests are discussed where banks were subjected to "severe but plausible adverse scenarios," and banks appeared to be resilient to the

---

[25] See IMF, United Kingdom Financial Sector Assessment Program, Supervision and Systemic Risk Management (June 2016),www.imf.org/external/pubs/ft/scr/2016/cr16156.pdf

[26] See www.imf.org/en/publications/cr/issues/2016/12/31/united-kingdom-2016-article-iv-consultation-press-release-and-staff-report-43979

[27] A central counterparty is a clearing house that stands between buyers and sellers in financial contracts. It collects money from both parties to the trade, guarantees that the contract will be honored (i.e., that the trade will be completed), and thus reduces counterparty risk. After the financial crisis there was great pressure to ensure that derivatives would be traded through central clearing houses so that a long string of bilateral hedging arrangements could not be disrupted by a single failure to deliver.

TABLE 6.5 *Financial soundness indicators for major UK banks*
(percent)

	2000–2006	2011	2012	2013	2014	2015
Capital adequacy						
Basel III common equity Tier 1 capital ratio	. . .	7.2	8.4	10.0	11.3	12.6
Simple leverage ratio	4.8	5.1	5.1	5.6	5.9	6.7
Basel III leverage ratio (2014 proposal)	. . .	. . .	. . .	. . .	4.4	4.8
Asset quality 1						
Nonperforming loans net of provisions to capital	. . .	16.1	13.9	9.5	5.4	4.5
Nonperforming loans to total gross loans	. . .	4.0	3.6	3.1	1.8	1.4
Profitability						
Return on assets before tax	1.1	0.4	0.2	0.3	0.5	0.4
Price-to-book ratio	224.6	57.0	81.0	106.0	96.0	76.0
Liquidity						
Loans-to-deposit ratio	113.1	108.9	103.1	99.1	95.9	96.7
Short-term wholesale funding ratio	. . .	18.8	16.4	14.1	12.5	10.4
Average senior CDS spread	. . .	2.7	1.5	1.0	0.6	0.8

The coverage of banks is as defined in the Bank of England's December Financial Stability Report, except for asset quality indicators for which the coverage is as defined in the IMF's Financial Soundness Indicators. Data for 2015 were the latest available at the time of the IMF Report.
Source: IMF, 2016 (Article IV) Consultation Report for the United Kingdom

shocks. Separate analysis of the nonbank financial sector was relatively reassuring; but this analysis was not as comprehensive as that for banks, and the IMF saw scope to improve available data, analytical models, and risk-monitoring tools. More generally, while the resilience of individual institutions had improved substantially with the regulatory reforms that followed the financial crisis, there was still a potential for the interconnectedness across subsectors of the financial system to amplify and propagate destabilizing shocks. The IMF stressed the importance of developing analytical tools to assess these interconnectedness risks.

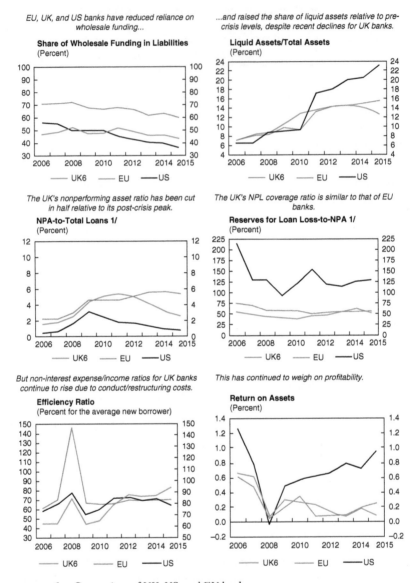

FIGURE 6.2 Comparison of UK, US, and EU banks

Source: IMF, 2016 Article IV Consultation Report for the United Kingdom

The *Report* discusses areas where progress still needed to be made, including (i) monitoring smaller financial firms, which, while not individually constituting systemic risk, might nevertheless impose systemic risk to the extent that their vulnerabilities are highly correlated; (ii) ring-fencing of core retail activities of large banks; (iii) ensuring the resolvability of large, complex, and interconnected financial institutions and the funding of firms in resolution; (iv) developing an effective resolution regime for insurance firms that could exert systemically important effects if they fail; and (v) dealing with potentially problematic differences in resolution regimes across jurisdictions.

With respect to macroprudential measures and indicators, besides discussing the raising of the countercyclical capital buffer, the *Report* pays special attention to the relationship between credit and housing markets (see Figure 6.3). Changes over time in lenders' loan-to-value and loan-to-income ratios were seen as useful indicators (and presumably could be more constrained in the event of excessive housing credit and a potential bubble).

Like all IMF consultation reports, that with the United Kingdom contains a risk assessment matrix, classifying risks by their likelihood and their impact, and then outlining possible policies to mitigate effects. Not surprisingly, given the date of the report, risks emanating from the financial sector were dominated (in both likelihood and impact) by those from a then-possible vote to leave the European Union. A final result in favor of Brexit (which subsequently came to pass) was seen as having myriad and important implications for London as a financial center.

Financial systems are in continuous evolution – situations change; new risks, opportunities, and incentives emerge; and economic agents find ways around unwelcome regulation – so policy will always be scrambling to keep up. The focus on the United Kingdom illustrates both the way a sophisticated regulatory and supervisory regime is assessed and the difficulties of monitoring vulnerabilities and risks in an advanced financial system facing potentially significant changes.

High-quality supervision entails imaginative stress scenarios, a constant attempt to see over the horizon to the next potential shock, and rigorous avoidance of complacency in seemingly benign circumstances. Problems of cybersecurity have recently added one new array of concerns but more such vulnerabilities will emerge over time. Regulation and supervision will always be a balancing act between risk mitigation on one side and efficient and innovative financial intermediation on the other. Supervision, at best, will be rigorous and imaginative; but it will never be perfect. The 2008

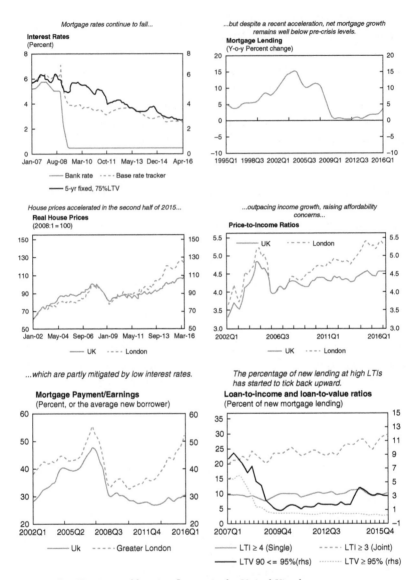

FIGURE 6.3 Housing and housing finance in the United Kingdom
Source: IMF, 2016 (Article IV) Consultation Report for the United Kingdom, www.imf
.org/en/About/Factsheets/Sheets/2016/08/01/16/14/Financial-Sector-Assessment-Program

financial crisis, which exerted detrimental effects for years thereafter, will
not be the last one.

5 Exercises

1 A potential investor has asked you to look at the balance sheet of a medium-size bank in a small country in the euro area. Its profitability has been relatively good, with a return on assets above the industry average, but the investor is concerned about vulnerabilities in its balance sheet. You are charged with assessing them. All assets and liabilities in the balance sheet are in euros, so there is no exchange rate risk. The only information you have initially is the simplified balance sheet shown in Table 6.6.

TABLE 6.6 *Simplified balance sheet of a medium-size bank in a small euro area country*

Assets (millions of euros)		Liabilities	
Foreign assets	100	Deposits	1500
Claims on the central bank	120	Loans from foreign banks	570
(currency plus reserves)		(unsecured)	
Loans to private nonbanks	2000	CET1	150
Loans to government	40	Other capital	80
Other assets	40		

(i) What is your initial view of the liability structure of the bank and its vulnerability to a run? What additional questions are relevant in this context and what prudential ratio would be useful as a standard for adequacy?

(ii) What is your initial view of the liquidity of the bank and its vulnerability to stress? How would you assess this and what prudential ratio would be useful?

(iii) How resilient or fragile is the solvency of the bank and what additional information would you need to answer this question?

(iv) What could be done to reinforce the bank's capital?

2 Suppose you learn a few additional things about the balance sheet above and the circumstances of the country. First, the country has recently joined the euro area and this has led to a drop in interest rates, a booming economy, and sharp increases in asset prices, particularly in real estate. Second, prior to joining the euro area the bank had no loans from foreign banks on its books and a much smaller portfolio of long-term mortgage loans. And, third,

this recent pattern of increased mortgage lending funded by loans from abroad was characteristic of most banks in the country. How would this information influence your view of the macroeconomic situation of the country and what policy tools may be useful to the financial authorities?

3 This is a political-economy question that calls for judgment. There is no one right answer; but, whichever way you answer, it is important that the case be sensibly argued.

Suppose a regional bank has the balance sheet shown in Table 6.7.

TABLE 6.7 *Balance sheet of a regional bank in the euro area* (in billions of euros)

Assets		Liabilities	
Foreign assets	1.0	Deposits	45.4
Claims on the central bank (currency plus reserve deposits)	1.2	Loans from other banks (unsecured)	3.0
Loans to private nonbanks	50.4	CET1	5.0
Loans to government	1.1	Other capital	1.6
Other assets	1.3		

This bank is not systemically important but it is the dominant bank in its region. Companies that account for about 60 percent of regional employment have their accounts with this bank; they represent most of the bank's lending and deposits, and most of the latter are too large to be covered to any significant extent by deposit insurance.

A large local company has made massive losses on speculative oil-derivative trading and has been forced into liquidation. This company is not a large employer and the government has ruled decisively against any direct bailout. But the company was highly leveraged: it accounts for €18 billion of the bank's private loan portfolio and the payout to creditors after liquidation will be only 20 percent of the loan values. The loss for the bank (the write-down of its loan portfolio) will amount to €14.4 billion, substantially in excess of its capital. Moreover, even if loans from other banks are written down to zero, an additional €4.8 billion would have to be covered by writing down the value of uninsured deposits. Such a write-down would threaten the solvency of a number of local companies that account for a significant proportion of employment.

What should the government do? What considerations should guide its actions? And how precisely should it carry them out?

CHAPTER 7

The External Accounts

In this chapter we establish a framework for analyzing how a country's economy interacts with the rest of the world. In focusing on how the domestic economy and monetary, fiscal, and financial sector policies influence and are influenced by the rest of the world, it draws on and provides some synthesis of the first six chapters of the book. The chapter covers four broad topics:

1 *Reading the external flow (balance of payments) accounts and noting the main influences on each of its principal components.*
2 *Considering the stock accounts (net international investment position) with special focus on external debt and official foreign exchange reserves.*
3 *Understanding five main types of macroeconomic issues for which external sector analytical tools are essential.*
4 *Analyzing external sustainability in terms of both a technical debt sustainability exercise and a broader consideration of the characteristics of debt, the adequacy of reserves, and the policy and institutional context.*

Most countries are separate units in terms of the currencies they use, their legal and institutional systems, and the priorities they assign to policy objectives. So understanding how an economy works internally – the main focus of the foregoing chapters – is important. But because individual economies operate in a global market, international interactions – always in the background of the analysis – have been impossible to ignore. Now we bring these interactions into the foreground, and we focus on how they influence activity, finances, opportunities, and vulnerabilities.

The importance of economic interactions among countries – *globalization* – has grown rapidly during the post-World War II era. The influence of the global economy is obvious for small countries where exports and imports are large in relation to purely domestic transactions. For large countries, such transactions may be a smaller proportion of the total, but external developments and shocks can still be highly consequential influences on domestic markets. Also, policies aimed at domestic objectives may have significant effects abroad, even if these are unintended.

External transactions – those between residents and nonresidents – can have important domestic implications. They may be:

- the source of long-term strength or weakness for a country's economic performance (e.g., through export market penetration as an engine of growth or through excessive dependence on foreign financing of budget deficits as a vulnerability);
- the origin of positive or negative shocks (e.g., from a sudden drop in the cost of a vital import or a jump in the risk premium in international markets on a country's bonds);
- an important shock absorber (e.g., through external financing of imports to cushion domestic absorption against a shortfall in harvests).

Therefore, clear analysis of transactions between residents and nonresidents is critical to understanding how a country is positioning itself to benefit from and to avoid setbacks from interactions with other countries.

The external accounts constitute an aggregation and netting out of individual sectoral accounts. They provide information that is at once distinct from, and yet critically complementary to, the analysis of individual sectors. This complementarity is evident in the different manifestations of financial crises that we have covered. In Chapter 4 we touched on monetary and exchange rate crises; in Chapter 5, fiscal crises; and in Chapter 6, financial sector crises. Each of these may have a different origin in misguided policy and a shock. Most of these crises, however, ultimately entail large and unsustainable outflows in the external accounts. The frameworks presented in this chapter are a window on vulnerabilities in a country's relationship to the rest of the world and how the external dimension of a crisis unfolds. They also provide insights on how external finances can be made more robust and crises can be forestalled.

1 Understanding the External Accounts

The external position of a country is represented in two kinds of accounts. The first, the balance of payments (BOP), records the *flow* of transactions (such as imports, exports, borrowing, and investment) between a country's residents and nonresidents. The second, the net international investment position (NIIP), records the stock of foreign assets owned by residents minus the stock of domestic assets owned by nonresidents (typically at the end of a period covered by the flow accounts).

Recall the distinction between flows and stocks. Flows are transactions that occur over a time period. For example, we record consumption or investment, government expenditure or revenues over a year or sometimes shorter periods like a quarter or a month. Stocks are aggregates measured at a point in time. We record various monetary and debt aggregates at the end of a year, quarter, or month.

A flow gives rise to a change in the stock between the end of the previous period and the end of the current period. Let's say I owed my bank $300 at the end of year 1, and I borrowed another $100 (the credit flow) in the course of year 2 (and made interest payments but no principal repayments). At the end of year 2 the level, or stock, of my indebtedness would be $400. The analysis is more complicated, however, if in addition to flows there are also valuation changes in existing stocks of assets or liabilities. This is the case in the external accounts where changes in exchange rates affect any transactions or stocks involving foreign currencies: transactions are recorded at the exchange rate on the date they occur, but stocks of foreign assets and liabilities are recorded at the exchange rate at the end of the period when they are measured.

To see the importance of this point, consider a country that has a zero flow balance in external financing in year t – i.e., financial inflows from abroad exactly match financial outflows to other countries. If the country's external financial assets are held in dollars while its liabilities are denominated in euros, and the euro appreciates against the dollar during the course of the year, the NIIP would show an increase in net indebtedness relative to year $t - 1$.

The IMF usually records external accounts in dollars (a dollar "numeraire") when it assesses BOP and stock developments, though it uses euros for euro area countries and sometimes even for other countries where euro transactions are a large share of the total. Many of the IMF's presentations also focus on both flow balances and stock aggregates as ratios to GDP, just like in the domestic expenditure or fiscal accounts, because the ratio provides scale. Again, however, the exchange rate makes things trickier. Changes in the exchange rate between the numeraire currency and domestic currency change these ratios even when flow balances are zero and the exchange rates between other currencies are constant. Thus, in the example above, even if the euro/dollar exchange rate were unchanged over year t so the stock of debt in dollars was constant, a depreciation of the domestic currency against the dollar (and the euro) during the year (by more than the rate of growth of nominal GDP) would raise the ratio of external debt to GDP for net debtors. If the country was a net creditor, the depreciation would increase the ratio of its net foreign assets to GDP.

A few other conventions in the external accounts are important to know:

- A transaction is considered "external" if it takes place between a resident and nonresident, where a nonresident is defined as an entity (person or business) that has resided outside the country for more than a year. In other words, residency rather than citizenship matters.
- A country's general government is defined as a domestic resident.
- External transactions are recorded on an accrual rather than cash basis and are valued at market prices.
- Merchandise exports and imports are usually recorded "free on board" (f.o.b. – i.e., excluding the cost of transportation and insurance) in the trade account, and the payments for transportation and insurance services related to trade are recorded in the services account.

Beyond these basic conventions are thousands of definitions and classifications that guide how categories of transactions and investment positions are recorded. An authoritative source on these definitions and classifications is the IMF's Balance of Payments and International Investment Position Manual, which is periodically revised to address the growing complexity of transactions.[1] The following discussion picks up key aspects of the accounting framework but the objective is a general understanding not an exhaustive exposition.

a Flows of Goods, Services, Income, and Financing

The BOP covers all transactions of a country with the rest of the world. Because it encompasses all trade (in goods and services), factor income flows, and the financing of these transactions, it sums, by construction, to zero in every period. The standard presentation of the BOP groups transactions in categories with similar characteristics, and balances are shown for analytically useful subsets of these groups. Each group is a starting point for examining specific questions about a country's relationship with the rest of the world. Macroeconomists focus on four main groups (and a statistical discrepancy), the sum of which is zero.

---

[1] See 6th edition, *Balance of Payments and International Investment Position Manual*, www .imf.org/external/pubs/ft/bop/2007/bopman6.htm. Definitions in this section conform to this manual.

$$CAB + KAB + NFB + E\&O + RT = 0 \qquad (7.1)$$

CAB = current account balance (+ = surplus) measured in nominal (or current price) terms

KAB = capital account balance (+ = surplus)

NFB = net financial balance excluding changes in official reserve holdings (+ = net inflows)

E&O = net errors and omissions, the net sum of statistical discrepancies in the other balances

RT = net reserve *loss* of the central bank. (Note, most BOP presentations show a reserve *loss* as a positive number as reflected in this equation.)

If a country has a negative current account balance and a zero capital and financial balance, it would lose reserves. This reserve loss would be the financing item for the current account deficit. It would be recorded as a positive number in equation (7.1). Note that RT here is usually equal to the change in net foreign assets in the central bank accounts of Chapter 4, albeit with the opposite sign and expressed in terms of foreign (as opposed to domestic) currency.

This section serves as a reference for the definition of each of these balances. The balance of payments table for Poland (Table 7.1) illustrates the conventional presentation.

The *current account* summarizes the balance of transactions in goods and services and of income flows. It encompasses:

- The *trade account* (receipts from goods exports minus payments for goods imports).
- The *services account* (receipts minus payments from trade in services such as transportation, insurance, tourism, legal, and medical services).
- The *primary (or "net") income flows* (net incomes from the temporary use of labor, financial resources, or nonfinancial assets). Examples are labor income from residents temporarily abroad; interest, dividends, or retained earnings on investments abroad; rental income on foreign property owned by a resident; and most types of aid (i.e., grants for development assistance).
- *Secondary income flows (or "current transfers")* are mainly gifts in kind, remittances of workers living abroad permanently, and payments to meet obligations to international organizations.

TABLE 7.1 *Poland: balance of payments*
(billions of US dollars unless otherwise indicated)

	2015	2016
		estimate
Current account balance	−2.9	−1.4
Trade balance	2.5	2.2
Exports of goods	191.0	195.6
Imports of goods	188.6	193.4
Net services	12.1	15.2
Net primary income	−16.6	−17.6
Net secondary income	−1.0	−1.2
Capital account balance	11.3	4.9
Financial account balance	−0.4	21.7
Foreign direct investment (net)	9.8	5.0
Portfolio investment (net)	−3.3	3.8
Financial derivatives	0.9	-0.1
Other investment (net)	−7.9	13.1
Errors and omissions	−6.9	−2.6
Overall balance	1.1	22.7
Change in reserve assets (minus is an increase)	−1.1	−22.7

Source: IMF, Republic of Poland, 2017 Article IV Consultation, www.imf.org/en/
Publications/CR/Issues/2017/07/17/Republic-of-Poland-2017-Article-IV-Consultation-
Press-Release-Staff-Report-and-Statement-by-45090
Note: Components do not always sum to totals due to rounding

In most summary BOP presentations, some large items, mainly exports and imports of goods, are shown as gross flows and then combined in the trade balance. However, most other categories of transactions are shown as net flows only. Data on the gross flows underlying these net magnitudes are available but, because they are usually composed of a large number of fairly disparate transactions, it is not practical or particularly useful to view the gross flows separately.

The *capital account* includes a smaller range of transactions of two main types:

- *Unilateral transfers* from or to nonresidents that change the stock of the recipient country's financial or real assets (most commonly official grants – development assistance – given with an obligation that the recipient use the funds for fixed capital formation). Debt forgiveness, when it is intended to improve the condition of the recipient rather than recognizing that the debt cannot be paid, is also included in the capital account.

- *Acquisition or disposal of nonproduced, nonfinancial assets.* These include certain types of transactions involving the ownership of land, mineral resources, leases, and marketing assets such as brands.

The *financial account* comprises all transactions between domestic residents and foreign residents involving the exchange of financial instruments.[2] Such transactions can be classified in many ways – e.g., by type of instrument, by maturity of the instrument, or by currency of the instrument. The most common, "functional," presentation is designed to help identify specific characteristics of financial flows relevant to basic questions about the sustainability of the flows and their impact on the economy of the recipient country.

The functional presentation comprises four broad categories of financial flows: direct investment, portfolio investment, financial derivatives (other than reserves) and employee stock options, and a catch-all of "other" investment. Reflecting the complexity of cross-border financial flows, the description of the four categories given here is adequate to inform macroeconomic analysis but does not provide exhaustive definitions:

- *Foreign direct investment* (FDI) includes all transactions where a resident of one country makes an investment that gives an individual or a business control or a significant degree of influence over the management of an enterprise resident in another country. Control or a significant degree of influence is defined as requiring that the investor has a voting share in the entity greater than 10 percent. Direct investment can also include debt flows from the investor to the enterprise if the enterprise is a direct investment affiliate of the investor. Defining direct investment is complicated insofar as it depends on the interpretation of cross-border ownership structures. But the basic objective is to identify financial transactions where investors tend to have a relatively stable and lengthy position in the recipient country. Also, most direct investment, in contrast to most other items in the financial account, does not change a country's gross external debt.
- *Portfolio investment* covers cross-border transactions in debt or equity securities other than those included in direct investment or reserve

---

[2] The central bank is either included as a distinct entity or, more usually, excluded from the financial account because changes in its assets and liabilities are assumed to reflect monetary or exchange rate policy decisions.

assets. The distinctive feature of these securities is that they are relatively easy to trade in fairly liquid markets. Thus portfolio investors have a largely anonymous relationship with the issuers of the securities, and they can, in principle, add to or liquidate their positions quickly. In practice, finding a counterparty if the market for a bond is in turmoil can slow things down.

- *Financial derivatives (other than reserves) and employee stock options* includes a variety of financial transactions with the common characteristic of being motivated by risk transfer rather than the investment of funds. Transactions related to forward contracts and options trading are important components of this type of financial flow. For these two types of transactions, gross positions are much larger than net flows (which consist, in the simplest case, of the initial premium payment and subsequently any cash value at the time of settlement). Employee stock options – which are motivated primarily by cross-border compensation of employees rather than pure trading of risk – are included in this category because of the option feature of the payment. In many presentations, financial derivatives and employee stock options transactions are not shown separately but are included in the category described next, "Other investment".

- *Other investment* is a residual category that covers financial transactions not included elsewhere in the financial account. Major entries include direct lending and borrowing, trade credits, currency transactions, IMF credits (although these are sometimes treated as part of official reserve transactions), and allocations of special drawing rights (SDRs), which are reserve assets created by the IMF, and other equity (e.g., nonsecuritized ownership rights of less than 10 percent).

Official reserve flows are changes in the reserve position of the monetary authority (in almost all countries the central bank). Official reserve assets include the whole range of assets that are controlled by the monetary authority and are available to meet BOP financing needs and to influence the exchange rate through purchases and sales of foreign currency for domestic currency. Official reserve asset flows are recorded separately from other financial transactions because they result from policy decisions (foreign exchange market intervention, discussed in Chapter 4).

Net errors and omissions is a balancing item. In principle, the sum of all transactions on the current, capital and financial accounts, and the net reserve loss equals zero. In practice, given the complexity of the data and data sources, imperfections (stemming from both recording of detailed transactions and inaccuracies in compilation) are inevitable. So adding up is not exact. The sum of these imperfections is recorded as net errors and omissions. The sources of errors and omissions can be simple shortcomings in data collection, particularly when transactions like workers' remittances or border trade are made in physical cash. Errors and omissions may also reflect unrecorded capital outflows motivated, perhaps, by portfolio considerations in the presence of capital controls.

The *overall balance* is the net sum of all "autonomous" or "above-the-line" external transactions (i.e., transactions other than those involving official reserves). Usually, it is shown as an aggregate balancing item (as in Table 7.1). It results from shifting RT (in equation (7.1)) to the right side of the equation (and changing the sign). It is an important aggregate for countries that fix their exchange rate or have a commitment to maintaining their exchange rate in a band, because it shows how much foreign exchange the central bank has to buy or sell in order to meet the net supply of or demand for foreign exchange resulting from above-the-line transactions.

As we saw in Chapter 4, these central bank transactions ("official intervention") indicate the pressure on the exchange rate and potential risks of reserve depletion or of externally–induced excess money creation and inflation. If the exchange rate is floating freely, the overall balance is likely to be close to zero – differing primarily by interest earning on central bank reserves.

b Judging the Credibility of Balance of Payments Projections

The main balances in the accounts – current account, capital account, financial account, and overall balance – are typically relatively small numbers. But they represent differences between large gross flows, which are subject to a set of determining influences. Standard relationships guide our interpretation of the behavior of the gross flows and are the basis for forecasting the balance of payments. While actual modeling may address highly disaggregated components of the BOP, we cover here only those flow variables that are most important. Because BOP projections are central to external risk assessments, having a simple framework for judging the plausibility of projections is important.

How we project the volume of exports (exports measured in terms of constant dollar prices) depends on a country's size and the composition of exports. Exports of a large diversified producer respond positively to world trade growth, negatively to increases in costs relative to those of competitors (i.e., reduced competitiveness), and positively to domestic excess supply capacity. Small countries, or even more definitively exporters of a relatively homogeneous commodity (say copper) that do not have any monopoly power, are typically characterized as facing infinite foreign demand at the existing world price. Their export function is essentially a supply function: exports are determined by their costs and their capacity to produce exports profitably at or below the world market price. The relationship between profits on the production of nontraded goods or import substitutes versus those on export production is also important to the supply of exports, as are capacity constraints.

Merchandise imports are sensitive to aggregate domestic demand and competitiveness. Stronger domestic demand raises the volume of imports (again, at constant dollar prices), both because the demand for the specific goods provided by foreign producers rises and because, when demand exceeds production capacity, excess demand must be met through imports. Competitiveness – measured as some price or cost index for domestically produced goods relative to that for foreign-produced goods – also affects imports; demand for foreign goods rises if they are relatively less expensive.

The previous two paragraphs address the *volume* of trade – i.e., trade in real (constant dollar price) terms. The nominal value of imports and exports depends on price developments as well. Obviously, volumes have to be adjusted for prices to get the values that enter the BOP. But for macroeconomic analysis, trade prices (often called *unit values*) are also summarized as the terms of trade – the ratio of the average price of a country's exports to the average price of its imports. For all but the largest countries the terms of trade are exogenous – i.e., beyond the control of domestic producers or governments. Even if a country experiences stable growth of export and import volumes, a sharp increase in the price of its exports (say, an increase in the world price of copper for a large copper exporter) while the prices of its imports remain constant means that the trade balance improves. Large terms-of-trade gains and losses – most prevalent in countries with narrow production bases and dependence on primary commodities – are highly consequential for macroeconomic equilibrium: without any change in the volume of domestic production, a country with a sizable terms-of-trade gain will have (at least temporarily) a greater capacity to consume and invest.

Other current account entries are even more country-specific. Primary income flows depend on variables such as the number of nationals working abroad or the number of foreign nationals working domestically. At any given time these are likely to be known variables (within a relatively small margin of error), though over time workers' remittances are responsive to employment opportunities and wage differentials at home and abroad. Similarly, net investment income depends on the residents' stock of foreign investments less nonresidents' stock of investments in the home country and the rates of return on each (often proxied by the interest rate). Over time the stock of investments abroad and nonresidents' investments in the domestic economy respond to a host of influences such as changes in competitiveness, yields on portfolio instruments, perceived risks, and other factors affecting the attractiveness of a country as a production platform.

Aid inflows (included in the secondary income account) are usually subject to prior commitments by foreign donors; however, it is often difficult to predict when these commitments will actually be disbursed. The latter may depend on political developments or the ability/willingness of the recipient country to meet prerequisite conditions.

Understanding the forces at work on items in the financial account is even more difficult than on the current account. For FDI, there are a few regularities such as the influence of competitiveness (specifically, the relative attractiveness of a country as a platform for production). But these are often overwhelmed by myriad other influences particular to individual countries, such as tax incentives, political stability, and characteristics of supply chains. FDI often reflects multiyear projects or commitments but the timing of disbursements is unpredictable. It is usually possible to forecast the direction of FDI (i.e., positive or negative net flows) but forecasting the size of gross flows (and, more so, net flows) is treacherous.

Portfolio investment and loans are typically quite responsive to changes in yield differentials between the domestic economy and the rest of the world. However, like FDI, they are influenced by many other factors, such as changes in investor sentiment, exchange rate expectations, and even the size and loyalty of a diaspora. Government borrowing and amortization schedules are usually reflected in budgets and therefore reasonably tractable.

Derivatives and other inflows are yet more difficult to interpret/forecast. The same goes for errors and omissions, usually set in projections at zero or some average of recent years if there is an established pattern. Net amounts under each of these headings can swing widely from year to year. The main value of examining these flows carefully is to appreciate when swings are unusually large and may indicate either a problem with data collection or some deviation from normal developments.

c External Stock Accounts: Looking Beyond the Flows

Flows of goods, services, and financial assets are central to analysis of a country's ongoing economic relationships with the rest of the world. But economists are also concerned about the implications of those flows for creditor and debtor positions between domestic and foreign residents. These are summarized in the balance sheets of various sectors – government, financial and nonfinancial businesses, and households – and the character-istics of these positions – debt or equity, currency of denomination, and (for debt) maturity. The focus on these relationships has intensified as the source of economic and financial crises has shifted from the current account to the financial account. External stock accounts described in this section are complementary to the stock accounts presented in previous chapters for the central bank, banking sector as a whole, and government.

Conceptually, the assessment of stock positions starts with the NIIP, an inclusive statement of a country's net claims on nonresidents. It is a conceptually simple aggregate but in practice subject to many complica-tions in measurement. The data needed to measure valuation changes on all stocks of assets and liabilities accumulated in previous years are exacting. When assets are traded publicly – e.g., on equity or bond markets – valua-tion is relatively straightforward, but when they are not, the complications are immense. Another complication is that the residence of asset holders is often not easy to determine. Thus the process of systematically reporting the NIIP for all countries is still in its infancy, and, except for the countries with the most sophisticated collection of financial sector data, the net NIIP is not available with accurate supporting detail.

The data underpinning the NIIP do not always appear in IMF Article IV consultation reports, which are the most complete IMF assessments and sources of data for individual countries. In any event, in practice, the IMF's analysis of stock positions or balance sheets tends to focus on the two aggregates of most direct interest to assessing external sector vulnerabilities: external debt – total (public and private) gross and net debt to nonresi-dents – and foreign exchange reserves (the gross and net foreign assets of the monetary authority). The description here of these aggregates foreshadows the discussion of vulnerability and sustainability later in the chapter.

(i) External Debt

The external debt of the country as a whole is a consolidation of the external debt of each individual sector of the economy – households, nonfinancial companies, the government, the banking system, and nonbank financial institutions. Why is external debt of interest in addition to a sector's overall debt (the focus of the fiscal and financial accounts)?

First, the basic arithmetic is important. Borrowing between residents equals lending between residents (thus netting to zero), so *net* external debt (residents' debt liabilities to nonresidents less nonresidents' debt liabilities to residents) is a complete statement of the potential impact on a country's balance sheet of events outside its control. In practice, however, a country's *gross* external debt typically commands more attention. One reason is that the holders of foreign liabilities and assets are not usually the same, so offsets in the event of setbacks are not meaningful.

Second, the importance of external debt stems from the defining characteristics of country units. National boundaries delineate an economic bloc in which agents use the same currency and are subject to a single legal and political framework. Borrowing and lending among residents is subject to interest rate and default risk. But foreign borrowing and lending adds the additional considerations of changes in political relationships between countries, different legal frameworks at home and abroad, exchange rate risk, and disparate macroeconomic developments and policies that influence risk premia, interest rates, and exchange rates.

Third, external debt always has an exchange rate dimension. If the debt is denominated in domestic currency, foreign investors bear the exchange rate risk; if it is denominated in foreign currency, domestic issuers bear the exchange rate risk. Mitigating factors such as a natural hedge (Mexican exporters to the United States may want to borrow in US dollars because their earnings are in dollars) may exist, but even then the exchange rate is an active consideration.

Different legal frameworks across countries are an important influence. A country targeting foreign investors and issuing in a major international currency will usually issue in foreign markets governed by foreign, usually UK or US, law. The terms of debt issued under domestic law can be altered by domestic legislation but those of debt issued under foreign law cannot; therefore, the latter type of debt will be more attractive to foreign investors. The law governing debt obligations is important in debt crises where debt restructuring or default becomes relevant. Because UK and US laws are rigorously enforced by the courts, issuance under foreign law protects creditors against arbitrary restructuring or default. Now, however, sovereign bonds issued under the law of a major country usually incorporate *collective actions clauses* (CACs), which allow a specified majority of bondholders to agree to a change in the terms of a bond. The purpose of CACs is to provide for orderly restructuring negotiations should a government be unable to meet the original terms of its debt.

As we will see in section 3, analysis of a country's external debt is a central part of the assessment of its vulnerability to setbacks that could end in crisis.

(ii) Central Bank Reserves

Reserves of the central bank comprise assets that are readily available to and controlled by the monetary authority for meeting BOP financing needs and influencing the exchange rate through direct intervention in foreign exchange markets. Judging the adequacy of reserves is an important part of any vulnerability analysis. Metrics for such judgments are discussed in section 3.

Both gross and net reserves play a role in external risk assessments. Gross reserves of the central bank are the total foreign exchange assets readily available for use.

$$Gross\ reserves = FXH + MG + SDR + RPF + OA \qquad (7.2)$$

FXH = foreign exchange holdings (usually in US Treasury bills or a comparably liquid short-term asset)

MG = monetary gold holdings

SDR = special drawing rights issued to the country by the IMF[3]

RPF = reserve position in the IMF (foreign currency amounts that a member country may draw from the IMF at short notice)[4]

OA = other short-term assets in foreign currency[5]

Net reserves take into account a central bank's foreign exchange liabilities. Net international reserves are defined as[6]

$$Net\ reserves = Gross\ reserves$$
$$- central\ bank\ foreign\ exchange\ liabilities$$
$$(7.3)$$

This measure, which obviously is either identical to (because a central bank has no foreign exchange liabilities) or smaller than gross reserves, tends to feature less prominently in external risk assessments than gross reserves.

---

[3]   SDRs are international reserve assets the IMF created to supplement the reserves of IMF member countries. SDRs are allocated in proportion to a country's voting quota at the IMF. They may also be obtained from another country through the IMF.

[4]   Comprises an undrawn "reserve tranche" (or the amount of a country's subscription to the IMF paid in hard currency) and lending to the IMF that is readily available to the country.

[5]   Examples are marked-to-market values of financial derivatives positions and central bank lending to nonbank, nonresidents.

[6]   Partly in response to the Asian crises of the late 1990s, where information on reserve assets in the runup to the crisis proved seriously inadequate, the IMF has put the definitions and data collection for reserves under the microscope. In so doing, it has significantly expanded the detail of coverage of reserve assets and liabilities. See www.imf.org/external/np/sta/ir/IRProcessWeb/pdf/guide.pdf. In most of the IMF's own country reports, however, a relatively simple definition of gross and net reserves continues to appear.

2 The Main Objectives of External Account Analysis

The external accounts summarize all interactions of the domestic economy with the rest of the world and can provide insights on the economic strength of a country and the risks that it faces. In particular, information from the external accounts helps in the analysis of five broad issues: domestic growth; smoothing of economic activity in the face of a temporary shock; competitiveness; repercussions from global imbalances; and vulnerability to crises. This section explains how the external accounts are used in each of these aspects of macroeconomic analysis.

a Domestic Growth

For many (especially small and low-income) countries, analysis of the external accounts is central to the consideration of a country's growth model – i.e., its strategy for raising income and living standards. Recalling the definition of GNDI from Chapter 2, it is obvious that trade provides two direct avenues for long-term growth: import-substitution and export-driven growth.

$$GNDI = C + I + X - M + NFI + TR \qquad (7.4)$$

During 1950–1980, many countries tried an import substitution route. The idea was that by establishing high tariff or quota barriers to imports, countries could develop their own industries to meet domestic demand and thereby achieve rapid growth. Many saw some initial success. Over time, however, the shield from external competition meant that domestic efficiency and productivity growth suffered, export growth was anemic, and, therefore, the effects of shocks (like increases in the price of imported energy or in foreign interest rates) could not be offset by raising exports. During the past few decades, the merits of export-driven growth models (to a large extent the model that fast-growing Asian countries have followed) have come to be seen as superior to import substitution.

For most countries, external markets for goods and services are a source of growth that is effectively boundless within a country's potential capacity to produce exports. As we saw in Chapter 3 (and specifically Box 3.3), for countries that are small producers of products with large global markets, a broadly accurate characterization of export performance is a simple supply function that posits production (or sales) as a function of domestic costs relative to the world price (an indication of the profitability of export production). Cyclical conditions (excess capacity in the domestic economy) can also temporarily affect exports – with larger excess capacity tending to raise exports – but the cumulative cyclical effect should be zero over the cycle. For countries that are potentially large producers relative to the global market, an important consideration in an export-driven growth strategy is the effect on the world price of significantly increasing supply.

The success of a country's export-driven development strategy depends on the country's price and cost competitiveness (discussed in Chapter 3) but also on the extent to which the country's policies and institutions motivate the creation and expansion of export industries. These latter components are much debated and often controversial insofar as they can involve policies that distort investment decisions in inefficient ways. On the less controversial side are policies that open an economy to FDI (and the accompanying technology transfer) and avoid protection against imports so as to allow needed imported inputs and prevent any import-substitution bias. On the more controversial side are tax and subsidy policies that encourage investment in export industries and may not be cost-effective.

Measuring the success of an export-driven growth strategy involves close examination of the external accounts against domestic and external developments. A key measure is export market penetration (the ratio of a country's exports to world imports).[7] Aggregate exports can be compared to world trade growth. Or, more meaningfully for most export-driven growth strategies, exports of manufactured goods can be compared to world imports of manufactured goods or to imports of manufactured goods in the main markets to which the country exports. For example, during the transition from centrally planned to market economies, most Central and Eastern European countries had export-driven growth strategies. The penetration of EU markets for their exports was a good indicator of success. Figure 7.1 shows the (exceptionally strong) evolution of this ratio for Poland.

Alongside rising export ratios, the country might also hope to see a positive contribution of trade in goods and services to growth. The argument here is that export growth may be rapid, but if it entails or is accompanied by rapid import growth it may not be contributing much to overall income growth. For example, a country may be pursuing an export-led growth strategy that requires large increases in imported inputs for export production. Export growth alone might suggest that the export strategy is having a large effect on GNDI. If the increase in imported inputs is taken into account, however, the contribution of *net* exports (i.e., exports – imports) may be far smaller. Similarly, if rapid export growth is achieved by diverting resources from the production of goods and services for domestic consumption, imports will replace at least part of that drop in production.

---

[7] The analysis, obviously, could be more granular: i.e., one could look at the exports of particular products relative to global imports of these products.

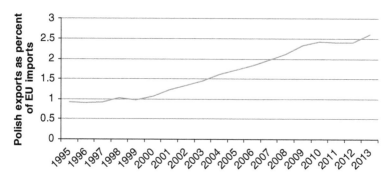

FIGURE 7.1 Poland: export market penetration, 1995–2013
Source: IMF, Direction of Trade, various issues

As noted in Chapter 2, the (percentage point) contribution of net exports of goods and services to GNDI is calculated as

Contribution of net exports to growth

$$= [(CAB_t - CAB_{t-1})/GNDI_{(t-1)}] \times 100 \quad (7.5)$$

This measure is not reflective of whether a country has a current account surplus or deficit. A positive contribution of the current account to GNDI can occur when a country goes from a larger current account deficit to a smaller one, when it moves from a deficit to a surplus, or when the surplus gets larger.

This *contribution of net exports to growth* is, however, a crude arithmetic measure that is meaningless without context. As elaborated in the next section, a drop in the current account balance may reflect a growth-positive surge of imports to support investment.

Export growth can drive domestic production, and current account surpluses can result in an accumulation of financial wealth – frequently two policy objectives, especially of EMs. But any wise export-driven growth strategy must, at some point, allow for substantial increases in domestic demand as residents reap the benefits of higher incomes.

b Domestic Stability and Use of Foreign Savings

Whether a growth strategy is "export-driven" or "import-substituting," it sometimes leads to the (mistaken) view that success can be more or less equated with falling current account deficits or rising surpluses (often mis-leadingly called an "improving" current account position). But the opposite (what is often called a "weakening" current account position) can help cushion negative shocks to the economy and allow for more gradual adjustment to the shock than would be possible with a constant or "improving" current account position. Current account deficits can also provide resources for investment and future growth. Just as deficit financing in the government accounts can help stabilize expenditure in a recession or provide resources for good investment opportunities, external current account deficits can reflect a country drawing on foreign saving for beneficial purposes.

Say a country has been pursuing an effective manufactured-export-driven growth strategy and is suddenly hit by an increase in imported energy prices. A larger import bill and current account deficit is financed by borrowing abroad and/or a drop in central bank reserves. The current account deficit – effectively a drawing on foreign resources – cannot continue indefinitely. But if energy price shocks over time are both positive and negative and are relatively short-lived, foreign resources (or use of reserves) can be useful in mitigating these shocks.[8] Even if such shocks are permanent, foreign resources can help phase in the adjustment in a gradual and more sustainable manner. (Box 7.1 elaborates on a terms-of-trade shock in the context of Chile and Peru.)

Box 7.1 Chile and Peru: Responses to the 2012–2016 Copper Price Fall

Chile and Peru are heavily dependent on copper production: in 2011 it accounted for over 15 percent of GDP and over 50 percent of exports in each country. The sharp drop in the world copper price that began at the end of 2011 followed a 10-year rise that had seen prices rise fivefold (albeit with a sizable dip in 2007–2009). The over 40 percent drop in the price from the end of 2011 through 2016 was, therefore, a partial reversal of the earlier rise.

Table 7.2 summarizes the size of the shock (scaled for its effect) for Chile and Peru and key aspects of the policy and private sector responses. Bear in mind that (as is typically the case in assessments of a shock), developments in 2012–2016 reflect not only the impact of and response to the shock but also an array of challenges affecting the global economy (the continuing recovery from the 2008 recession) and political economy issues in the countries themselves.

---

[8]   This is the consideration at the heart of the central bank's intervention decision described in Chapter 4.

Box 7.1 (*continued*)

TABLE 7.2 *Chile and Peru: summary assessment of the world copper price shock, 2011–2016*

	Chile						Peru					
	2011	2012	2013	2014	2015	2016	2011	2012	2013	2014	2015	2016
Shock measures												
Terms of trade (% change)	1.5	−6.6	−2.9	−2.0	−4.1	−1.7	7.0	−2.3	−5.2	−5.4	−6.4	−0.7
Annual tax equivalent*		−2.1	−3.0	−3.7	−5.3	−6.4		−0.5	−1.9	−3.3	−5.3	−5.9
Policy space, response												
General gov't balance	1.4	0.7	−0.5	−1.5	−2.1	−2.9	2.0	2.1	0.7	−0.3	−2.2	−2.3
General gov't structural balance**	−1.0	0.0	−1.0	−1.5	−2.0	−2.2	1.2	1.4	0.1	−0.2	−1.7	−1.9
Public sector external debt	2.9	3.1	3.4	3.8	4.3	4.9	7.2	10.0	9.0	8.7	11.1	10.3
Gross international reserves***	42.0	41.6	41.1	40.4	38.6	38.6	48.9	64.0	65.7	62.4	61.5	61.7
Exchange rate (home currency/US$)	483.7	486.5	495.3	570.4	654.1	676.8	2.75	2.64	2.70	2.84	3.19	3.38
Private response												
Private S-I****	−2.6	−4.2	−3.1	0.3	0.2	1.0	−4.5	−5.5	−5.8	−5.0	−3.5	−0.7
Private external debt	36.7	42.4	45.2	54.0	60.4	59.8	14.5	17.8	18.2	21.9	23.5	23.2
Outcomes												
Current account	−1.2	−3.5	−3.7	−1.3	−2.0	−2.2	−1.9	−2.7	−4.4	−4.4	−4.8	−2.7
Real GDP (% change)	6.1	5.3	4.0	1.9	2.3	1.6	6.5	6.0	5.8	2.4	3.3	4.0

*Change in overall export price from 2011 times previous year volume minus change in overall import price from 2011 times previous year volume.
**In percent of potential output.
***Includes effects of changes in the exchange rate on valuation.
****For Peru, private and government S-I balances do not sum to the current account balance because of omitted public enterprises and different data sources.
Source: IMF staff reports, central bank websites, and authors' calculations.

With that proviso, several observations emerge from the data:

1 The terms-of-trade loss was very large, reaching a tax equivalent of over 5 percent of GDP annually in 2015–2016 (relative to the terms of trade at the previous peak in 2011).
2 From the outset, both countries had ample policy space (general government surpluses, low external debt, and sizable foreign exchange reserves) to smooth the immediate effects of the shock on absorption. The question for policy was: how long and how deep would the price change be and how should policies balance protecting traded goods (especially metals) producers vs. protecting domestic consumption and nontraded goods producers.

(*continued*)

Box 7.1 (*continued*)

3 Chile intervened minimally to smooth the path of its peso, although during the greatest exchange market pressures in 2015 it leaned against the wind by stepping up its sales of reserves. Peru, which in the first half of the period was still intervening against a surge in capital inflows, resisted depreciation more strongly in the second half of the period. Accordingly, Chile's peso depreciated over the five years by 40 percent and the Peru's sol by 23 percent.

4 Fiscal policy actively contributed to cushioning the drop in domestic absorption in both countries. Over the period both countries experienced a swing in the general government balance of some 4.5 percentage points of GDP. Automatic stabilizers (mainly through a drop in fiscal revenues from mining) accounted for most of that weakening in Chile; a large shift in the structural balance from surplus to deficit dominated the weakening of the overall fiscal balance in Peru. Still both countries ended this very difficult period with structural deficits of only about 2 percent of GDP.

5 The private sector initially increased foreign borrowing significantly but the private S-I balance rose strongly in the second half of the period.

6 The drop in the government S-I balance was larger than the increase in the private S-I balance; thus the current account deficit (relative to GDP) widened by almost 1 percentage point in Chile and almost 3 percentage points in Peru through 2015. (In Peru, a sharp increase in the current account balance in 2016 was influenced by a jump in metal export volume as a large capacity expansion came on-stream.)

7 Real growth remained positive throughout the period. By the end of the period, fiscal and external positions remained well within the limits of sustainability.

Another common example of the expenditure-smoothing role of variations in the current account arises in the case of a crop failure in a developing country with a narrow export base. It may make sense to accept a wider current account deficit to cushion the effect of the crop shortfall on consumption if the shock is of reasonably short duration.

In both of these cases wishful thinking on the part of policymakers that can obscure realism is a danger: if the scope for foreign borrowing is limited by already high debt and risk sentiment in global financial markets, allowing full flexibility of the exchange rate to equilibrate the balance of payments may be much the wisest option.

An even more important consideration is whether a country should borrow abroad to finance profitable domestic investment. Productivity gains in manufacturing may require investments in plant and machinery beyond what can be financed by domestic saving. As is clear from the real resource constraint derived in Chapter 2 (albeit expressed here in nominal terms), foreign savings transferred through the current account increase the resources available for investment.

$$I = S - CAB \tag{7.6}$$

The country may borrow abroad and, even as its export growth picks up sharply, see a substantial widening of its current account deficit as it imports investment goods. Foreign investors have a financial claim on future domestic income (interest and repayment of loans or dividends on equity). However, as long as the rate of return on the investment exceeds the cost of borrowing, the initial inward resource transfer is beneficial.[9]

The point to take away from this discussion is that the external accounts contain a great deal of information about recent and prospective developments for the growth and stability of income and expenditure. But they must be interpreted carefully with an understanding of the growth potential of exports, shocks and cyclical influences on the external accounts, and the effects of resource transfers (and external financing) on supply conditions and potential output.

c Competitiveness

In Chapter 3 we discussed several price and cost measures of competitiveness – i.e., real effective exchange rates (REERs). They show changes over time in competitiveness but do not provide a clear signal of whether the *level* of competitiveness is satisfactory. For the latter, the measures developed in Chapter 3 must be viewed against analysis of the external accounts, from which we can judge whether changes in REERs are adequate to produce a sustainable current account position. The risk of reaching the

---

[9] Note, however, that distorted relative prices, such as an unsustainable real exchange rate, will lead to unwise and potentially problematic borrowing and investment decisions.

wrong conclusions from an assessment of REERs alone is especially high when a country experiences structural change or structural shocks.

Let's consider a few common examples where the BOP accounts provide critical context for measures of competitiveness.

Suppose REERs appear to be in a competitive range vis-à-vis recent historical experience.[10] But if the growth of exports is not keeping up with that of external markets or the current account deficit is widening, we would want to delve deeper into the external accounts to understand the roots of the disappointing export growth. We might see that lower global export prices have led to a deterioration in the terms of trade. This change would both lower the nominal value of a given volume of exports and, by reducing profit margins on exports for given domestic production costs, act as a drag on export supply. Such a finding would lead us to the conclusion that relative price or cost measures of competitiveness cannot merely stay on a par with recent levels but must actually improve in order to restore adequate competitiveness given the worsening of the terms of trade.

Another example where analysis of the current account could influence conclusions on competitiveness is when shocks to nontrade items are expected to result in lasting changes to the current account position. Take a country that has been a major beneficiary of inflows on the primary and/or secondary income accounts, owing to large inward workers' remittances. If remittances are coming from a part of the world that suffers a major lasting recession, they will drop, as will the current account balance. The country needs to find new sources of foreign receipts. This means cost and price competitiveness will need to strengthen to boost exports, contain imports, and attract investment to the traded goods sector.

A common way that superficial analysis of price measures of competitiveness leads to wrong conclusions occurs when rising per capita GDP, owing to export-led growth and productivity gains in the traded goods sector, leads to large increases in domestic demand for both traded and nontraded goods, and higher prices for the latter (the Balassa–Samuelson effect).[11] In such circumstances, the BOP accounts bring an essential perspective to an assessment of competitiveness: the diminution in competitiveness as measured by traded-nontraded goods prices is not only benign,

---

[10] Recall from Chapter 3 that competitiveness may be measured by the price of traded goods relative to that of nontraded goods (with this measure usually proxied by a REER based on broad price indices at home and abroad corrected for exchange rate movements), or by relative unit labor costs at home compared with those abroad, again with a correction for exchange rate changes (i.e., a ULC-based REER).

[11] This is the Balassa–Samuelson effect illustrated in Box 3.5.

it is actually essential to achieving equilibrium. One should not be concerned about some apparent loss of CPI-based competitiveness, or even some drop in the current account balance, as long as export growth remains robust and the balance of payments overall remains reasonably strong.[12]

What all of these examples have in common is a structural change or real shock that changes the equilibrium REER, whether measured in terms of relative ULCs, aggregate price indices, or ratios of traded to nontraded goods prices. Insofar as these measures of competitiveness do not have any benchmark or structurally neutral level, they are commonly judged relative to recent historical levels, an inappropriate comparator in the event of a change in real circumstances. But regardless of whether these measures change or stay the same, any analysis of competitiveness must be backstopped with an examination of the external accounts.

d Global Imbalances: Symmetry Considerations

Concerns about external current account imbalances are typically asymmetric – large or persistent deficits give rise to far more concern than large or persistent surpluses. Our illustrations of external current account analyses thus far speak to this asymmetry and point to the reasons that it exists: large or persistent deficits lead to a depletion of reserves and/or a buildup of debt (unless they are financed by FDI inflows); if uncorrected, they place a country at high risk of a debt crisis. Large or persistent surpluses may also not be sustainable indefinitely, though there is typically no decisive event like a crisis to stop the flow.

These basic facts create a problem for BOP analysis. The global zero balance constraint (the sum of all countries' current accounts, abstracting from measurement errors, is zero) means that all deficits must be matched by surpluses in other countries. Current account deficits large enough to be worrisome in one or a small number of countries can be matched by small surpluses spread over a large number of countries, and this configuration would rightly raise concerns focused only on the deficit countries. But when large deficits are matched by large surpluses, each concentrated in one or a small number of countries, it is reasonable to ask whether the imbalances are being driven by policies and conditions in the surplus countries or in the deficit countries, and where the burden of adjustment should fall. If policies in a particular surplus

---

[12] We should be concerned, however, if this change in relative prices overshoots any plausible equilibrium. This usually entails very rapid increases in some nontraded prices – most commonly real estate – that elicits substantial, credit-fueled investment as discussed in Chapter 6.

country were driving the developments in deficit countries, placing the onus of adjustment on the deficit countries would force restrictive policies on these countries and thereby depress global economic activity.

Such circumstances have been at the center of the concerns about global imbalances, especially during 2004–2008 when the current account imbalances of several large countries or regions rose very rapidly. The main features of these imbalances (shown in Figure 7.2) were large deficits in the United States and large surpluses in oil exporters, China and other emerging Asian countries, Japan, and Germany.

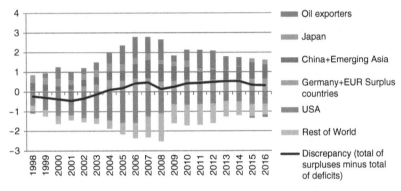

FIGURE 7.2 Global current account imbalances (percent of global GDP)
Source: IMF WEO, April 2016

Broadly, two perspectives dominated the debate. Some argued that the problem resided with the surplus countries, especially China and some European countries. In this view, for instance, official Chinese purchases of dollars, which were invested to a large extent in US Treasury bills, were artificially holding down the value of the renminbi, giving Chinese exporters a competitive advantage. The weak renminbi constrained real wages and thus domestic demand, increased profits and saving in the export sector, and, together with China's roughly balanced fiscal position, sustained upward pressure on the Chinese current account position. In addition, Chinese purchases of US Treasury bills kept downward pressure on US interest rates, which spurred domestic demand in the United States. European surpluses were seen as an intra-European problem as they were largely matched by deficits of European countries.

Others argued that the global imbalance problem stemmed from the United States. US fiscal deficits were large and growing, private saving relative to GDP was falling, and the US current account deficit was a reflection of those domestic imbalances. Moreover, in this view, China should not be faulted for accumulating reserves to serve as a safety net in the event of a future crisis and, as the reserve currency country, the United States should accept that effort.

Still others argued that the imbalances were primarily the result of differences in structural characteristics and stages of development between China and the United States. This group pointed to several factors that probably contributed to the imbalances and would with time reverse or subside. China had a large underemployed rural population that kept downward pressure on wage costs and thus the real exchange rate as these workers joined the industrial economy. Also, China's demographic profile had a far greater aging of the population on the horizon than that of the United States, so a very high saving rate made sense.

The imbalances have been the source of much concern and discussion for two main reasons. First, the persistence of the imbalances was seen as evidence that policy intervention in the foreign exchange market was thwarting equilibrating exchange rate adjustments (appreciation in the surplus countries and depreciation in the deficit countries). In the absence of such exchange rate movements, resources were being misallocated by false market signals. For fear of a sharp and costly correction, surplus countries would be locked into policies that sought to sustain the disequilibrium conditions and global imbalances. Second, there was a strong view that the imbalances could not continue indefinitely and that, without policy actions to curtail them, there would eventually be an acute discontinuity ("disorderly adjustment"), probably entailing a collapse of the dollar and a disorderly reallocation of resources in both surplus and deficit countries in response to the sharp change in relative price signals.

This example – and the differences in views as to its origins – are representative of the difficulty of pinning down the causes of large global imbalances and of agreeing on what should be done to remedy them before they produce disorderly adjustments. In general, global imbalances become large (and therefore the focus of attention) when one or a few countries are accumulating reserves rapidly – typically to prevent an exchange rate from appreciating but also in some cases to establish a safe level of reserves. The reserve currency country (or countries) will usually need to run a current account deficit in these circumstances.

It is almost definitional that when large countries have large imbalances, both the surplus and deficit countries need to adjust – either by allowing market forces to play a larger role in determining exchange rates, or by changing other policies in one or both countries. But how to apportion the burden of adjustment is an exceptionally difficult – and highly political – question without an unambiguous framework for analysis. (Box 7.2 describes an exercise in the IMF that attempts to determine how adjustment burdens can be made consistent with global and domestic stability.) Policy prescriptions for addressing persistent payments imbalances need to address several considerations: the effects of sizable exchange rate changes on growth, employment, resource allocation, income distribution, saving, and investment; the special position of the reserve currency country; and the influence of structural characteristics, including demographic features, that differ between countries.

Box 7.2 The IMF's External Balance Assessment

The IMF – in what is called the External Balance Assessment (EBA) model – has created one approach that aims to identify the sources of global imbalances and the policies that will be most effective to address them. An econometric exercise establishes a relationship between the current account and a list of variables that influence it for as many countries as data availability permits. On the structural side variables include influences that are not subject to policy manipulation or ones for which policies tend to change slowly: measures such as productivity in each country relative to some benchmark country, an indicator of global risk aversion, a measure of home bias in the investment preferences of a country's residents, demographic variables, the terms of trade, growth potential, and trade openness. On the policy side, variables include measures of fiscal policy, official foreign exchange intervention, monetary policy (such as short-term interest rates and credit growth) and capital controls. To the extent possible, explanatory variables are measured as differences relative to world averages (or some other common benchmark) so that the influences of own-country variables and of foreign variables are both captured.[1]

The estimated parameters can be used to provide a categorization of structural and policy influences on current account positions for each country. In principle, this categorization allows analysts to assess when a substantial deviation of a country's current account position from balance stems from influences largely out of a country's control – such as demographic factors that influence the saving rate – and when it is the result of deviations of policies from sustainable (or what the IMF

Box 7.2 (*continued*)

calls "desirable") positions – such as excessive fiscal deficits or large-scale foreign exchange intervention to influence the exchange rate. Such a classification could serve as a basis for reaching views on whether global imbalances in current account positions result from policy choices in a deficit or surplus country or are the result of structural aspects of one or more economies that are not amenable to policy correction. With this classification in hand, calculations of over- and undervaluation of exchange rates can be derived. For example, a country that is shown to have a large current account surplus stemming from policy influences would by implication have an undervalued currency. The exercise is used to derive quantifications of over- and undervaluations of major currencies.

In practice, many problems mar the execution of this approach. Data deficiencies are a major concern. At least as serious are problems with the conceptual framework. Current account positions, real exchange rates, and many macroeconomic policy decisions are closely intertwined so that separating those influences into endogenous and exogenous factors is laden with problems. Also problematic is the need to establish some "desirable" stance of policies from which to measure deviations of actual policies. While the exercise has value in providing an empirically-based measure of the source of imbalances (and by extension over- and undervaluation of currencies), it does not have the conceptual or empirical rigor to provide an explanation of the source of imbalances that is robust to serious challenges from authorities in countries experiencing the imbalances.

[1] IMF, External Balance Assessment (EBA) Methodology: Technical Background (June 2013).

e Vulnerability to External Financing Crises

Most economic crises arise from vulnerabilities of domestic origin, as described in Chapters 4–6 – defending an exchange rate fixed at the wrong level, profligate fiscal policies, inadequate prudential regulation or supervision of banks, and/or excessive leverage in the nonbank private sector. For most countries such crises ultimately spill over to create unsustainable developments in the external accounts. Less frequently, crises initially unfold in global capital markets: usually such circumstances involve a global shock (such as an increase in global risk aversion) or a regional event that sets off "contagion" to a region or asset class. (Contagion, the term applied to large, usually negative, changes in market perceptions about one country spilling over to affect another country or a group of countries, is described in detail in Box 7.3.) It stands to reason, therefore, that we should scour the external accounts to anticipate (1) whether a domestic vulnerability poses a threat to the external accounts and (2) whether the safety margin in a country's external position is adequate to withstand global or regional shocks.

Box 7.3 Economic Contagion: What Is It and How Can It Be Addressed?

The focus on contagion dates back to Thailand's financial crisis in mid-1997, when substantial financial outflows and a speculative attack on the Thai baht were seen as the genesis of crises in other countries in the region (South Korea, Indonesia, Malaysia, and the Philippines) and ultimately further afield. While contagion is now widely accepted as a serious threat to stability, consensus on a precise definition, the channels through which it operates, and what can be done to limit it remain somewhat controversial.

The term international economic contagion (hereafter "contagion") almost always refers to the transmission across countries of negative financial shocks. Some researchers or commentators see contagion as encompassing any situation where a shock in one country also affects others, though most use the term in a narrower sense to differentiate it from (a) common shocks (i.e., shocks that affect two or more countries directly in a similar way), and (b) spillovers (a high, but predictable, influence of a shock in one country on other countries). Spillovers may also constitute common shocks and vice versa.

An example of a common shock would be the effect of an increase in US interest rates on all indebted EMs (and this would also be a spillover from the United States to these countries). An example of a spillover would be the effect of a policy-induced drop in China's copper imports on Chilean exports; this would be a shock common to other copper exporters.

Contagion in the narrow and more precise sense is an unexpectedly rapid or large co-movement of asset prices across countries. For instance, an event that makes investors nervous about their financial exposure to Brazil might elicit a critical reexamination of exposure to

Box 7.3 (*continued*)

various other EMs that leads to a jump in risk premia in all of these countries. Such an abrupt transmission of volatility could trigger crises in the more vulnerable countries affected.

For policymakers a key question is why some countries are more vulnerable than others to contagion. Most agree that vulnerability rises with insufficient buffers (e.g., low official reserves) and greater fragilities (e.g., high external debt, large gross financing requirements, low domestic saving and thus reliance on foreign financing). Perhaps most importantly, the main victims of contagion in the 1990s intervened significantly to limit the flexibility of their exchange rates thus encouraging foreign currency exposure in the private sector. An asset price shock in another country heightened market awareness of the risk that the central bank did not have adequate reserves (or the will to raise interest rates sharply or impose financial market restrictions) to defend the exchange rate, so conditions were ripe for a speculative attack.

Actions to reduce the risks of contagion take two forms. First, policies that make countries vulnerable to contagion need to be avoided. The IMF has thus increased its attention to identifying vulnerabilities in fiscal policy, banking regulation, and external indebtedness. It also views exchange rate flexibility as a significant strength in reducing the risk of contagion.

Second, an international lender-of-last-resort facility may mitigate contagion-generated crises. An analogy with banks helps explain this notion. For bank crises, one makes the distinction between liquidity and solvency problems; the central bank's lender-of-last-resort function can be highly effective in the former, when banks are solvent but need temporary funding to restore market confidence. Similarly, countries with sound policies and robust buffers that nevertheless get caught up in a wave of contagion should be able to ride it out if they have access to adequate resources to reassure markets about underlying sustainability. Such resources might be used passively (simply as a signal to markets that resources are adequate to fully service government or banking sector debt) or even actively to limit extreme volatility in foreign exchange markets. Importantly, however, an international lender-of-last-resort facility can help only countries with fundamentally sustainable policies – not countries that have basic weaknesses such as an overvalued currency or excessive debt.-

(*continued*)

Box 7.3 (*continued*)

After the 2008 financial crisis, the IMF established lending facilities that seek to reduce the risk of contagion by providing lender-of-last-resort-type assurances. Under the IMF's *Flexible Credit Line* (FCL), countries with fundamentally strong policies – i.e., sound public finances with easy sovereign access to markets, low inflation, a well-regulated financial system, external sustainability, and data integrity and transparency – can receive, in noncrisis conditions, the IMF's stamp of approval and preapproved access to large-scale financing in the event of a contagion episode. Three countries – Mexico, Poland, and Columbia – have entered into FCL agreements as of 2018. Two other countries – Macedonia and Morocco – have entered into *Precautionary and Liquidity Line* (PLL) agreements (which provide preapproved, rapid, contingent financing in a contagion episode subject to somewhat less rigorous initial qualifications but with targeted conditionality to address policy weaknesses).

What we look for in the external accounts is driven by our views of how crises unfold. In the past 70 years, those views have changed markedly. In the 1950s–1960s, when global financial markets were small, crises tended to evolve slowly. Countries with current account deficits financed them from official aid, official foreign lending, or (temporarily) drawing down official foreign exchange reserves. Crises took the form of current account deficits that could no longer be financed from these sources – what would be called flow imbalances. So vulnerability assessment focused on the size of a current account deficit and adequacy of reserves.

The crises experienced by Turkey from the late 1950s through the late 1960s are good examples. Large fiscal deficits and rapid credit growth pushed up domestic demand, stoking inflation, and thereby reducing competitiveness. Trade deficits rose, and the foreign exchange reserves of the central bank (which was defending a fixed exchange rate) fell. When reserves reached a critically low level, the IMF would provide financing to bolster reserves while measures were put in place to tighten monetary and fiscal policies and, in some instances, to devalue the lira. These flow account crises were slow-moving but chronically recurrent.

As international financial markets grew, a new breed of crises was born. Since the late 1970s, crises have increasingly played out through the external financial account.[13] Countries that had relied on foreign financing for current account deficits over many years became highly indebted to foreign creditors. In such circumstances, a sudden change in risk assessments by global investors could shut off financing sources and then produce devastating financial outflows. The emphasis in vulnerability assessments shifted to countries' debt profiles.

A major puzzle in financial account crises is why they often occur so abruptly. A typical precrisis scenario is one where a country is pursuing policies (fiscal, monetary, and financial sector) that are not flagrantly bad but raise questions about sustainability. Nevertheless, the country is experiencing reasonable growth, has low inflation, and borrows abroad to finance a current account deficit without much difficulty. The country may even have had a recent surge in financial inflows if, for instance, global risk tolerance had risen. The surge may have eased domestic credit conditions (especially if the central bank was purchasing dollars to resist an appreciation of its currency) and pushed up consumption or investment. But then a sudden jump in the market perception of risk – e.g., from contagion or a political development – sparks sizable outflows from residents sending funds abroad and nonresidents repatriating maturing loans. At this point, most countries make emergency policy adjustments to deal with the crisis – typically increasing the policy interest rate (to reflect the jump in the market perception of risk) and/or allowing a depreciation of the currency. If these policy adjustments are not adequate to restore confidence or themselves raise market concerns about their balance sheet effects, the crisis may expand to engulf all entities in the economy – banks, corporations, and the government – that rely (directly or indirectly) on foreign financing.

The question in such circumstances is what triggered the crisis so abruptly? Why did the country not experience a gradual, and therefore more tractable, transition from relative stability to market turbulence to crisis? Why, when nothing of note had changed in the country, did the market's assessment of risk suddenly change? The effort to answer these questions has spawned a number of stylized models characterizing the causes and triggers of BOP crises. These models in turn have driven methodologies for vetting the external accounts for vulnerabilities to crisis.

Models of external financial account crises have many permutations but they all have one basic point in common: when a country is heavily exposed

---

[13] Such crises are typically called "capital account crises" reflecting old terminology where the financial account was called the capital account. Following current definitions they should be called "financial account crises."

to international capital markets – especially through short-term external debt – changes in sentiment (including increases in uncertainty about future policy choices) can move asset prices and financial flows with lightning speed. The trigger may be a change in government, a shift in average expectations about future policy choices, a suddenly apparent financial problem in a major bank or corporation, or a new perception that large market participants have lost confidence in the country's ability to sustain exchange rate stability. Contagion from some other country's setback is also a common trigger.

The key point from this characterization of crises is that countries need to keep a close eye on vulnerabilities of the external position to crisis and adjust policies preemptively to mitigate risks. Such assessments need to consider the sustainability of external financial flows and risks in the composition of such flows. Debt sustainability analysis – the subject of the next section – is an essential tool. Safety cushions against sudden reversals in financing – especially international reserve holdings which are also discussed in more depth below – are important, both in themselves and in order to maintain the confidence of creditors.

3 External Vulnerability and Risk Assessment

The assessment of external vulnerability – like fiscal sustainability, a task that is most systematically carried out in IMF Article IV consultations – in many respects tracks the methodology of fiscal sustainability analyses. The similarities stem from the fact that a key part of the analysis concerns whether the debt ratio (in this case the external debt ratio) is expected to be stable or to stabilize over the medium term. But also the government's external debt is often a large or even dominant part of total external debt, so government debt dynamics may drive problems in external debt sustainability.

However, differences are also significant. In assessing fiscal sustainability we saw that the analysis had to go beyond a simple calculation of whether plausible projections would stabilize the ratio of government debt to GDP. But external sustainability entails even more nuanced judgments.[14] Factors

---

[14] This is reflected in the IMF's treatment of fiscal and external debt sustainability. External sustainability figures prominently in Article IV consultation reports (most reports have an annex on external sustainability) but in practice it tends to take something of a backseat to fiscal sustainability. Moreover, a finding of a high probability of fiscal sustainability going forward is one of four essential conditions a country must meet before receiving large-scale ("exceptional access" to use the jargon) IMF financing in near-crisis or crisis conditions.

such as the adequacy of official foreign exchange reserves and the potential for non-debt-creating inflows (especially foreign direct investment in the private sector) to finance external deficits figure importantly in external DSAs.

In this section we review the basic external debt sustainability condition and then discuss some of the more nuanced features of the external DSA.

a The External DSA

The external DSA, the centerpiece of external sustainability, asks the following question: For realistic projections of GDP growth, the exchange rate, inflation, interest rates, and foreign financing options, will a country's future external borrowing needs allow the ratio of external debt to nominal GDP to stabilize at a level that can be financed without jeopardizing potential growth? The algebra is similar to that for public debt sustainability. We write it out here for completeness.

The external debt ratio is constant if the percentage change in debt is equal to the percentage change in nominal GDP.

$$\Delta D_t / D_{(t-1)} = \Delta Y_{n,t} / Y_{n,(t-1)} \tag{7.7}$$

D = domestic currency value of gross external debt of all sectors of the economy[15]

We assume (for simplicity and as an approximation of actual external debt in EM and low-income countries) that all debt is denominated in US dollars.[16] The currency dimension of external debt makes the external DSA slightly more complicated than the fiscal DSA insofar as the exchange rate must be explicit in the calculation. So while in Box 5.6 we saw how the exchange rate *could* enter the calculation of fiscal sustainability, it almost always does for external sustainability.

$$D = D^\$ E \tag{7.8}$$

$D^\$$ = the dollar value of external debt
E = domestic currency price of dollars

---

[15] For notational simplicity, "D," which is used to symbolize government debt in Chapter 5, is being used in this chapter to symbolize total (public + private) debt to nonresidents, i.e., external debt.

[16] In actuality, most countries have debt to nonresidents in more than one currency, and many also have such debt in domestic currency.

Define GDP measured in dollars as $Y^\$ = Y_n/E$ so that

$$(1 + gr_t^\$) = (1 + g_{n,t})/(1 + \varepsilon_t) \tag{7.9}$$

ε_t = the percentage change in the exchange rate in period t

The change in the stock of external debt in period t is

$$\Delta D_t^\$ = i_t{}^w D_{(t-1)}^\$ - NDCAB_t \tag{7.10}$$

i^w = effective dollar interest rate on external debt

NDCAB = noninterest current account balance plus net non-debt-creating financial inflows, all measured in dollars.

In most countries non-debt-creating financing consists chiefly of foreign direct investment and portfolio investment in equities. It may also include the use of the official reserves of the central bank if such use is envisaged.[17]

In order to stabilize the external debt ratio, the growth rate of debt must equal that of nominal GDP, both measured in the same currency. This gives us the sustainability condition. Dividing equation (7.10) through by $D_{t-1}^\$$ and setting it equal to the growth of GDP (measured in dollars) yields

$$\Delta D_t^\$/D_{(t-1)}^\$ = i_t{}^w - NDCAB_t/D_{(t-1)}^\$ = (1 + gr_{n,t})/(1 + \varepsilon_t) - 1 \tag{7.11}$$

Rearranging this equation we get

$$(NDCAB_t/Y_t^\$)(Y_t^\$/D_{t-1}^\$)(D_{t-1}^\$/Y_{t-1}^\$)$$
$$= (D_{t-1}^\$/Y_{t-1}^\$)[i_t^w - \{(gr_{(n,t)} - \varepsilon_t)/(1 + \varepsilon_t)\}] \tag{7.12}$$

This can be simplified to

$$ndcab_t[(1 + gr_{(n,t)})/(1 + \varepsilon_t)] = (D_{(t-1)}^\$/Y_{(t-1)}^\$)$$
$$\times [\{i_t^w(1 + \varepsilon_t) - gr_{n,t} + \varepsilon_t\}/(1 + \varepsilon_t)] \tag{7.13}$$

or

$$ndcab_t[(1 + gr_{(n,t)})/(1 + \varepsilon_t)] = (D_{(t-1)}^\$/Y_{(t-1)}^\$)$$
$$\times [\{i_t^w(1 + \varepsilon_t) - gr_{n,t} + \varepsilon_t\}/(1 + \varepsilon_t)] \tag{7.14}$$

---

[17] In projections underpinning the DSA, changes in official reserves may be projected to be zero (if reserves are at a desirable level) or may be included in NDCAD if a change is part of the plan. The neutral assumption is for both errors and omissions in the balance of payments accounts and the use of official reserves to be zero.

or

$$ndcab_t = (D_{(t-1)}/Y_{(n,t-1)})[\{i_t^w(1 + \varepsilon_t) - gr_{n,t} + \varepsilon_t\}/(1 + gr_{(n,t)})]$$
$$where \quad ndcab_t = NDCAB_t/Y_t^\$ \qquad\qquad (7.15)$$

The message from this sustainability condition is similar to that from the fiscal sustainability condition. A higher interest rate on external debt and a depreciation of the domestic currency mean that the inflow of nondebt financing plus the noninterest current account balance needs to be higher in order to stabilize the external debt ratio. But more rapid growth reduces the level of nondebt inflows required.

The value of the sustainability condition is that it gives us a forward-looking framework for considering how close a country's actual noninterest current account balance is to a sustainable level. If the actual balance is below the level consistent with a constant external debt ratio, markets will be wary unless the country is taking steps to strengthen it. But even if it is above the debt-stabilizing level, market assessments of the country's vulnerability (and thus the all-important risk premium on debt) will factor in how close to this level it is and the risk that shocks will drive it lower.

To carry out a DSA, we make assumptions about the medium-term path of all the variables on the right side of equation 7.15 – real growth, the GDP deflator, exchange rate movements, and interest rates, as well as non-debt-creating flows (essentially foreign direct investment and any portfolio equity inflows), and the scope for using official reserves for financing (more on this below). As in the fiscal DSA, two indicators for judging sustainability emerge. First, we can look at the trajectory for the debt ratio to see whether it is stable or it stabilizes at some point on the medium-term horizon. Second, we can calculate the debt-stabilizing noninterest current account balance (for given growth, interest rate and exchange rate conditions) which can then be judged against projections based on the current stance of domestic policies. If prospective current account financing needs exceed debt-stabilizing levels, so that the trajectory shows a rising external debt ratio, there is a prima facie case for policy adjustments.

As with fiscal DSAs, these projections are increasingly uncertain as the time horizon lengthens, so sensitivity analysis of the effects of different trajectories for the critical variables is necessary. Typically we shock individual variables in the DSA by two standard deviations of their averages over the past 10 years or some combination of variables – say growth, the yield on domestic debt, and the exchange rate – by one standard deviation for each variable. We can then see how sensitive the sustainable position is to a range of plausible shocks. If the baseline projection for the current account deficit is so close to the calculated sustainable path that a plausible combination of shocks leads to an unsustainable situation, then policy action (e.g., tightening fiscal and/or monetary policies to contain demand, or structural reforms to raise potential growth) is needed to establish a safer margin and reduce vulnerability.

Even sensitivity analyses leave many questions about judgments. A critical difficulty is capturing dynamic effects. For example, feedback loops from shocks to confidence effects and further shocks are exceptionally difficult to capture. Often structural parameters – like the openness, size, or existence of a diaspora, regional stability, or level of development – are important to the judgments.

In external risk assessments, several issues beyond the DSA are critical. Two broad types of considerations stand out: the characteristics of debt and debtors, and the size of the reserve buffer against shocks.

b Characteristics of Debt and Interrelationships of External Debt Holders

Because these considerations are usually qualitative – i.e., they do not have very precise criteria – they tend to lead to less definitive judgments than the public sector vulnerability analysis usually reaches. A summary of the central questions about the characteristics of a country's external debt profile is as follows:

- *What is the prospect of non-debt-creating financial inflows supplanting debt-creating inflows?* For most countries, FDI is the main non-debt-creating inflow, and it is sensitive to economic policies and conditions. FDI entails no fixed interest obligations, and thus risk is shared between foreign and domestic investors. It is typically characterized by stable and long-lasting links between the investor and the recipient country. The greater the share of FDI in future external exposures the less worrisome is a given external position.
- *Do we have a good basis for judgments on whether the private sector is holding excessive external debt?* A view popular in the late 1980s (known as the Lawson Doctrine after the then-Chancellor of the Exchequer in the United Kingdom) held that the external debt of the private sector produced nowhere close to the same risks as that of the public sector: essentially, the latter was the responsibility of government and could affect taxpayers while the former was not

and could not. In effect, if private borrowers became insolvent, their assets would be liquidated according to processes prescribed by bankruptcy and liquidation laws. The losses would be borne by private equity holders and creditors, not by taxpayers. It was, moreover, difficult to determine a safe level of private external debt – private borrowers might be naturally hedged against exchange rate risk through export earnings or holdings of foreign assets.

This theory lost favor during the Asian crises in the late 1990s which were effectively sparked by excessive private borrowing (sometimes with implicit government guarantees) either by corporations so large that their liquidation would have had profound macroeconomic effects, or in countries where bankruptcy laws were absent or inadequate. These examples extinguished the notion that private external debt does not matter. Moreover, the analysis in Chapter 6 highlights the risks stemming from linkages between the nonbank private sector and banks: these make foreign borrowing by banks common and risky. Still, as demonstrated in Chapter 6, it remains difficult to pass judgment on whether aggregate nonbank private external debt is excessive.

- *Are net external debt positions an adequate representation of exposure to exchange rate risk?* For most countries, a sizable part of foreign assets and foreign liabilities are denominated in major foreign currencies – US dollars, euro, sterling, or yen – but the currency composition of assets may differ from that of liabilities. Changes in the exchange rate between the major currencies as a group and the domestic currency are always important. However changes in exchange rates between major currencies (which can be large and sudden) may be almost as important. In other words, while the external DSA presented above assumed all borrowing was in dollars and all assets were held in local currency, in fact the currency composition of assets and liabilities can be consequential.

- *Does the maturity structure of external assets and liabilities entail illiquidity risks?* Significant maturity mismatches between external liabilities and assets leave the domestic holder of net liabilities vulnerable to changes in interest rates and rollover risks.[18] The external vulnerabilities stemming from maturity mismatches are similar to those described for the public sector in Chapter 5

---

[18] While one usually hears the term *maturity mismatch*, as noted in Chapter 6, the real issue is liquidity rather than maturity. If short-term liabilities are matched by long-dated assets that can be easily liquidated *without significant* loss there is no mismatch problem.

and the financial sector in Chapter 6 but they also apply to house-holds and nonfinancial businesses in the external vulnerability analysis.

- *How important is the concentration and interconnectedness of major foreign currency debtors?* A concentration of external debt in a particularly vulnerable sector exacerbates risk. Interconnectedness, too, can be problematic. For example, banks collectively and indivi-dually may have small or no net foreign liabilities but long-term government debt might be a large share of their assets. And the government itself might have large net foreign liabilities. If foreign holders of government bonds suddenly change their view on whether the government can repay (or the likelihood of a significant deprecia-tion) then an increase in the risk premium on government debt raises secondary market interest rates. Banks would then experience either significant losses or substantially reduced liquidity.[19] If such losses are so large as to require government support for bank recapitalization, doubts about fiscal sustainability would rise. Disentangling such inter-connections requires scenario analysis to work through the effects of a specific shock.

c The Role of Official Foreign Exchange Reserves in Vulnerability Analysis

Central bank holdings of foreign exchange reserves are an important buffer against external sector vulnerability to shocks. This is obvious for countries that fix or allow little movement in their exchange rates. But it is even important for countries with flexible exchange rates; any country can encounter setbacks of domestic or external origin that would result in exchange rate volatility that might best be limited by intervention. Moreover, markets view the level of reserves as a signal of a country's ability to service debt even in the face of setbacks. Empirical studies indicate that the intensity of a crisis and the setback to domestic absorption during crises is less, the higher the level of a country's official reserves. No single metric exists for judging reserve adequacy so several are commonly used:

---

[19] The accounting conventions (examined in Chapter 6) on whether banks have to show these losses on their books – i.e., on whether they must mark assets to market as opposed to holding them at constant book value – depends on whether the assets are held in the "banking book" or the "trading book." But even if banks are not required to mark to market, any attempt by banks to sell these bonds to meet liquidity needs would entail realizing losses. Thus the government bonds may become effectively illiquid.

- *The number of months of imports that existing reserves would cover.* Three months is usually the bare minimum. The logic is not complicated: should some event profoundly disrupt a country's export capacity, reserves indicate how long the central bank would be able to finance essential imports to support supply chains and basic needs. In the age of large-scale international capital mobility, this measure is less relevant than it was in the mid-twentieth century, but it still commands attention.

- *The ratio of reserves to a country's total external short-term debt.* The rule of thumb is that reserve assets equivalent to 100 percent of short-term external debt place a country in a safe position: the logic is that amortizations could be covered for a year if it proved impossible to roll over maturing debt. The relevant concept of short-term debt includes total (public and private) debt up to one year in original maturity and medium- and long-term loans with remaining maturities of a year or less.

- *The ratio of reserves to the money supply.* This metric is especially relevant in countries that have committed to both fixing the exchange rate vis-à-vis a major currency and not restricting private capital or financial transactions. In such a country, the central bank has pledged to buy any amount of domestic currency with official reserves at a fixed price on demand, so the entire domestic money supply represents a potential drain on foreign reserves.[20] There is no rule-of-thumb target ratio but the metric helps assess the vulnerability of the exchange rate fix and the open capital account to a diminution of confidence in the currency.

- The IMF's *Analysis of Reserve Adequacy* (ARA) metric.[21] This metric was developed in the aftermath of the 2008 crises. The IMF sought a measure that maximized simplicity, completeness, and comparability across countries. Using a large sample of episodes of exchange market pressures in EMs, the methodology creates a probability density function of the size of each of four principal types of drains on the balance of payments in such episodes: short-term debt outflows, other external liability outflows, export losses, and liquid domestic assets outflows (proxied by the change in broad money).

[20] In a "crawling peg" regime the authorities fix a path, rather than a level, for the exchange rate. But this entails similar obligations to exchange foreign currency for domestic currency on demand at a pre-set exchange rate.

[21] For the most recent update on the IMF's approach to reserve adequacy and references to the substantial history of related work see www.imf.org/external/np/pp/eng/2014/121914.pdf

These probability densities are used to assign risk-based weights to each type of potential drain, and the four types are aggregated into an overall metric against which to assess reserve levels (in a way analogous to the risk-weighting of bank capital for regulatory purposes). Reserve holdings of 50 percent of this metric were found to be sufficient to cover 95 percent of the episodes in the sample. Along with other empirical work, this helped identify a range of 100–150 percent of the metric as a recommended level of reserves for precautionary purposes. In IMF vulnerability analysis, this metric has become an additional standard to the three conventional measures (specified above) for EM countries.

External vulnerability generally, and reserve adequacy in particular, are viewed in light of two types of policies.

First, a country's exchange rate policy – the more flexibility, the less likely is the central bank to intervene to limit volatility or counteract changes and the less likely are borrowers to be complacent about exchange risk. A given level of reserves that is judged to be inadequate for a country that limits exchange rate flexibility might be considered adequate in a country that has a flexible exchange rate. Because the formal description of a country's exchange rate policy does not always accurately match actual practice, care is needed in defining a country's exchange rate policy.[22]

Second, a country's history of capital controls (or, in IMF parlance, capital flow management [CFM] policies) plays into judgments about the adequacy of reserves. Countries with such measures in place or a history of using them might be judged, depending on the efficacy of such measures, to need lower levels of reserves.

4 Exercises

Many of the exercises in earlier chapters had aspects that could be addressed more fully once the reader had covered material in subsequent chapters. Some of these raised questions about the balance of payments, external debt, and foreign exchange reserves. It might now be worth revisiting these exercises after completing the two below.

1 A developing country in 2018 has low and steady inflation, output close to potential, and a growth rate that is closing the income gap with more

---

[22] The IMF publishes annually its classification of every member's exchange rate policy. See www.imf.org/external/pubs/nft/2014/areaers/ar2014.pdf

advanced countries. The country has a managed floating exchange rate, and the central bank intervenes to forestall what it regards as temporary or unwarranted changes in the exchange rate. It is a large producer of copper. Copper already accounts for 40 percent of exports, and exploration suggests that discoveries of new deposits may be imminent. The United States is its main trading partner and also a source of remittances from workers employed in the United States. Its trade deficit is significant but financed largely by these remittance inflows and by FDI. Foreign borrowing is very small. Reserves are at a comfortable level.

A summary balance of payments for 2018 (all figures in percent of nominal GDP) is shown in Table 7.3; omitted items (e.g., "net services" or "portfolio investment") are zero. While it is unusual to present a balance of payments table all in percent of GDP (rather than in dollars or euro or some other currency), we present them like that here to provide a sense of scale.

TABLE 7.3 *Summary balance of payments 2018* (percent of GDP)

Current account balance (CAB)	−5
Exports of goods and services	35
Imports of goods and services	45
Net primary income (NPI)	5
Capital account balance (KAB)	0
Net financial account balance (NFB) of which	5
Foreign direct investment (FDI)	4
Other investment (net) (LOANS)	1
Overall balance	0

Let's consider three hypothetical sets of developments in 2019: Case 1, Case 2, and Case 3.

The exercise entails inferring the circumstances that might have led to these outcomes for each of the cases. There may be more than one valid inference in each case – i.e., various stories about how the change came about – and you need only give one plausible explanation. Given your narrative about the circumstances that produced the outcome in each case,

TABLE 7.4 *Summary balance of payments 2019* (percent of GDP)

	Case 1	Case 2	Case 3
Current account balance (CAB)	−13	2	−15
Exports of goods and services	28	38	35
Imports of goods and services	47	42	55
Net primary income (NPI)	6	6	5
Capital account balance (KAB)	0	0	0
Net financial account balance (NFB)	9	−8	20
Foreign direct investment (FDI)	2	0	12
Other investment (net) (LOANS)	7	−8	8
Overall balance	−4	−6	5

outline your policy prescriptions and what they are contingent on.

The three alternative balance of payments summaries are given in Table 7.4, with numbers once again expressed as percentages of GDP.

2 Consider a country characterized by the following data. The home currency is the rupee and the inflation rate is 6 percent in 2018 and is projected to remain at that rate through 2020. The corresponding foreign inflation rate (in US dollars) is a steady 2 percent.

The authorities let the exchange rate float but it has tended to depreciate just enough – by 4 percent a year – to offset inflation differentials, so that there has been no appreciable change in the real exchange rate. External debt is all denominated in US dollars and carries an interest rate of 5 percent throughout the period under examination.[23]

The figures in Table 7.5 are actual data for 2018 and projections for 2019 and 2020.

Despite the planned central bank intervention in 2020 to build up reserves, the exchange rate is projected to continue to depreciate to offset inflation differentials – a happy coincidence that will stabilize the real exchange rate. Omitted flows are zero.

(i) Fill in the debt and debt/GDP figures for 2019 and 2020. Given projections for FDI of $3 billion in each year and an increase in NFA of $2 billion in 2020, what current account balance would

---

[23] While we measure inflation and depreciation on an end-of-period basis – i.e., December over December – obviously converting rupee nominal GDP (a flow variable) into dollars should require dividing by the average rather than the end-of-period exchange rate. However, for simplicity, when considering the external debt ratio we look at the dollar debt level at the end of year *t* divided by nominal GDP in year *t* divided by the end-of-year exchange rate.

TABLE 7.5 *Summary of key external sector data, 2018–2020*
(billions of US$, except where indicated)

	2018	2019	2020
Current account balance (CAB)	−6.0	−8.0	−14.0
of which			
Net interest receipts [*]	−5.0	−5.15	−5.4
Foreign direct investment (net)	3.0	3.0	3.0
Other investment (LOANS)	3.0	5.0	13.0
Overall balance (ΔNFA) [**]	0.0	0.0	2.0
Memorandum items			
Exchange rate (Rs per US$, eop)	8.0	8.32	8.65
GDP (in US$)	200.0	209.6	219.8
External debt (US$, eop)	103.0	. . .	. . .
External debt/GDP (in percent)	51.5	. . .	. . .

[*] Note there are no private interest receipts, and to simplify we are ignoring interest earning on foreign reserves. Therefore, these numbers are the product of the stock of debt at the end of the last period and 5 percent interest on that debt.
[**] This is the change in net foreign assets of the central bank. Note that to build up reserves for prudential reasons, the central bank is projected to intervene in the foreign exchange market in 2020 to increase its net foreign assets by $2 billion.

      stabilize the debt ratio in 2020? Show how this is consistent with the DSA mechanics in this chapter.

(ii) The increase in the current account deficit in 2020 is striking: it is projected to rise from 3.8 percent of GDP in 2019 to 6.4 percent of GDP. How would the composition of domestic demand influence your concern about this increase?

(iii) After the projected increase in reserves in 2020, the gross foreign exchange reserves of the central bank would amount to $70 billion. The central bank's reserves are highly liquid. It has no short-term foreign liabilities and longer-term foreign liabilities are low (only $2 billion). How would the maturity structure of external debt influence your concern about the level of reserves in 2020?

(iv) The authorities claim to follow a managed floating exchange rate regime, and it appears that (aside from the planned purchases of foreign exchange to build reserves in 2020) they have eschewed intervention to influence the exchange rate. What bearing does the exchange rate regime have on the adequacy of reserves? How might the characteristics of private foreign borrowers influence exchange rate policy and the vulnerability of the economy to shocks?